000375

MEMORIAL UNIVERSITY

WITHDRAWN

MAY 6 2021

LIBRARY

OF NEWFOUNDLAND

D1416007

Science Fiction and Organization

Science fiction can be seen as a diagnosis of the present, and a vision of possible futures. As such, it forms an excellent tool of interrogation for both contemporary organizing processes and organizations as institutions. To date, however, the marginal activity of science fiction has been largely ignored in writing on organizational theory. This international collection is the first book of its kind to explore how science fiction can enrich organizational studies by drawing on perspectives across the arts and social sciences.

Key themes include:

- Examining the interrelation of organizational theory and developments in science fiction.
- Showing how immersion in science fiction can alter the reader's perspective and how this, in turn, feeds an understanding of organization.
- Discussion of how the exploration of popular themes in science fiction (such as identity, the nature of reality, the place of technology, the all-powerful corporation, the creation and maintenance of meta-narratives) corresponds to approaches taken to similar themes within organizational theory.

The range of sources and theoretical perspectives included in this text will ensure its importance for academics in the fields of organizational and social theory, particularly those interested in the relationships between art, theory and literature.

Warren Smith is Lecturer in Organization Studies at the Management Centre, University of Leicester.

Matthew Higgins is Lecturer in Management at the Management Centre, University of Leicester.

Martin Parker is Reader in Social and Organizational Theory at the University of Keele.

Geoff Lightfoot is Lecturer in Accounting at the University of Keele.

Routledge Studies in Human Resource Development
Edited by Monica Lee
Lancaster University

HRD theory is changing rapidly. Recent advances in theory and practice, in how we conceive of organizations and of the world of knowledge, have led to the need to reinterpret the field. This series aims to reflect and foster the development of HRD as an emergent discipline.

Encompassing a range of different international, organizational, methodological and theoretical perspectives, the series promotes theoretical controversy and reflective practice.

1 Policy Matters
Flexible learning and organizational change
Edited by Viktor Jakupec and Robin Usher

2 Science Fiction and Organization
Edited by Warren Smith, Matthew Higgins, Martin Parker and Geoff Lightfoot

Also available from Routledge:

Action Research in Organisations
Jean McNiff, accompanied by Jack Whitehead

Understanding Human Resource Development
Edited by Jim Stewart, Jim McGoldrick, and Sandra Watson

HD
31
S3428
2001

Science Fiction and Organization

**Edited by Warren Smith,
Matthew Higgins, Martin Parker
and Geoff Lightfoot**

London and New York

First published 2001
by Routledge
11 New Fetter Lane, London EC4P 4EE

Simultaneously published in the USA and Canada
by Routledge
29 West 35th Street, New York, NY 10001

Routledge is an imprint of the Taylor & Francis Group

© 2001 Edited by Warren Smith, Matthew Higgins, Martin Parker
and Geoff Lightfoot

Typeset in Baskerville by RefineCatch Limited, Bungay, Suffolk
Printed and bound in Great Britain by St Edmundsbury Press,
Bury St Edmunds, Suffolk

All rights reserved. No part of this book may be reprinted or
reproduced or utilized in any form or by any electronic,
mechanical, or other means, now known or hereafter
invented, including photocopying and recording, or in any
information storage or retrieval system, without permission in
writing from the publishers.

British Library Cataloguing in Publication Data
A catalogue record for this book is available from the British Library

Library of Congress Cataloging in Publication Data
Science fiction and organization / edited by Warren Smith . . . [*et al.*.]
      p.   cm.
   Includes bibliographical references and index.
   1. Organization.   2. Science fiction.   I. Smith, Warren, 1967–
HD31 .S3428   2001
302.3′5 – dc21   2001019498

ISBN 0–415–21588–9

Contents

* For the world is hollow and I have touched the sky, etc. are titles of episodes of *Star Trek*
   – The Original Series, 1966–9

Notes on contributors

David Boje, Professor of Management at New Mexico State University, has published numerous articles in *Administrative Science Quarterly*, *Academy of Management Journal*, *Management Communication Quarterly* and other journals. He edits the *Journal of Organizational Change Management* and is founding editor of *Tamara: The Journal of Critical Postmodern Organization Science*. He serves on the editorial board of *Academy of Management Review*, *Management Digest*, *Organization*, *Journal of Management Inquiry*, *Management*, *Organization Studies*, *EJ-ROT* and *Emergence and Management Communication Quarterly*. Recent books include *Narrative Research Methods for Communication Studies* (London: Sage, 2000) and *Spectacles and Festivals* (Hampton Press, CA, 2001). Vita is at http://cbae.nmsu.edu/mgt/dir/faculty/vita/boje/.

Daniel F. Coleman (Ph.D., State University of New York at Buffalo) is a Professor and Dean at the Faculty of Administration, University of New Brunswick, Canada. His current research interests are the causes and consequences of organizational commitment, employees' responses to privatization and leadership. He teaches courses in Organizational Behavior, Organization Design, Motivation and Leadership.

Martin Corbett is Senior Lecturer in organizational behaviour and industrial relations at the University of Warwick Business School. His interest in researching, understanding (and perhaps transcending) the dualism of the social/organic and technical/mechanical has led to a number of papers and books over the past fifteen years. Currently Book Review Editor of the journal *Organization*, Martin dreams of becoming cyborg but has yet to own a reliable motor vehicle or demonstrate even rudimentary mastery of the modern personal computer.

Christian De Cock is a Lecturer at the School of Business and Economics, University of Exeter. He received his first degree from the University of Antwerp (lic. T.E.W.) and M.Sc. and Ph.D. degrees from the Manchester Business School, University of Manchester. Prior to joining Exeter University he worked as a research fellow at Manchester Business School and as a lecturer at the University of London. Christian is Associate Editor of the journal

Creativity and Innovation Management. His research has appeared in such journals as *Asia Pacific Business Review, Interfaces, International Journal of Organizational Analysis, Organization Studies, Journal of Management Studies,* and *Journal of Management Inquiry.* He has also written several book chapters and teaching cases. Christian conducts research on organizational change, organizational creativity and organizational storytelling.

Maria Aline Ferreira has a first degree from the University of Oporto and a Ph.D. from the University of London (Birkbeck College). Since 1987 she has worked at the University of Aveiro, where she is now an Associate Professor. Recent publications include 'The Foreigner Within: Teaching The Rainbow with the Help of Cixous, Kristeva and Irigaray', 'Approaches to Teaching D.H. Lawrence', 'Myth and Anti-Myth in Angela Carter's *The Passion of New Eve*' in the *Journal of the Fantastic in the Arts,* 'D.H. Lawrence and Hélène Cixous: Unexpected Contiguities' in *Études Lawrenciennes* and 'Another Jouissance: Secular and Mystical Love in Kate Chopin's "Two Portraits"', *Literature and Psychology.*

David A. Fitchett is currently preparing for submission of his Ph.D. thesis on the fiction of J.G. Ballard at Brunel University. His primary areas of interest include apocalyptic science fiction and utopian island spaces in British literature of the twentieth century.

James A. Fitchett was awarded his Ph.D. from the University of Stirling in 1998. His research draws on social theory to consider issues including experiential consumption and the culture industry. He has published work on illicit recreational drug consumption, the relationship between consumption and environmentalism and consumer citizenry. He currently holds a lectureship in marketing and consumer research at the University of Exeter, UK.

Christopher Haley is currently at the Department of History and Philosophy of Science in Cambridge, where he is engaged in doctoral research concerning nineteenth-century æther physics. Besides this, one academic interest is the philosophy of physics – specifically, the attempts to reconcile quantum mechanics with special relativity. A further interest is the public understanding of science, and to this end he may be found working in the Whipple Museum of the History of Science on occasion. He enjoys the fiction of Iain M. Banks.

Matthew Higgins is a Lecturer in Management in the Management Centre at the University of Leicester. His Ph.D. at Keele University explores issues of morality and engagements with marketing. Current research interests include critiques of marketing and cultural movements, ethics and marketing in the not-for-profit sector.

Donncha Kavanagh is Lecturer in Management in University College, Cork. His research interests include the pre-modern, the history of management thought, actor-network theory and the sociology of technology.

Kieran Keohane Ph.D. (York, Canada, 1993), Statutory Lecturer in Sociology, National University of Ireland, Cork, is the author of *Symptoms of Canada* (Toronto: University of Toronto Press, 1998).

Carmen Kuhling Ph.D. (York, Canada, 1998), Lecturer in Sociology and Womens' Studies, Department of Government and Society, University of Limerick, is the author of *The New Age Ethic and the Spirit of Postmodernism* (Creskill, N.J.: Hampton Press, forthcoming). She is interested in the philosophy of the social sciences, postmodern theory, the relationship between creativity and subversion, and the relationship between popular culture and social transformation.

Chris Land is an ESRC-funded research student at Warwick Business School. As part of his Ph.D., he is currently researching post-structural perspectives on the relationship between organization and information technology. This work brings together interests in actor-network theory, cyborg studies, popular culture and Deleuze and Guattari. Other significant research interests include information warfare, time, cybernetics, William Burroughs and South Park.

Geoff Lightfoot is Lecturer in MIS and Accounting at Keele University. His current research interests include the use of Darwinist metaphors in management and accounting literature and futures trading (both on capital markets and SF collectors' fairs). Sadly, however, the weight of his own collection of SF books, videos and collectibles recently caused his house to overbalance. Although this does make getting in and out rather difficult, the postman is happier as he no longer has to make regular deliveries from Amazon.

David McHugh is a Senior Lecturer in Organizational Behaviour in the Department of Management at the University of Central Lancashire. He is a keen member of the International Brotherhood of Tooth Fairies and a staunch proponent of lecturer-centred teaching. He has an abiding interest in the issues of subjectivity and workplace identity but would rather read SF than organization theory. He is the co-author of a well-regarded critical organization studies text and very little else. He lives near Liverpool, is married to Chris Corcoran and has two daughters named Roia and Anya. Between them they have responsibility for a number of rats, tropical fish and a parrot called Goodison. Dave is an avid collector of SF books for which he gets no end of domestic gyp and will read or watch any old crap that can be remotely regarded as SF. He is a passable singer but an atrocious guitarist and would like to hear from anyone who has solid empirical evidence of the media conspiracy against Everton Football Club.

John Monin is Associate Professor and Head of the Department of Management and International Business at the Auckland campus of Massey University, New Zealand. He read humanities subjects for his initial degrees, majoring in Latin, and his doctoral studies were in information systems. He has contributed chapters in books on a range on topics including information management, network analysis and philanthropy. He has co-authored books on project management and business and society, but his abiding interest is that of the language and discourse of management.

Nanette Monin lectures in Massey University's Department of Management and International Business, Auckland, New Zealand, where she teaches papers on Business and Society and Corporate Citizenship. Her research interests are centred around management rhetoric and narratology and she is currently engaged in a deconstruction of foundational management theory. She holds degrees in English literature and in management, has published work on business ethics and metaphor theory, and is the editor of *Narratives of Business and Society: Differing New Zealand Voices* (Auckland: Longmans, 1999).

Martin Parker is Reader in Social and Organizational Theory at the University of Keele, and used to work in the sociology department at Staffordshire University. He mostly writes about culture and organization. His most recent books are *Ethics and Organization* (edited, London: Sage, 1998), *The New Higher Education* (edited with David Jary, Stoke-on-Trent: Staffordshire University Press, 1998) and *Organizational Culture and Identity* (London: Sage, 2000).

Erik Piñeiro was born in Madrid in 1970 and carried out his undergraduate studies at the School of Telecomunication Engineering in Madrid, the Royal Institute of Technology in Stockholm and TELECOM Paris. He still owns 33% of the company he helped to build in Madrid between 1995 and 1998. In May 1998 he was offered a Ph.D. studentship post at the Royal Institute of Technology in the Department of Industrial Management and Organization, led by Professor Claes Gustafsson. His thesis is currently evolving around the concept of The Aesthetics of Instrumental Action (basically why Redondo's move in the semi-final in Old Trafford is beautiful). He was led astray by friends and ended up publishing an article in the Swedish journal *Kommunal Ekonomi och Politik* (September 1999). His alter-ego, Rike Reipino, has been known to carry out time-travelling experiments with moderate success.

Warren Smith works at the Management Centre, University of Leicester (previously Leicester University). He wishes to thank Martin Parker for suggesting a coda for his article. All articles should have one.

James M. Tolliver (Ph.D., Ohio State University) is a Professor of Management at the Faculty of Administration, University of New Brunswick, Canada. He teaches Organizational Behaviour and Leadership and has received the University's award for outstanding teaching. He has more than a passing interest in science fiction.

Introduction

More amazing tales

Matthew Higgins

'The seeds of doom'

We can all find cultural artefacts that depict a particular age, things that anchor a stage in our growing up. These artefacts depend upon personal or social influences and the generation in which you were born. As a child of the seventies, one of the things that offered pleasure was the escapism found in science fiction (SF). SF offered the possibility of temporarily standing outside of this world, looking up to the stars and imagining anywhere but the here and now. The stories created a space within which a vision could be inserted. Series such as *Star Trek*, *Flash Gordon*, *Blake's 7*, *Dr. Who*, and comics such as the *Eagle* (handed down) offered a projection of a future world that appeared both eerily alien and securely familiar. In later life you realize that this juxtaposition was achieved through accentuating and generating a dialogue with existing social conditions, but at the time . . .

It was the 50th birthday celebrations for Dan Dare, he of the boy's action comic *Eagle* (2000), Dan Dare, the all-British hero, seems to epitomize a period that could place faith in tomorrow. Those initial stories in April 1950 offered the possibility of 'seeing' the future, to be able to imagine strange tomorrows. These were worlds of intergalactic warfare, God-fearing heroes and rotund jovial sidekicks. Whilst appreciating the post-war jingoism within Dan Dare, we seem to be living in very different times, a time when the œuvre of science fiction is all-pervasive but yet we find difficulty in imagining a tomorrow divorced from today. Future projections of time seem unable to escape the imagination of the perpetual present and a strong dose of millennial pessimism. Divisions between future, past, present, and science fiction and science fact appear susceptible to slippage. Through evocation of science fiction themes, the future is already present. Biospheres, once tended light years away by Freeman Lowell in *Silent Running* (1971), can now be seen in the £79m Eden Project at St Austell, Cornwall.[1] These vast domed greenhouses, which resemble the lunar cities depicted in science fiction, are now part and parcel of the Cornish environment. The gaffe over the inclusion of genetically modified seed in oil-seed rape has produced a story-line and paranoid rhetoric not dissimilar to that found in *The X Files*. The thrusting future found in Dan Dare may no longer hold resonance with contemporary society, but SF retains a strong influence upon how we engage with the present and anticipate the day after tomorrow. The recent box office success of films such as *X-Men* (2000), *Lost in Space* (1998) and *The Matrix* (1999) is testament to the fact that SF, rather than being a marginal figure, is part and parcel of the modern lived environment. In short, within and through SF we can find things to say about contemporary society.

In light of this it is hardly surprising that some relatively enterprising academics should seek to flow with this *Zeitgeist*, to explore management through the tool of science fiction. Mixing the familiarity and entertainment value of science fiction with the 'scholarly' popularity of management is surely a crowd-pleasing recipe? The predictable debate will start revolving, 'innovative study' or 'dumbing down'? Some academics may find self-comfort by accusing us of 'cashing in and selling out', pandering to juvenile obsessions, but obsessions with rather valuable PR worth. Appearances in the *Guardian* newspaper[2] may carry with them accusations of rampant careerism within the ivory towers of academia and I accept that defence against such accusations is difficult. I am guilty as charged unless I rely upon some mutual faith in the value of what science fiction can offer. However at the back of my mind there is always the nagging thought. Where else are you able to find employment that allows you to get away with talking about your personal hobby/interest within the context of your area of study? We as editors are after all four fully-grown *men*, gainfully employed, for the time being, in fairly respectable universities. Are we admitting a curious instrumental dilettantism? Or are we hiding our light under a bushel?

Any claim that I may want to make for science fiction's ability to offer some perspective on management must stumble over the conventional low culture tag that SF drags with it. Despite the projections of science fiction within the present, the consumption of SF remains conveniently presented as an escape from the mundanity of everyday life. Such portrayals reinforce a popular image of science fiction: pulp fiction, mass-produced trash with lurid covers. However, despite this tag, the value of studying science fiction has not been lost even within commercial organizations that utilize different criteria for assessment of value. In the late 1970s Sperry Univac, a large IT company, sponsored a series of seminars exploring the potential social consequences of contemporary science fiction with a view to enhancing their new product development (Malik 1980). Indeed the European Space Agency is studying science fiction for ideas and technologies that could be used in future missions.[3]

Even within academia what we are doing is not particularly new. For over two decades the hard and social sciences have seen science fiction as a valuable means of expression and comprehension. The physical sciences have seen science fiction as a source of ideas, even lawyers have utilized the keywords of science fiction to spice up their academic output (see Corcos *et al.*. 1999, Effross 1997). However, it is perhaps in the arena of sociology, cultural and media studies that the initiative has been seized. Laz (1996), Greenberg *et al.* (1975) and Ofshe (1977) have written about or provided collections of science fiction stories for sociology students. These are designed to sharpen social awareness via comprehension and discussion exercises. They claim that science fiction is a useful tool in the sociology of teaching, due to its ability to make strange whilst encouraging critical and reflexive accounts.

Science fiction: so what?

So the oddity of this collection is not the appearance of science fiction within an academic context, but rather that science fiction is being discussed within a field of study, namely management and organization, that revels in performativity. This produces an entertaining scenario where 'the intellectual dandyism of cultural studies collides with the grey functionality of management science' (Parker *et al.* 1999: 579). Despite the popular press stories of City bankers dressing as Spock (amongst other scandalous activities) at weekend retreats, and unlike many other forms of social science, organization and management studies do not seem to have fully appreciated the rich resource that science fiction would appear to offer.[4]

So have we found a niche that is all ready for exploitation? Well partly yes, but I do not want to be perceived to be blazing a trail on some new frontier. This is far from our intention. Management and organization have enjoyed their fair share of one-night stands, fads and fancies, from micro marketing to knowledge management. Instead of introducing this year's debutante we want to make apparent what is already present, to highlight existing tendencies and themes within the study of organization and management. To develop this point further, some explanation is necessary on the evolution of this science fiction and organization 'project'.

The origins of this particular edited collection can be traced back to the Management Department at Keele University around 1996–7 where all four editors worked. The idea of *doing something* on science fiction and management grew from the bantering that was produced by our shared interest in science fiction. We decided to see what we could do with this interest and we speculatively approached publishers. Somehow we managed to convince the editors of the journal *Organization* to take us seriously, wangling the opportunity to edit a special edition of the journal on science fiction and organization. A call for papers was released; the response to which was pretty surprising. We received nearly thirty submissions, including three full-blown fictions. From this list we published six papers in a special edition of *Organization* (Vol. 6, No. 4, 1999) with the hope that we could find a further publisher who was willing to publish an edited book collection. That publisher proved to be Routledge who initially saw great potential in this project. With such enthusiasm we decided to probe further into the academic psyche to see how many more anorak wearers we could 'out'. To this end we arranged a conference imaginatively titled 'Science Fiction & Organization' for which the call for papers read:

> Although popular accounts of the actions of organizations frequently call upon tropes developed within science fiction, the marginal (and seemingly non-academic) nature of science fiction has meant that it has been largely ignored in the serious business of writing organizational theory. Nevertheless

science fiction can be seen as a diagnosis of the present and a vision of possible futures. As such it provides a contemporary resource with which to interrogate both contemporary organizing processes and organizations as institutions. This international collection aims to explore how science fiction can enrich studies of organizations by bringing together a number of papers by different authors based around the theme of organizations and science fiction. The papers assembled in the book will draw upon perspectives from across the arts and social sciences and will encompass innovatory approaches to both organizational theory and of the reading (and writing) of science fiction.

Once again the response to the call for papers was reassuring. Despite the occasional rant denouncing the futility of SF in the serious business of management, the messages of support and the number of confirmed conference attendees ensured the conference was viable.

Our original call for papers for the special issue of the journal had ensured that we were largely able to avoid face-to-face contact with the authors. Any idiosyncrasy or eccentricity on the side of either party could mostly be hidden behind the typed page or electronic communication. This safety was not afforded in the conference environment. This required total submersion into the messiness of physical human interaction. Within popular urban mythology science fiction conventions and gatherings are notorious meeting places for obsessives and anoraks; what Tulloch and Jenkins (1995: vii) call 'pimple faced nerds in rubber Vulcan ears or wrapped in multifaceted scarves, overweight women clutching collectibles and dolls'. However, rather than the Vulcan-eared delegates, we were faced with an international audience who actually wanted to raise and discuss issues surrounding SF and organization with a relatively straight face. Could it possibly be that other people shared a belief in the scholarly value of submerging science fiction within management?

The hidden agenda

Within the initial introduction of the Special Issue of *Organization* we spelled out the terms of our engagement with science fiction and organization. For those readers who are not acquainted with the arguments it is worthwhile covering that ground again. We were keen from the beginning to try to avoid simply viewing science fiction as another resource from which management can survey and plunder. Applied science fiction, the type occasionally found in airport bookshops for the 'quirky and creative manager' does not really appeal to us. It lacks a fundamental appreciation of the potentiality science fiction possesses as an analytical tool. Our project is concerned not with what science fiction can do for management but rather what science fiction will do to studies of management.

One way of approaching science fiction is to view SF as morality tales, warning of possible futures, playing through the means necessary for them to be avoided or rectified. These reflectionist accounts of science fiction attempt to 'read' science fiction for a social purpose. The assumption is that science fiction produces evidence that can be read as critiques of contemporary society and its possible future directions. Isaac Asimov (1971: 285), for example, argues that science fiction offers a mode of thought to question and imagine change, 'We've got to think about the future now. For the first time in history, the future cannot be left to take care of itself; it must be thought about.' His work could be seen as a form of 'social science fiction', a means to speculate, extrapolate and moralize over the effects of technological, political and sociological change. Such 'purposeful' science fiction is therefore a forum where alternative realities are presented which reflects the social trends and preoccupations of the time.

Organizations and ways of organizing feature prominently in science fiction. Films such as *Rollerball* (1975) and *1984* (1984) moralize over the role and prospect of the human within organizations. The darker side of commerce and government found in the industrial-military complex are subjected to interrogation in films such as *X Files* (1998), *Aliens* (1986) and *Robocop* (1987). *The Running Man* (1987), *Videodrome* (1983) and *eXistenZ* (1999) focus upon the media conglomerates and their grip on public perceptions of reality. The response or solution to the moral danger changes according to the contemporary social concern at the time of writing. When once science and rational government offered the hope of a peaceful future, now it is the lone individual who is able to summon a vision of revised humanism. In films such as *The Matrix* (1999), human value is reduced to its biological entity. Science and technology has enabled the development of artificial intelligence (AI). AIs shackle the human body into pods, adopting intensive human farming techniques to generate energy. The hero Thomas A. 'Neo' Anderson must seek spiritual enlightenment to be the 'one', the saviour of a lost human consciousness. Here SF offers warnings, explanations and solutions to contemporary social concerns.

However, whilst we may provide readings of science fiction and reflect these back on our understandings of organizations, this only goes so far. Reflectionist accounts, whilst providing resources for critical theorists within organizational studies, maintain the disciplinary comfort boundary between the study of organization and the production of science fiction. Instead we sought to unsettle this comfortable boundary, to begin to appreciate the fluidity within and between science fiction and organization, a 'neo-disciplinarity' (Parker *et al.* 1999: 583). SF has always been a key constituent of organizational studies, but usually dressed up in respectable literary terms. Thus the grounded fictions presented in the future worlds forecast by Drucker, Bell, Handy and Toffler are little more than fantastic fiction, nicely packaged for managers and management academics.

Obviously such an argument rests on notions of legitimacy credited to forms of knowledge, in particular the primacy of scientific modes of knowing within Organizational Science. This is not to suggest that adopting scientific method in the study of organizations is itself misguided. It is the simple appreciation that the scientific method used in the study of organizations is not the only form of knowledge that can be utilized. The work of Paul Feyerabend and his book *Against Method* (1993) seems highly pertinent here due to his criticism of restrictions placed upon forms of knowing. Feyerabend warns that claims for truth based only upon epistemological criteria are misleading because they fail to appreciate the socio-historical specificity of the claims. Scientific rationalism is but one means to generate knowledge and according to Feyerabend not particularly the best way. This is not to deny that scientists discover novel facts; however it requires claims of 'progress' and 'development' to be tempered and appreciated within a wider socio-historical context. This 'anarchistic theory of knowledge' necessitates a realization of the context-riddled specificity of all claims. With such an acknowledgement, spaces open up within and between disciplines, creativity provokes a pushing and blurring of disciplinary boundaries. It is within this mood of wanting to encourage a plurality of approaches within the study of organizations and management that this present collection should be seen.

'The greatest show in the galaxy'

The thirteen stories before you were chosen because they all in different ways seek to grapple with the potentialities and views that science fiction offers the reader of organization and management studies. The thirteen chapters within the book are ordered into four parts, each with its own approach to discussing organization through the language, imagery and themes of science fiction. In Part 1, 'For the world is hollow and I have touched the sky' some contextual footwork is undertaken. The domain and themes of science fiction are discussed. Two papers seek in different ways to offer prospective routes through which we can begin to engage management with science fiction. A fan of literary science fiction, David McHugh, opens this section with a partisan appreciation of SF with ' "Give me your mirrorshades": science fiction "methodology" meets the social and organizational sciences'. Marching the reader through the definitions, domains and 'history' of science fiction, McHugh offers his perspective on the pleasures, benefits and insights that a devotion to science fiction offers the social science academic. McHugh suggests that adopting a reflectionist approach to science fiction offers only a partial, indeed negligible, contribution to our understanding of organization or management. The strength of science fiction lies not so much in the message that it carries, but instead upon its distinctive method. It is upon the nature of this SF method that McHugh focuses the majority of the chapter. Contrasting it to the method found in other literary forms, McHugh argues that SF encourages an openness of thought, provoking a confrontation of issues and raises the potentiality and attraction of subversion and change. The chapter concludes with caution over the motive and manner with which organizational theorists are embracing SF.

Chapter 2, 'Science fiction and the making of the laser' by Christopher Haley, highlights the fluidity between science fiction and science fact, a point briefly raised earlier in this introduction. Using Ronald Reagan's 'Strategic Defence Initiative' (SDI) as a starting point Haley begins to unravel the manner in which SF offered a presentational focus and helped shape the development of what became dubbed the 'Star Wars project'. Haley argues that the development of

SDI owes greatly to the fictional 'death ray projector' which featured in the 1940 film *Murder in the Air*, starring Ronald Reagan. Here we can witness Feyerabend's exposure of the rational hypothetical deductive model and cultural specificity as fantasy drives the development of military hardware.

Viewing science fiction as a refuge or platform from which writers can espouse radical ideas or make scathing commentary on the contemporary society has a particular resonance. Our second part, 'Mirror, Mirror' seeks to interrogate texts that provide reflections on our lived experience of the social world. *Metropolis*, alongside Charlie Chaplin's *Modern Times* is frequently employed as a cultural resource through which the inequalities of the class system and bureaucratic organizational structures can be criticized. In 'Metropolis, Maslow and the Axis Mundi' Jim Tolliver and Dan Coleman ask us to consider *Metropolis* as a mythical film, which is anchored within a root metaphor. They believe that through such reanalysis we can subsequently reappraise our understanding of organizational structure.

Whilst Tolliver and Coleman may believe that metaphor has effects within discourse, they possibly did not envisage the nature of the repercussions that can be found in the second morality tale. 'The rape of the machine metaphor' by Nanette Monin and John Monin, argues that as virtual reality plays an increasing part within real life we need to be aware of potential convergence and the threat of alienation. Through the use of Chad Taylor's cyberpunk tale 'The man who wasn't feeling himself', Monin and Monin argue that a metaphor may initiate 'pathological perceptions' which in turn may encourage real life actions. It is within this context of metaphor as social challenge that Monin and Monin spin their morality tale.

Science fiction is traditionally associated with boys' bedrooms and sweaty anoraks. Taylor's tale of the rape of a woman by a computer epitomizes this masculine bent of the presentation of technology within SF. However, following Haraway's interjection and the theoretical fertility of the cyborg, science fiction has become an arena for writers interested in gender. In 'Organizing men out in Joanna Russ's *The Female Man* and Fay Weldon's *The Cloning of Joanna May*', Maria Ferreira offers a feminist critique of existing patriarchal modes of organizational ordering through readings of the two influential stories. Using the contemporary corporate concern with the environment and social well-being as background, Ferreira argues that Weldon and Russ offer us both a critique of the existing male order and a manifesto for change.

Whilst Ferreira finds hope in SF, the fourth morality tale within this episode, 'Drowned giants: science fiction and consumption utopias' by James Fitchett and David Fitchett, details the ambivalent relationship between science fiction and consumer society. From the Golden Age of science fiction and its representations of a futuristic society filled with stainless steel dreams, to environmental catastrophe, science fiction, according to Fitchett and Fitchett, offers contradictory readings of the pleasures of consumption. Through a reading of Ballard's short story 'Drowned giant', Fitchett and Fitchett comment upon the allegorical message about the human condition and consumer society. They bemoan the consequences of the colonization of the future and our fleeting engagement and long-term disenchantment with the spectacular.

In 'Spectacle and inter-spectacle in *The Matrix* and organization theory', David Boje asks whether we could be missing something. Could the nightmare scenarios of nanotechnology, biotech genetic re-engineering, virtual technology and the expansion of information technology, forewarned in popular science fiction films, be shaping our future? Could a more critical reading of organizational theory injected with an appreciation of science fiction encourage us to face up to living in an inter-spectacular society? Extending Debord's Society of the Spectacle, Boje seeks to offer insight into the areas within Plato's cave usually covered by shadow.

Part II sought to elicit lessons from science fiction; Part III, 'Is there in truth no beauty?' utilizes science fiction to explore tensions and lesions within social and organizational theory. 'Reading *Star Trek*: imagining, theorizing and reflecting on organizational discourse and practice' by Donncha Kavanagh, Kieran Keohane and Carmen Kuhling, introduces this part with an examination of the parallels and intersections between *Star Trek* and contemporary management discourse. Kavanagh *et al.* argue that the four series represent an 'ideal type' of the dominant organizational ethos of their time; thus seeing SF as 'data' allows us to make sense of theory and practice and imagine alternatives. In 'From the Borgias to the Borg (and back again): rethinking organizational futures' Chris Land and Martin Corbett continue the *Star Trek* theme with an interrogation of the liberal humanist principles that they claim lie behind organizational studies. Utilizing a reading of the Borgias and *Star Trek*'s Borg in order to ground interpretations of humanism, they argue that current fads in organization theory (OT) such as knowledge management reveal the limitations of thinking through the human/technological dualism, hence they question the suitability and sustainability of humanism in a technologically driven age.

Trying to understand how to conceptualize the lived experience within OT is a theme developed further in Christian De Cock's 'Of Philip K. Dick, reflexivity and shifting realities: organizing (writing) in our post-industrial society'. De Cock poses a fundamental question, one that is often passed over by contemporary scholars of organizations. Why, when we proclaim to be living in new times and express concern over our sense of unease about our claims on the nature of 'reality', do we seek to speak with such lucidity and coherency? Why do we continue to believe in the singularity of authorial structure? De Cock takes us into the messiness of complexity and tenuous realities via an evolving personal obsession with Philip K. Dick and his writings.

A sense of living in changed times, a sense of loss, a questioning of an assumed stable identity are themes explored by Warren Smith in his paper ' "I am a man, and nothing human is alien to me": alienation and freakishness'. Using the theme of the body and notions of the 'other' Smith seeks to analyse how changing conceptions of alienation depicted through contemporary science fiction can find resonance with the freak show. The freakish alien, Smith suggests, is no longer a distant creature from which we recoil in horror. We must labour at making sense of its presence because the alien moves within us.

The final part, 'The gamesters of Triskelion' tries to present some order to the questions that arise throughout this collection. However rather than wrapping up the proceedings in a comfortable package, Martin Parker's chapter, '"Repent Harlequin!" said the Ticktockman: digesting science fiction' seeks to revolt against this very possibility. Searching to find a space within which to protect the sanctity of triviality from the encroachment of performativity, Parker invokes Bataille and Baudrillard and the metaphor of digestion. The fear of the *coloniza*-tion of SF by management and organization studies, rendering SF useful, encour-ages within Parker the desire to make SF indigestible or at the very least to rid it of nutritional value.

And finally, a real fiction. Erik Piñeiro's cautionary tale, 'Cyberpunk manage-ment', takes us almost two decades into the future. The Science Fiction and Organization project has colonized SF, a new breed of capitalism has taken over in the virtual frontier, opening up the possibilities for a select few initiated into Firmnet, a mysterious, fictional group of elite managers. Successful author, Bridgitte Yan Lopez has completed her latest virtualOpus 'Winning the race', in which she offers advice for the prospective supermanager who wants to join the elite. Piñeiro introduces the story with a response from 'The art of management' to a review on Lopez's vOpus by a lowly Ph.D. student, Rike Reipino. Rike dares to question Lopez's interpretation of the 'classics' and society's unquestioned preference for style over substance.

'The space pirates'

The writing of the introduction is traditionally the last thing to get considered. It gets written shortly after the editors and contributors have become tired of the whole project. Accordingly it has similarities to the final lunge of the long-distance swimmer, the consequences and pace of the race having been decided some time back and the pre-race butterflies and excitement no longer figuring. The book is now almost complete and the question still begging is why did we start this all off?

There is something very 'lad-ish' about putting together an edited collection that features science fiction. It is not so much that science fiction is taboo. But bringing SF into the office from the darker realms of personal taste is for some reason frowned upon. Colleagues and friends register a polite smile when you inform them of your current work. You can see them wondering whether this professional interest in science fiction is merely the latest manifestation of a mid-life crisis, a longing for the romanticized safety of the juvenile bedroom. 'Now, tell me about your mother', they think. Heads of Departments wonder about the direction of future research output, praying that this is merely a temporary side-line to be indulged. Some believe that you are desperately seeking a means to be young and trendy. Others feel uncomfortable in the presence of a proud 'geek'.

Why couldn't we be happy simply maintaining a friendly conversation about SF in Martin 'Furry Bundle' Parker's office? Couldn't we have performed a simi-lar service to organization science through a study of horror flicks, *Carry On* movies, the songs of Hoagy Carmichael . . . 'All thought is immoral. Its very essence is destruction. If you think of anything, you kill it. Nothing survives being thought of' (Lord Illingworth in Wilde 1990: 464). Is it maybe time to return to the 'seriousness' of management and organizational studies and leave our foibles where they can be thoughtlessly cherished? See what you think.

Acknowledgments

We would like to express our thanks to our benevolent benefactor, Professor Peter Jackson from the University of Leicester, who provided the encouragement, resources and financial support to ensure that the conference and this book were more than pipe dreams. Darth 'Alf' Rehn at the Royal Institute of Technology in Stockholm, Sweden, was instrumental in designing and hosting the Science Fiction & Organization Web Page. We would finally like to thank all of the contributors to this edited collection and to those who submitted work . . .

Notes

1 Wednesday, 24 May 2000, 'Botanic garden proves a hit', www.news.bbc.co.uk
2 John Grace, 'Aliens ate my MBA', *Guardian Education Supplement*, 9 May 2000.
3 Mark Ward, 'Science fiction powers space research', BBC News Online, Thursday, 11 May 2000, 09:24.
4 Corbett (1995) and Parker (1998) provide rare examples of work that seeks to engage with science fiction themes and motifs.

References

Asimov, I. (1971) 'Social science fiction', in D. Allen (ed.) *Science Fiction: The Future*, New York: Harcourt Brace Jovanovich, pp. 263–91.

Corbett, J.M. (1995) 'Celluloid projections – images of technology and organizational futures in contemporary science-fiction', *Organization*, 1995, Vol. 2, Nos 3–4, pp. 467–88.

Corcos, C., Corcos, I. and Stockhoff, B. (1999) 'Double-take: a second look at cloning, science fiction and law', *Louisiana Law Review*, Vol. 59, No. 4, pp. 1041–99.

Effross, W.A. (1997) 'High-tech heroes, virtual villains, and jacked-in justice: visions of law and lawyers in cyberpunk science fiction', *Buffalo Law Review*, Vol. 45, No. 3, pp. 931–74.

Feyerabend, K. (1993) *Against Method*, London: Verso.

Greenberg, M.H., Mislead, J.W., Oleander, J.D. and Warwick, P. (1975) *Social Problems Through Science Fiction*, London: St Martins Press.

Laz, C. (1996) 'Science fiction and introductory sociology: the handmaid in the classroom', *Teaching Sociology*, Vol. 24, No. 1, pp. 54–63.

Malik, R. (1980) *Future Imperfect: Science Fact and Science Fiction*, London: Francis Pinter.

Ofshe, R. (1977) 'Introduction', in R. Ofshe (ed.) *The Sociology of the Possible*, 2nd edition, New Jersey: Prentice Hall.

Parker, M. (1998) 'Judgement day: cyberorganization, humanism and postmodern ethics', *Organization*, Vol. 5, No. 4, pp. 503–18

Parker, M., Higgins, M., Lightfoot, G. and Smith, W. (1999) 'Amazing stories: organization studies as science fiction', *Organization*, Vol. 6, No. 4, pp. 579–90.

Tulloch, J. and Jenkins, H. (1995) *Science Fiction Audiences: Watching Doctor Who and Star Trek*, London: Routledge.

Wilde, O. (1990) 'A woman of no importance', in O. Wilde (1990) *Complete Works of Oscar Wilde*, London: Collins, pp. 431–82.

Part I

For the world is hollow and I have touched the sky

1 'Give me your mirrorshades'

Science fiction 'methodology' meets the social and organizational sciences

David McHugh

The faster you travel the more forward visibility you need.

(Sutcliffe, 1996)

Introduction

Although SF has been characterized by Clute and Nichols (1993) as a genre mainly determined by publishers, this chapter deals with SF as a paraliterature (see below) that embodies an *SF methodology* which James (1994) argues mainstream authors often fail to handle adequately. This notion of an SF methodology is founded in the very beginnings of science fiction and will be central to any possible articulation of SF and the field of organization. In support of such projects, this chapter aims to examine the reciprocal conceptualizations that have been produced by SF and the social sciences and in particular organization and management theory. One of the editors of this volume said that this was in danger of becoming a 'fan's paper'; well it is and I am. I am a fan of SF and of organization theory and I think both can enrich and illuminate the world. Our job here is to explore the limits of how they might do this together.

Before looking at what the social and organizational sciences want from SF this chapter will explore the provenance, conceptions, attractions and domain of SF. First though, we need to ask whether there is a relationship between SF and social science at all? For myself the question is very simple, the relationship is in me and in the way in which both domains have informed my worldview. The synergistic influences on the directions my interests have taken are something I will try to document as we go along. I will later examine previous attempts to analytically link the two domains. These have not had any great success and have more often come from those with an interest in SF than social science. On a superficial level both are inclusive of science, though much SF contains little recognizable science and many (especially in the organization field) don't like the appellation social '*scientist*'. A more pertinent question is whether SF has a consistently different relationship to social science than does literature in general? My own experience here is germane in that for a number of years I ran a course in which students were encouraged to explore a literature of their choice, seeking metaphors, illustrations and insights into social and organization theory. The products ranged from managerial rationalizations as seen through Miller's *The Crucible* to a very funny piece on divisions of labour in the *Thomas the Tank Engine* books. A recent book by Brawer (1998) subtitled 'Insights on management from great literature' only approaches SF tangentially in briefly looking at efficiency experts through Twain's (1889) 'A Connecticut Yankee at King Arthur's Court'. Though I have no intention of trying to do it here, there is no doubt that we could take an organizational process such as leadership and find exemplars in SF stories for every facet of its study from group and task maintenance to managerial styles and social networks. The problem is that there is no consistent SF take on this and we could do the same with mainstream literature even in the use of extreme cases, Conrad's *Nostromo* and *Heart of Darkness* (and of course Coppola's *Apocalypse Now*) being examples that Clute and Nichols (1993, 260) argue have 'more than once served as a model for modern SF writers'. What SF can do is to draw on a greater range of resources and alternatives for its extrapolations than mainstream literature can muster. For example we might take the consideration of community consciousness, as in the repeated focus on the Borg in this volume. What the social and organizational sciences might do with such concepts is moot, but we can imagine how we might project the evolution of the Borg as an organization. What would they do if they won? When everyone and everything has been assimilated and their goals achieved, might they not turn their attention back on themselves? In examining their origins they might rediscover and perhaps recreate the very subjectivity and cultural differentiation the lack of which makes them one of the most alienating alien races found in media SciFi since the Daleks. The important point here is that lessons and illustrations can be found anywhere, but my argument is that the *method* implicit in SF provides us with lessons that can move us beyond reflexive analysis. Finally, as a counterpoint to the theme of SF methodology I will raise the notion of whether it is really SF *style* which is behind the current interest in SF in the organization/critical management field.

SF – provenance and conceptions

Historically, both social science and SF go back as far as the particular commentators you care to credit. In general, social science as a term tends to be traced back to the 1830s with Comte and Spencer as the first notables. SF as a term goes back to 1851 (Wilson in James, 1994, 7–8) though it was not in common use until the 1920s. Those such as Aldiss (1986) cite Mary Shelley as the first SF author with Frankenstein in 1818. I tend to favour Lambourne *et al.*.'s (1990, 3) identification of Johannes Kepler's 'Somnium' (1634) as the seminal SF story on the basis that it was the first to explicitly utilize what came to be seen as an SF methodology. Though linked to myth (specifically that of Icarus) 'Somnium' 'was intended to demonstrate and propagate Copernican notions' within an allegory which pits science against ignorance. This heuristic has been a familiar theme in SF ever since. H.G. Wells travelled the same territory, though with an explicitly social perspective, in *The Time Machine* (1895).

Regardless of provenance, conceptions of SF abound and range from the popular to the pompous. For example, what do most people associate with SF? (i.e. the 73 per cent that don't read it: SF is estimated at only 1 per cent of library borrowings and sells less than fantasy). The most repeated images are the lurid and highly sexist covers associated with the pulp magazines of the so-called 'golden age' of SF from the late 1930s to the mid-1940s. A lot of SF short stories also found their way onto the 'top shelf' because *Playboy* and their ilk paid more per word than genre publications. Lurid covers are certainly one of the things that attracted me to SF, but by the same token that is why I picked up the first paperback edition of Margaret Mead's *Sex and Temperament* (1950), which used grass skirts and naked breasts to exactly the same effect as any pulp publication.

The sensationalist style of both SF and social science were equally formative influences for me, the difference lying in that I tended to read the SF books all the way through. Beyond its sensational origins we have the general media conceptions of SF, which come mainly from what are termed 'SciFi' films and popular media programmes. This chapter does not address SciFi film in the main, one reason being that according to Barber (1995), 'Media SF tends to consist of old, stale ideas reworked from books that came out 30 years ago'. It appears to me that too much of the commentary and analysis of SF tends to focus on media SciFi and not on literary SF, which is where most of what I value in the genre resides.

Conceptions of literary SF often tend to the grandiose. For example J.G. Ballard writing twenty years ago (cited in Barrett, 1993, 44) claimed that, 'All literatures other than science fiction are doomed to irrelevance. None have the vocabulary of ideas and images to deal with the present, let al.one the future.' In a similar vein Scholes and Rabkin (1977, vii) assert that 'For the past century and a half, writers of what we have learned to call "science fiction" have been trying to create a modern conscience for the human race'.

Perhaps such claims lead the critics of SF to be as dismissive in their put-downs as the advocates are grandiose in their claims, from damning with faint praise as a 'mildly embarrassing form of popular culture' (Luckhurst, 1991, 360), to the old saw about SF being 'fairytales for adults'. More vitriolic characterizations see SF as a *subliterary genre* with an assumed homogeneity of audience, doubtless consisting of gangs of spotty males (gang as in *g.a.n.g.* – green anorak no girlfriend, Barber, 1995). The level of caviling might be likened to cross-paradigmatic debates in social science except that the vitriol is more likely due to the terminal smugness of both parties. A better analogy might be to the name-calling between the more dogmatic followers of 'serious' and 'popular' music. Whatever the case, the proponents of SF are seldom reluctant to present it as an exemplar of what is current in other areas. Csicsery-Ronay identifies cyberpunk as the 'apotheosis of postmodernism' (1991, 182) and McHale (in Luckhurst, 1991, 360) asserts that, 'Science Fiction ... is to postmodernism what the detective novel was to modernism'.

In all, getting close to SF is like looking at a fractal. It appears to be the simple reiteration of a theme but at the same time embodies increasing levels of complexity as your level of resolution (or analysis) increases:

> Science fiction is an anomalous genre because what is required to maintain its characteristic attitude to the world is not repetition ad infinitum of a series of stereotyped exemplars but a supply of images which gradually change so as to appear novel while never becoming truly strange.
>
> (Stableford, 1979, 36)

These broad conceptions of SF do not however help us to get any nearer to a relationship between SF and social science, though the elaboration of definitions over time is itself instructive. Indeed, the developmental stages of SF as a genre are viewed by commentators such as Collick (1997) as tantamount to paradigm shifts. Though there may be a case to be made for such a view it is probable that such basic shifts of worldview have generally been reflective of paradigmatic crises in the philosophical, scientific and cultural spheres rather than coming from within SF. The only paradigm shift SF can realistically lay claim to is the one it presumably went through itself when it became distinguishable from fantasy, when it discovered that it had a voice which was educative as well as entertaining. Though 'Somnium' got there first it was Gernsback's 1926 definition from the pulp era of SF as 'a charming romance intermingled with scientific fact and prophetic vision' (Collick, 1997, 3), which first consciously recognized that there might be method underlying the monsters and mayhem that characterized the SF of that era. This 'supplying instruction and knowledge' was of course linked directly to the development of a market for SF short stories from the popular science and electronics magazines of the day. At the same time though, Gernsback's rival John Campbell explicitly connected this view with scientific methodology and the production of images of future human societies. So from early on there has been a notion of SF as embodying some kind of methodology directly analogous to the 'thought experiments' that underwrote the real paradigm shift being fashioned by the physicists of the nascent atomic era.

Clute and Nichols (1993) contrast the optimism of the early ideas on SF to the 1960s New Wave appeal to literary status, though it was a more pessimistic approach dealing with issues more socio-psychological than technological. Reflective of post-war cultural shifts, probably better exemplified by rock'n'roll, and of existentialist ennui with science, in its anti-materialistic, anti-conventional and speculative stance, the New Wave rejected any rigorous methodology. But such rejection is itself a reflection of the 'critique as method' stance, which was the legacy of the Frankfurt School. From today's standpoint both suffered the same eventual fate, being overwhelmed (but not drowned) by the floodwaters of global capitalism. The outcome for SF at least was a more moral cultural tone which was the genesis of the kind of 'modern conscience for the human race' notions propagated by those such as Scholes and Rabkin (1977, iv).

The idea of romance was still there in the New Wave. For example, Aldiss in the 1970s, despite his contribution to the dystopias of the time, defined SF as 'the search for a definition of mankind and his status in the universe which will stand in our advanced but confused state of knowledge' (Aldiss, 1986, 30). Aldiss does however make this a literary definition which specifically linked SF to Gothic fiction. I actually prefer Aldiss' more flippant definition which identifies SF as, 'Hubris clobbered by nemesis … by which count, ordinary fiction would be hubris clobbered by mimesis' (30). The implication here is that in mainstream literature human agency is problematized by everyday occurrence whilst in SF it is problematized by stronger forces. As far as literary definitions go I find that Suvin's notion that, 'basically, SF is a developed oxymoron, a realistic irreality, with humanized nonhumans, this worldly other worlds and so forth' (1979, viii, in James, 1994, 11), is more a description of SciFi film and TV than of literary SF itself. This definition is appealing, however, in that it raises the image of an oxymoron, a 'pointed foolishness', becoming the object of serious and heated debate in academia and elsewhere.

The combination of more modern notions of SF as an 'elite, technocratic fiction' (Mendlesohn, in James, 1994, 3) with the dystopian sentiments of the New Wave leads us almost directly to 1980s cyberpunk, though again I prefer Spinrad's appellation of 'Neuromantic' for its pun on the fate of punk as a musical/social movement. Resonant mainly of the long-delayed impact of uncertainty theory on the social sciences, cyberpunk celebrated the impact of the chaotic and complex in both personal and cultural terms. Though its concerns were essentially onto-logical and epistemological, in methodological terms cyberpunk falls back on the kind of *soft determinism* espoused by Scarborough and Corbett (1992) as a way of understanding technology in relation to organizations. They see technology as no more than 'suggesting' the forms of action and change that can take place because use of technology is mediated by issues of power, meaning and know-ledge. So in the cyberpunk world the fallout at street level of the strategic, inter-necine struggles of the political-military-industrial complex 'suggests' the shape of our lives in the interstices between contingencies exemplified by the resources we can command, borrow or steal. At this juncture definition of SF becomes almost a sterile issue. It is the debate over how definitions are enacted in culture which is of import and which is exactly what might be expected from the 'apotheosis of postmodernism'.

There has long been an undercurrent of feminism in SF, though it was just as marginalized as feminism was elsewhere until the 1970s (see Clute and Nichols, 1993, 424–5, for an excellent explication). *Feminist SF* has had basically the same relationship to mainstream SF that feminism in general has had to 'normal social science'. It has widened the range of internal and external critique available to both fields and has provided a theoretical and methodological counterbalance to the rabidly patriarchal and positivistic assumptions they lived comfortably with for many a long year. Recurrent motifs in what has almost been a genre within a genre include strong anti-hierarchical and often ecological themes. Though not all women SF authors write recognizably feminist SF (Clute and Nichols (1993) cite a neat typology from Martin) some of the most noted female authors, such as Doris Lessing, Ursula Le Guin and Marge Piercy, are sometimes credited with opening up a new appreciation of issues of culture, community and interpersonal relationships to the field.

In recent years we have had the return of what Csicsery-Ronay (1991) calls the *expansionist mode* of SF with some excellent hard science fiction: Kim Stanley Robinson's *Mars Series*, for example, and the type of 'Universe' novels currently constructed and explored by Iain M. Banks, David Brin and Peter F. Hamilton to name but a few. As well as the literary legacy of cyberpunk (e.g. Neal Stephenson and Jeff Noon) we also have the highly developed markets for series SciFi (e.g. the *Star Trek* and *Babylon5* books) and board and computer game tie-ins (e.g. *Battletech*). What seems to be extant now is a blending of cautious optimism about the possibilities of science with pessimism about the ability of our political and socio-cultural institutions to handle change. Frederick Pohl (1993, 48) asserts that 'SF is the literature of change' and that the literary devices used in the SF method itself change with the latest notions in science. This is another reason for notions of change in SF being analogous to, or more correctly reflective of, paradigm shifts. Collick (1997, 1) links such shifts to the continuous 'inscription and rein-scription of different histories of the genre' with each new generation of critics. Likewise James (1994, 1) connects changes in definitions of SF to the self-interest of critics and makes a very useful distinction between academic debates about the role and content of SF compared to the 'disposability of the product'.

Even the conception of SF as a subliterary genre has been appropriated and subverted by SF commentators such as Suvin and Delaney to become the notion of a paraliterature, modeling, reflecting and paralleling what Delaney terms *mundane* literature without accepting its conventions or limits. Delaney even presents SF as a 'modular calculus', essentially a modeling technique which would, 'itself be a model of what the mechanism of science fiction might be if SF were truly the bridge between science and literature' (Broderick, 1995, 130). Delaney also raises issues over the marginalization of SF and James (1994, 5–6) speaks of the ghet-toization of SF and SF authors, though at the same time he reminds us of the cultural richness often found in ghettos. Taken together these conceptions begin to resemble debates over the relations between social science and 'natural' (or should we start calling it mundane?) science.

Personally I find much literary criticism of SF to be fairly sterile because it is often restricted to arguments about the relations of SF to the concept of the 'fantastic' or the 'marvelous' in mainstream literature, or to the finer distinctions between utopias and dystopias. The former distinctions are I feel answered by what might now be seen as a paradigm shift away from myth and fantasy once the methodology of SF had become established. The latter debates tend to ignore the kind of experience that students of organization are intimately familiar with, the panoply of putative managerial utopias that were far less so for their participants, scientific management and downsizing being but two. That one person's dystopia can be another's utopia, that some people like war, that some thrive in totalitarian and oppressive systems may be one of the factors that makes SF possible, the vicissitudes of current existence legitimating the suspension of disbelief necessary for the SF method to work.

In any case debates over the content of the genre are of reduced import to SF when considered as a paraliterature, since it apes everything found in other genres from 'high' art to pop culture. For example I swear I actually have read an SF horse-racing detective novel, though I can't remember where. In the end the boundaries of SF are probably best apprehended through experience, e.g. in the frustration felt in sorting through the horror and fantasy titles in secondhand bookstalls to find SF books you haven't read.

The attraction of method

It is certain that much popular SF (especially media SF and series SF) is simply formulaic escapist fiction, though as Stableford (1979, 36) points out, SF has a wider range of characteristic resolutions than 'mundane' literature, which is an attraction in itself. In essence though, SF is no *more* fictional or escapist than any other literature and much less than some. A point I will return to later. The enjoyment of the escapist element is generally linked to the *sense of wonder* or *otherness* which Clute and Nichols (1993, 1084) liken to 'a sudden opening of a closed door in the readers' mind', though others link this to a quality of estrangement as embodied in the Romantic concept of the *Sublime* (Robu, 1988) or even a *sense of loss* (Robu, 1995). Whatever this sense is, it is found everywhere in SF and links the oft-found fascination with cosmic destiny in writers like Stapledon and Van Vogt to that with *technology* in Verne's 'extraordinary voyages' and their successors (see Lambourne *et al.*, 1990, 9). The allure of 'marvelous flying machines' (see Corbett, 1995) and other embodiments of technology lead us to the well documented notion that many are attracted to science through SF (e.g. Lambourne *et al.*, 1990, Pohl, 1993). Indeed Bainbridge (1976, 198) notes that SF was 'the popular culture of the Spaceflight Movement'. Though Bainbridge downplays the current relationship of SF to astronautics, I would argue that this is more likely to be a result of the bureaucratization and professionalization of the space industry and I would bet that the present-day entrepreneurs who want to break into it are or were SF fans. For myself, though not much of a scientist, I can cite Asimov's psycho-history from the *Foundation Series* and the Bene Gesserit priesthood from Frank Herbert's *Dune Series* as productive of my own interest in psychology.

Bainbridge also argues that SF's major *role* is in the spawning of deviant social movements and as a *cultural redoubt* (1976, 233) for concepts rejected or not yet accepted by science. This link to deviant subcultures (as with the notions of marginalization and ghettos above) provides another major attraction of SF that I think of as a *capacity for subversion*. According to James (1994, 3), SF is more subversive than other popular fiction in that it more often offers both imaginative alternatives and criticism. SF is a redoubt for deviant ideas and those who hold them and provides us with a sense of 'otherness without alienation' (*Economist*, 1995).

Another attraction of SF is often seen in its *predictive capacity*, though this tends to be denied from within the genre in that in futurological terms SF authors are as often wrong as right (Miles, 1993). Prophecy is essentially irrelevant to SF as it is more about 'what could be' than 'what will be'. As I have intimated previously, SF is much more about reflexivity to current social trends/structures than about the kind of 'foresight planning' which is of increasing concern to trading and technology companies. The notion of SF as a 'new look at ourselves' (Radford, 1978) could actually be seen as contradictory to SF as futurology in that SF methodology does not necessarily involve prediction of the future but rather its assimilation into current understanding. At the same time there are themes in SF which are of particular relevance to those of us interested in the future of organization and management. The theme of self-management and co-operatives in opposition to the domination and despoliation of corrupt politics and global capitalism is probably best exemplified today in Kim Stanley Robinson's *Mars Series* and the even more recent *Antarctica* (1999). Likewise, though seldom if ever receiving any consideration in the critical literature on SF, the notion of how work will change is almost as much a constant in SF as FTL travel, providing the background on which future societies can be painted. This latter theme on work is one of many examined in Stableford and Langford's fictional future history *The Third Millennium* (1985) which is a distillation and synthesis of the whole canon of futurological SF. On a personal level my own interest in the area of identity in the workplace was greatly informed by Samuel R. Delaney's *Stars in My Pocket Like Grains of Sand* (1984), which did for notions of multiple careers and the split between occupations and socially necessary work what he earlier did for notions of lifestyle, aggregate families and transsexuality in *Triton* (1976). The ramifications of future work and lifestyles have of course been endlessly revisited in more or less tangential fashion in the extensive literature on robots and machine intelligence. Karel Capek's *R.U.R.* (1921) is generally identified as the genesis of the robot (or at least the word), though Asimov *et al..* in their excellent compendium on robots and computers, *Machines that Think* (1984), argue for Ambrose Bierce's *Moxon's Master* (1894) about a chess-playing machine as the first story to raise the issues 'about the relationship between mechanistic and living systems' (1984, 16). Once again it is the explicit use of a heuristic methodology which leads to Bierce's story being singled out as SF from the numerous tales of automata common in the nineteenth century. The relevance of this strand of SF to modern organization theory is signified in the current popularity of the cyborg as both an analytic object and cultural icon. The cyborg, which according to Clute and Nichols (1993, 290) first raised its (ugly?) head in E.V. Odle's *The Clockwork Man* (1923) is so ubiquitous today in SF and media SciFi as to be almost passé. Nevertheless it is a motif which neatly parses the problems of military and social organization as in Walter Jon Williams' *Hardwired* (1986) and Marge Piercy's *Body of Glass* (1992). Cyborgs are examined in more detail elsewhere in this volume, though McCaffery's (1991) *Storming the Reality Studio* and Gray's (1995) *Cyborg Handbook* contain some seminal analysis.

The final attraction of SF I wish to note is that I think of it not just as a literature of change à la Pohl but a literature that *confronts* change. SF does not merely raise tensions between ignorance and science, free will and determinism, it does not simply explore differences or contradictions, it confronts us with them in a way that the social and organizational sciences are loath to do. This for me is the abiding theme of SF; whatever the domain or subgenre we deal with there is always confrontation (though not necessarily conflict) between every combination of person, organization, culture and environment you can imagine. SF methodology for Pohl consisted of, 'looking at the world around, dissecting it into component parts, throwing some of those parts away and replacing them with invented new ones – and then reassembling that new world and describing what happens in it' (1993, 1). Effectively then, SF makes variables out of what everyday life often treats as ontological and epistemological 'fixities'. Through the appropriation of potential realities as thought experiments SF is able to examine the implications and iterations of ideas and their applications as *strong determinants* of psycho-social, politico-economic and ideological/cultural gestalts. Then by confronting us with what oppositional constructs might imply if they were strong determinants of reality it forces us to think outside of the bounds of acceptable knowledge or conventional wisdom, as good analytical research should. The use of Darwinian and Marxian determinism in Wells' *The Time Machine* (see Scholes and Rabkin, 1977, 19–20, 148 and James, 1994, 28) should leave us in no doubt as to the efficacy of the method.

The domain of SF

What does SF consist of? Bainbridge and Dalziel (1978) attempted to map the domain of SF as understood by fans by locating authors in relation to hard science, the New Wave and fantasy (see Figure 1.1). Though almost as memetically seductive as Maslow's Baleful Triangle, Bainbridge and Dalziel's work is probably best seen as an example of the disjunctures between conceptions of what SF represents. For example when I asked people to locate modern authors on Bainbridge's schema, I found four basic reactions:

1   OK, give me a go.
2   The locations given are wrong.
3   You can't do that with SF.
4   You can only do it by locating individual stories.

In response to the last three reactions I then tried to do something similar to Bainbridge by web-searching for the topics taught in the increasing number of science fiction courses world-wide, which I roughly prioritized by frequency of occurrence with the results below:

- utopias/dystopias
- film and pop culture
- robots, cyborgs and technology
- counterfactuals and 'alternativities'
- history and genres

Figure 1.1 SF as seen by the fans – circa 1978

Source: Reprinted from Bainbridge and Dalziel (1978) by permission of the editor of *Science Fiction Studies*

- time travel
- *Star Trek*
- gender, sexuality and feminist SF
- Philip K. Dick *
- novels, poetry and criticism
- catastrophe and apocalypse
- mind and intelligence
- physics, space-flight, cosmology, astronomy
- religion, culture, racism, slavery, economics, class, Cold War

(*Though Philip K. Dick was the most cited author, the most cited novel was Ursula Le Guin's *The Dispossessed*, with Gibson's *Neuromancer* coming a strong second.)

What surprised me here was the lack of courses which dealt specifically with extrasensory phenomena, there appearing to be at least one set of ideas which, though snug in the redoubt of SF, are not so acceptable in its academic study. All the same, there is little about the domain of SF that is not mirrored in a fairly straightforward fashion somewhere in social science. After all, we are every one of us a time traveller. But commonality in objects of interest is not enough for a relationship, we might know that the concept of organization is where sociological and psychological sensibilities should be able to meet, but it doesn't stop the arguments. We need to consider further what social science and SF can *do* for each other.

Social sciences and SF

The social and organizational sciences might be said to be looking to areas such as science fiction for indications of how to escape from the 'normal science' which disciplines such as organizational behaviour (OB) have found themselves thrashing around within of late. As Stableford (1978, 117) has argued:

> science fiction is of especial interest to sociologists and of considerable potential value in that theirs is the science most confounded by problems of method and which thus stands to gain most from the creative use of the imagination.

Both Stableford and Suvin in the seventies tried to look towards a sociology of SF but these were essentially sociologies of literature applied to SF as paraliterature. Suvin's concerns were with genres and subgenera and a somewhat Kuhnian interpretation of how their norms and conventions regulate literary and hence cultural discourses. Stableford examined the functions of SF (using the media sociology of Hugh Dalziel) as:

- directive (instruction or prescription)
- maintenance (ideology)
- restorative (escape or 'respite').

Stableford's effort essentially reiterates much of the conventional wisdom about SF for a critical audience and work such as this has been largely superseded by feminist and postmodern interpretations of SF. More interesting perhaps are Stableford's (1978, 116–19) commentaries on works by Milstead *et al.*. (1974) and Greenberg *et al.*. (1975) which tried to approach the teaching of social science *through* SF. Stableford notes that SF writers must invent sociological rules and principles though 'imaginative leaps & hypothetical ventures', while social scientists are 'confined by caution'. Stableford sees social science as a 'frustrated science' though others have an even more jaded view. D.G. Compton (1970) in *The Electric Crocodile* puts forward the notion that having a science of sociology at all is an admission of failure. Stableford clearly dislikes the notion of 'sociology through SF', as he sees using SF to make social science more attractive to apathetic students as 'bad policy'. The kind of stories cited are not *about* social science and are interested in different questions, and even though there is still a 'kinship of creative method', the potential in SF for illuminating social science is incidental to the creative process. Worse still for Stableford, social science doesn't understand jokes and yet insists on trying to find a point in them. As with the domain of SF, no one will agree on which stories best illustrate what or what the same stories are about. What we appropriate and why becomes of more concern than explanatory or emancipatory power. For Stableford, SF must stand as literature and not as 'sociological data'. Social science should use its own perspectives and analytic procedures but in order to raise social science questions from reading SF, not 'try to pretend that a story is something which it blatantly is not'.

The relations of behavioural science to SF receive a more upbeat treatment from Radford in his review of Katz *et al.*. (1974, 121–3, in the same issue as Stableford above). He notes that SF deals with many psychological and pseudo-psychological phenomena and that SF encourages an interest in science and an 'active questioning approach'. However he would probably go some of the same way as Stableford in that he notes that 'on the whole the SF is better than the psychology' and again raises the notion that SF 'sugars the scientific pill'. The real problem for Radford though is the very subjectivity of psychology in that 'every explanation produced is itself an explicandum', and he concludes that for psychology and SF, 'reality is lost in an ever receding vista of reflections' (the fractals again). Unlike Stableford though, Radford does recommend the experience of trying to articulate psychology and SF, even in the face of suffering possible 'scientific vertigo' on the way.

The recurring theme of SF methodology must also be considered from the point of view of SF as a form of social science and the insights it may contain. Berger (1988, 35) for example, has documented the common threads found in stories dealing with the historical and social order in the pulp era as follows:

- scientific/technological determinism thwarted by irrational/emotional human fear
- most humans will succumb to such fear and to self-indulgence
- elites will either exile themselves or resort to authoritarianism
- elite control is the only route to stability – though not in the long term.

Although specifically located by Berger in the period from the 1930s to the 1950s I find that these threads are still common currency in modern SF. Westfahl (1996) similarly notes the historical tension between technological determinism and fear which is echoed today in the dystopian/utopian themes found in cyberpunk and much hard science fiction. As with my comments on cyberpunk above, SF has also routinely used uncertainty and indeterminacy (especially in time travel stories) as a deterministic mechanism for far longer than social science has even realized their import. This emphasis on confrontation with strong forms of determinism is one reason why SF is often portrayed as the only consistently critical literary genre. Though neither consistent nor necessarily coherent in approach SF does routinely mount critiques of political and socio-economic systems more resonant with everyday complaints about the 'system' than much of modern academic disputation. If I have a favourite story which exemplifies this it is Pohl and Kornbluth's *The Space Merchants* (1953) which brilliantly highlights the dependency of global capitalism on advertising technique for what we now call political spin and for enacting in our minds the market diversification and stratification which consumerism demands. 'The space merchants' led me directly to my fascination with the psychology of persuasion and thence onto critical social theory through the cultural criticism of the Frankfurt School as exemplified in Adorno's *Prisms* (1967).

Conclusion

What do the social sciences look for in SF? Both fields have problems with external validity and both are dependent to greater or lesser extents on the suspension of disbelief performed by audiences. Alfred Bester notes for example that what makes SF is the creativity of its reading public (Platt, 1987, 243) and the counterintuitive products of critical social and organizational science certainly rely on the exercise of what Goffman (1971) termed 'tact' when delivered to managerial audiences. Trends in science and culture (be they dominant, coming or speculative) supply the analytic and plot devices for social science and SF, both being fashion-conscious disciplines. That SF even aspires to a methodology makes it a *good companion* (in the fantasy/quest sense) in the heroic search for understanding of societies and organizations. Method also implies a learning process, just as learning burns new neural pathways in the brain (or hologrammatic images, or whatever is the latest notion on learning), so does SF – it is virtual experience rather than escapism. The modular calculus lives! A historical novel might also be virtual experience but is in effect much more escapist than SF as it ignores the assumptions which have to be made to allow the observation of historical events, even fictional ones. In SF on the other hand, the speculative explanation of time travel phenomena is bread and butter to both the fan and author. Likewise, though it is allowed in soaps like *Brookside*, for example, to present the most outrageous frequency and range of improbable events (in a probabilistic sense *Star Trek* may be more 'likely' than most soaps), you are still not allowed to bring in anything that is implausible to 'common sensibility'. SF is that other domain where such speculation is not only allowable but *de rigueur* if you want to be taken seriously, and being taken seriously is what SF has long wanted.

So if we can offer serious regard to SF, what do we get? First we get a *redoubt* for our deviant ideas; what we can't say in our mundane science can be pursued with gusto when bracketed with SF. Second, we get the ability to apply new and untried *resources* (for example the concept of the cyborg) to extend our capacity for subversion and to mount attacks on common sense from the security of new deviant subcultures. But it is not just the content and the method that attract us, it is the *style* also. The Terminator doesn't just want your clothing and your means of transport, it wants your sunglasses too. The hipness of cyberpunk and the solid extrapolation of hard SF are both commodities to be hungrily consumed by those who have endured the cycles of 'revolt into style' that characterize our own disciplines. SF handles this process much more consciously than social science because it in turn needs that creative leap to supply the next set of iterations on the theme. When as organization theorists we get bored with our latest fads our caution often overrides our desire to utilize what is hip just for the fun of it, or it may be of course that we are just desperate to be optimistic about something. This latter point links SF to the whole horror genre in that perhaps what SF tells us is that we aren't doing too badly in our mundane existence; it could be a lot worse. Conceivably though, it is the notion of SF method vs SF style which is of particular relevance to organization theorists, especially those of the critical 'genre' who often have no *real* voice for the audiences that they really need to address, i.e. managers and policy makers. Like the spotty SF fans who were ecstatic to swap their green anoraks for cyberpunk mirrorshades and go out in search of a girlfriend, critical management theorists look for the hip in order to impress those who have previously eschewed their lefty student image. Perchance this is no bad thing, SF being another route through which we can access the 'dark side' of our disciplines (see Corbett, 1994, 3) enlivening our respectability by hanging round with some disreputable-looking friends who wear dark glasses at night!

But the most seductive element of SF is that for all its irreality it is likely that it is the sense of *real* confrontation we can get from SF that brings us back to it time and again. For all that we have questioned and rejected modernist notions of progress, what we most often see in SF are the various manifestations of change and progress once more considered as strong determinants of reality. We know there is no 'one best way', but in SF at least there is the possibility that through confrontation by skill, intellect and belief then at least something might work out, that we can confront the evils of the world and maybe come out on top. SF tackles the problems that other genres can't reach.

The problematic here lies in the fact that in the end organization theory can only 'utilize' SF as metaphor or allegory and we have already discussed the faults inherent in trying to illustrate social science through SF. Even if it is bad policy to use SF to engage apathetic students, I feel that Radford's optimism about the value of SF exposing students to science still has some justification. A touch of scientific vertigo would do no harm to the many business and management students who use the methods and findings of scientific endeavour and yet are woefully ignorant of its history and philosophy. Opening our eyes to the scientific imagination and encouraging cross-disciplinarity are the legacy of Campbell's methods of instruction and can have significant benefits in expanding the range of categories and concepts available to us in deciphering the world. In keeping up with our own disciplines it is difficult for us to do the same in others, but we *can* have the latest notions on quantum computing, nanotechnology or the anthropic principle in cosmology distilled into a 'charming romance' for us, so that we may ponder their implications at our leisure.

I have not tried in this piece to consider social science as SF, to explore the fictions that we readily subscribe to, the notions of leadership, externally derived motivation and the efficacy of groups being notable examples. Many of the trite and alliterative 'models' used by management theorists and consultants are pure science fiction, variable factors considered as strong determinants of reality for analytic or heuristic purposes. I suspect that considering organization theory as science fiction puts us on the road leading back to Feyerabend's (1975) thesis on the legitimacy of 'anything goes' methodologies as the introduction to this volume avers. Though 'anything goes' is a principal component of SF methodology and is highly influential in the development of postmodern social theory, the tension between constructive anarchism of method and almost nihilistic deconstruction of normal science makes Feyerabend pretty strong fare for managerial audiences. This has the effect of making such concepts shy of venturing out from the kinds of redoubt that organizational science can fashion at present. I myself have often seen a kind of culpable incomprehension take root in managers when confronted with Feyerabend in research methodology seminars. Now, however, I can put the mirrorshades on and give them this volume in the hope that it may help set them on the kind of journey SF and organization theory have taken me on.

I want to end on a note of caution for those in the social and organizational sciences that want to use SF for whatever purpose. In the end it is science fiction as an *activity* that is of import, in that 'it comes from a whorehouse but it wants to break into the palace where the most sublime thoughts of human history are stored' (Lem, 1985, 59). If it is the reading and writing of SF which produces any desirable effects associated with it, then too much focus on SF as an analytic object may produce identifications deleterious to both the discipline making those identifications and to SF itself. Remember: 'The future happens when Junior discovers Nintendo, not when academicians decide to announce it' (Clarke, 1993).

References

Adorno, T.W. (1967) *Prisms* (trans. S. and S. Weber), Neville Spearman, London.
Aldiss, B. (with Wingrove, D.) (1986) *Trillion Year Spree: The History of Science Fiction*, Paladin, London.
Asimov, I., Warrick, P.S. and Greenberg, M.H. (1984) *Machines that Think: The Best Science Fiction Stories about Robots and Computers*, Allen Lane, London.
Bainbridge, W.S. (1976) *The Spaceflight Revolution: A Sociological Study*, Wiley, New York.
Bainbridge, W.S. and Dalziel, M. (1978) 'The shape of science fiction as perceived by the fans', *Science Fiction Studies*, Vol. 5, No. 15 (July), pp. 164–71.
Barber, R. (1995) 'Stand by for the alien invasion', in *The Independent on Sunday*, Metropolitan Life, 20 August.
Barrett, D. (1993) 'Science and fiction: blasting down the ghetto walls', *New Scientist*, Vol. 137, No. 1865 (March 20), p. 44.
Berger, A.I. (1988) 'Theories of history and social order in Astounding Science Fiction, 1934–55', *Science Fiction Studies*, Vol. 15, pp. 12–35.
Brawer, R.A. (1998) *Fictions of Business: Insights on Management from Great Literature*, Wiley, New York.
Broderick, D. (1995) *Reading by Starlight: Post Modern Science Fiction*, Routledge, London.
Clarke, J. (1993) 'Science and fiction: in pursuit of the modern', *New Scientist*, Vol. 137, No. 1865 (March 20), p. 45.
Clute, J. and Nichols, P. (eds.) (1993) *The Encyclopedia of Science Fiction*, Orbit, London.
Collick, J. (1997) 'Science fiction unbound: definitions and histories', in *Procyon: the academic website for science fiction and fantasy studies* (Note: this URL is now defunct).

Compton, D.G. (1970) *The Electric Crocodile*, Hodder, London.

Corbett, J.M. (1994) *Critical Cases in Organisational Behaviour*, Macmillan, London.

Corbett, J.M. (1995) 'Celluloid projections: images of technology and organizational futures in contemporary science fiction film', *Organization*, Vol. 2, Nos. 3/4, pp. 467–88.

Csicsery-Ronay, I. (1991) 'Cyberpunk and neuromanticism', in, L. McCaffrey (ed.) *Storming the Reality Studio: A Casebook of Cyberpunk and Postmodern Fiction*, Duke University Press, Durham, North Carolina.

Economist (1995) 'Loving the alien/hard and soft science fiction', Books, Vol. 336.

Feyerabend, P. (1975) *Against Method*, Verso, London.

Goffman, E. (1971) *The Presentation of Self in Everyday Life*, Pelican, Harmondsworth.

Gray, C.H. (ed.) (1995) *The Cyborg Handbook*, Routledge, New York.

Greenberg, J.D., Milstead, J.W., Orlander, J.D. and Warrick, P. (eds) (1975) *Social Problems Through Science Fiction*, St James's Press.

James, E. (1994) *Science Fiction in the Twentieth Century*, Oxford University Press, Oxford.

Katz, H.A., Warrick, P. and Greenberg, M.H. (eds) (1974) *Introductory Psychology Through Science Fiction*, Rand McNally.

Lambourne, R., Shallis, M. and Shortland, M. (1990) *Close Encounters: Science and Science Fiction*, Adam Hilger, Bristol.

Lem, S. (1985) *Microworlds*, Secker and Warburg, London.

Luckhurst, R. (1991) 'Border policing: postmodernism & science fiction', *Science Fiction Studies*, Vol. 18, pp. 359–66.

Mead, M. (1950) *Sex and Temperament in Three Primitive Societies*, Mentor, New York.

Miles, I. (1993) 'Stranger than fiction: how important is science fiction for futures studies?', *Futures*, Vol. 25, No. 3, pp. 211–15.

Miller, A. (1968) *The Crucible: A Play in Four Acts*, Penguin, Harmondsworth.

Milstead, J.W., Greenberg, M.H., Orlander, J.D. and Warrick, P. (eds) (1974) *Sociology Through Science Fiction*, St James's Press.

Platt, C. (1987) *Dream Makers: Science Fiction and Fantasy Writers at Work*, 2nd edn, Xanadu, London.

Pohl, F. (1993) 'Forum: two-way look at the literature of change – Frederick Pohl considers some ways in which science and science fiction overlap', *New Scientist*, Vol. 138, No. 1874 (22 May).

Radford, J. (1978) 'Alienists meet the alien', *Foundation*, 13 (May), pp. 121–3.

Robu, C. (1988) 'A key to science fiction: the sublime', *Foundation*, 42 (Spring), pp. 21–37.

Robu, C. (1995) *Twelve: A Romanian Science Fiction Anthology*, Sedona, Timisoara.

Scarborough, H. and Corbett, J.M. (1992) *Technology and Organization*, Routledge, London.

Scholes, R. and Rabkin, E.S. (1977) *Science Fiction: History, Science, Vision*, Oxford University Press, New York.

Stableford, B.M. (1978) 'Sociological fallacies', *Foundation*, 13 (May), pp. 116–19.

Stableford, B.M. (1979) 'Notes towards a sociology of science fiction', *Foundation*, 15 (January), pp. 28–41.

Stableford, B. and Langford, D. (1985) *The Third Millennium*, Paladin, London.

Sutcliffe, T. (1996) 'Don't believe what you read in the papers – it's pure science fiction', in the *Independent*, Arts, 20 July.

Suvin, D.S. (1979) 'The state of the art in science fiction theory: determining and delimiting the genre', *Science Fiction Studies*, Vol. 6, No. 17 (March), pp. 32–45.

Westfahl, G. (1996) *Cosmic Engineers: A Study of Hard Science Fiction*, Greenwood Press, Westport, CT.

2 Science fiction and the making of the laser

Christopher Haley

The development of technology was possibly the most significant economic, political and cultural force of the twentieth century. The sheer ubiquity of this second scientific revolution makes it of interest to a wide variety of academic concerns, including organizational studies, prompting the desire to understand the forces which drive and direct such development. This essay seeks to explore one impetus in particular – that of science fiction.

The rise of science fiction as a genre is intimately connected with the technological progress of the twentieth century, yet it has been neglected both as a resource for the study of the history and philosophy of science, and as a potent social force in itself. This omission has perhaps been due to the belief that one must first read the 'pulp fiction' seriously, requiring a suspension of disbelief which might seem in some way at odds with critical inquiry, or which may be mistaken for unhealthy credulity. This is something which academics have been reluctant to accept, but which is clearly unnecessary. Whatever the reason for the inattention, however, it is an aim of this paper – and indeed this compilation – to suggest that it should not continue.

Though fanciful and playful, much science fiction has sought to make perceptive comment about emerging technology and cultural tendencies. By describing alternative worlds it highlights that which is contingent – and thus open to change – within our own. As speculative fiction or *gedankenexperiment*, it offers possible visions of how technology may be used or abused, and what awaits us if social trends are regulated or left unchecked. To be sure, many of these expectations and fears already exist within the collective consciousness, but like a parabolic mirror SF reflects these whilst bringing them to focus. SF reifies otherwise nebulous notions, providing vivid examples which may warn or inspire. Unease concerning genetically modified organisms would surely have existed without the literature of Mary Shelley, for instance, but there is no doubt that the idea of Frankenstein's monster has been a helpful rallying point for environmentalists, just as Orwell's Big Brother has been for libertarians. Equally, many scientists will admit to being personally motivated by the more optimistic visions of technological utopia.

Through the crystallization of hopes and concerns, SF shapes the way in which research is directed and received, and pre-forms much of our technology. This is perhaps unsurprising, for even if one does not accept the hard sociological claim

that science is just another cultural enterprise, one cannot deny that much technology is produced in response to social needs and desires. Yet there remains a
reluctance to take this notion seriously. This appears to stem from two points. The
first is that whilst the idea is not novel, the majority of accounts are unfortunately
marred by a tendency towards the anecdotal or highly speculative. The second is
that such assertions appear to lie uneasily with other characterizations of post-war
science, such as the military-industrial complex. Surely such whimsical extra-
scientific influences are incompatible – or at best, comparatively insignificant –
with the political and commercial concerns of 'big science'? This essay aims to
resolve these objections. It argues that far from being in conflict, the military-
industrial complex has actually been disposed towards futuristic high-tech and the
reification of science fiction. The claim is illustrated using a concrete example –
the development of the laser.

Perhaps the most frequently cited example of an interplay between science
fiction and science fact is the Strategic Defence Initiative, Reagan's fantastic proposal for an orbiting anti-missile shield. From the start the public language used in
this project was self-consciously 'sci-fi'. The extremely ambitious scheme soon
acquired the nickname Star Wars, after the highly successful film by George
Lucas, and this association was played upon by Reagan himself: 'the Force is with
us', he pointedly remarked (Ben-Tov 1995: 3).[1] This much is neither controversial
nor particularly remarkable. Rather, what remains open to debate is the origin of
the idea. There seems little doubt that much of the impetus was due to Reagan
himself, who presented the idea to the public after little or no discussion about its
technical feasibility. As one of Reagan's science advisors later said, 'we were
stunned . . . the whole thing was just nutty, because it was content-free – it was a
challenge to the scientific community to go invent something' (Hunter 1992: 58).

Where, though, did Reagan acquire the notion? Some SF writers have recently
claimed that the idea was a direct product of their input into the Citizens'
Advisory Council on National Space Policy, which was convened in 1980 and is
alleged to have influenced much of the Reagan administration's space policy.
Others have made much of the possible connection with a 1940 Warner Brothers'
film entitled *Murder in the Air*. The trailer for this production promised the audience a gripping tale about 'the most deadly weapon ever known to man' – 'a
death ray projector', capable of knocking enemy aircraft out of the sky from a
considerable distance. In language that was to be echoed virtually verbatim forty
years later in defence of SDI, it was promised that this superweapon would make
the United States 'invincible in war', so ultimately proving to be 'the greatest force
for peace ever discovered', the 'hope and prayer of all thinking people regardless
of race, creed, or government'. The principal actor in this film was of course
Ronald Reagan.

Whilst the curious similarity between *Murder in the Air* and SDI has been much
noted before, and rumours abound concerning the role of SF writers like Larry
Niven and Jerry Pournelle, accounts appear divided between those which take it
as unquestionable proof of the power of science fiction, and those which dismiss
it out of hand. Most orthodox expositions adopt the latter view: 'The actual

origins of modern directed energy devices are considerably more mundane than the science fiction of H. G. Wells and *Murder in the Air*, claims Baucom's *The Origins of SDI*, before proceeding to a history of the maser (Baucom 1992: 107). However, this paper argues that even if SDI was solely a consequence of laser and maser development, the role of SF cannot be ignored, for these 'pure' technological achievements were themselves inspired by science fiction: from the first conception of the laser to Reagan's 1983 'Star Wars' speech, it was a case of fantasy pushing science; fact following fiction.

To appreciate this, we must first understand just how potent an icon the beam weapon has been in Western (and particularly American) culture, and the extent to which ray guns gripped public imagination. Returning to *Murder in the Air*, it is significant that although the film was ultimately advertised along such lines, with the device featuring prominently in posters and publicity stills, the death ray was originally intended to be only incidentally important. When the screenplay was first completed, the film was intended to be a caution against subversion within the United States, as part of an ongoing campaign by the Warner Brothers to 'restore the integrity of law enforcement', and a warning about the increasingly unstable situation in Europe (Vaughn 1994: 69). However, as the Second World War began, the script was revised to shift the emphasis onto the American 'superweapon'. To quote Vaughn, 'The idea undoubtedly owed much to popular culture of the time, and Warner publicity acknowledged that there had been considerable speculation on the radio and in comic strips about the possibility of a death ray device' (Vaughn 1994: 78). Vaughn notes that beam weapons had appeared in at least twenty major films and serials during the previous decade.

One event stands out in particular: the 1938 radio dramatization of H.G.Wells' *War of the Worlds*. As is well known, the broadcast inspired mass panic; thousands fled their homes – some even committed suicide – to escape the invading Martians and their death rays (Clarke 1992: 87). Significantly, many believed there to be a factual basis to the fictional technology: in the 1920s and 1930s, widespread rumours had circulated concerning the invention of marvellous rays and beams, news which was lent considerable credence by the respectable press.[2] The electrical pioneers Guglielmo Marconi and Nikola Tesla were just two of many inventors who were described as having produced electromagnetic beams capable of stopping internal combustion engines, giving shocks, killing mice or worse. The confiscation of Tesla's research papers by the FBI upon his death did nothing to dampen speculation. Whether or not there was any truth behind the stories, however, what such episodes demonstrate is the willingness of many to believe in such devices. And as war broke out in Europe once again, the military, too, took an interest in anything that might provide an edge over the enemy. The most successful of such outlandish ideas was, of course, that other science fiction device – the atomic bomb. However, whilst the science fiction associations of the bomb are striking – and were even implied by some of those involved – they warrant treatment elsewhere.

After the war, military research into beam weapons continued through *Project Defender*, a programme established under Eisenhower to investigate possible intercontinental ballistic missile defence (Broad 1986: 49). This was clearly a highly speculative project: the trade journal *Aviation Week* reported that the 'United States is stepping up the pace of its research on exotic weapons, broadly referred to as "X-Weapons", as a possible defense against ICBMs. These bear a slight resemblance to the "death ray" concepts of science fiction' (Klass 1961: 52). Along with plasma and particle beams, it was reported that the 'techniques now under investigation include the use of microwave energy to produce plasma discharge with the objective of producing artificial lightning balls'. The reports seem cautiously optimistic: 'Barring an unanticipated breakthrough, the present state of research suggests that any effective ICBM defense using X-Weapons probably is at least five years away, and perhaps a decade off.'

Masers and lasers

Defender was officially abandoned in the early 1960s, when Congress ordered a series of military spending cutbacks. Yet just as the programme was being killed off, new technology appeared towards which the military could switch attention. A few years earlier in 1951, a team at Columbia University led by Charles Townes had begun work on apparatus intended both as a source and amplifier of microwaves, using resonance in a cavity filled with deuterated ammonia. They were supported by the US Department of Defense because of the device's potential use in radar and microwave communications. By 1954, the team was able to produce a continual output of microwaves, at nano-Watt power. They called their creation the MASER (microwave amplification by stimulated emission of radiation). The radiation proved to have considerably less frequency variation than the most stable device previously available, making the maser very attractive for a high-precision frequency standard. For this reason, the US Army Signal Corps also funded some of the research. However, whilst the device was initially publicized as 'a unique atomic clock', it would not be perceived as a mere timekeeper for very long. In writing his report, Townes chose to explain the operation of his invention in terms of a nuclear chain reaction (Forman 1992: 108). Although scientists and reporters alike frequently use metaphors in the explanation of new phenomena, we should note that Townes' language seems considered and deliberate, and was repeated in such other articles as his patent application. This was, moreover, shortly after the successful demonstration of the hydrogen bomb. From the outset, his public presentation coloured the way in which his invention would be received.

The next few years saw intense activity in this field, although the number of groups involved remained low. Towards the end of 1957, both Townes (along with a colleague, Schawlow) and another researcher, R. Gordon Gould (working for the company Technical Research Group), began wondering whether a maser-like device could be made to work in the visible range of the electromagnetic spectrum. Such a device would clearly be called a LASER (light rather than microwaves). Then, around the same time in 1957, the Soviets launched the first artificial satellite, Sputnik I. The effect on American military research was dramatic. Sputnik drove home Soviet Cold War capability: the technology used to launch a satellite could equally launch ICBMs. American funding for military research and development virtually trebled, with the National Aeronautics and Space Administration (NASA) and the Advanced Research Projects Agency (ARPA) both founded the following year in direct reaction to the Sputnik crisis of confidence. Interestingly, ARPA states that its mission was, as it remains today, 'to investigate ideas and approaches that the traditional R&D community finds too outlandish' (DARPA 2000).[3]

Both Townes' and Gould's groups applied for military support to develop a laser – the former to the Air Force Office of Scientific Research (AFOSR), the latter to ARPA. Townes received a grant almost instantly: a member of AFOSR recalled, 'I think this was the shortest time between receipt of a proposal and the issuance of a contract in the history of AFOSR' (Bromberg 1991: 78). The Air Force anticipated applications in communications, range-finding and target designation, yet clearly had weaponry in mind also: speaking in 1959, before any working laser had yet been demonstrated, one USAF Lieutenant-General remarked that, 'the Air Force death ray program (sic) involves research in the possible use of radiation energy as the lethal technique in an Air Force weapon' (Klass 1961: 52). Gould's group was similarly well treated, receiving grants several times greater than they had ever dared ask for; and likewise, though they proposed applications similar to those suggested by Townes, were also asked to investigate the possibility of developing the laser as a directed-energy weapon, for use against ballistic missiles and possibly even satellites. As *Aviation Week* noted in 1962, 'the idea of using the optical maser as a source for a radiation weapon or death ray arose before the device was operated and has been the subject of widespread speculation' (Miller 1962b).

Faith and optimism

The first visible laser was actually demonstrated in June 1960 by Theodore Maiman of Hughes Research Laboratories, using a ruby rod. Later that same year, a team of three at Bell Laboratories produced the first continual laser beam with a helium-neon laser. If it had not already begun, interest in lasers now rocketed: research, both military and industrial, increased ten- or twenty-fold over the next three to four years alone (Bromberg 1991: ch. 4). The device is now so familiar that it is difficult to appreciate the intensity of the interest that its realization generated. Newspapers, playing with the popular fascination with ray guns, ran excited stories such as: 'Light of Hope – or Ray of Death?' (Manchester 1963: 138), and 'Light Ray – Fantastic Weapon of the Future' (US News 1962: 47), which claimed that 'the idea of "death rays" . . . has moved out of the realm of science fiction'. There were predictions 'of giant laser machines which will emit precisely aimed daggers of energy', and conjectures that 'the laser's "bullets of light" may usher in a new kind of warfare envisaged only in science fiction' (Manchester 1963: 139).

Being visible radiation, the laser had more obvious an impact than the maser. It is also clear that by now the nuclear metaphor of the maser had become a deeper association: 'There was so much that was unknown about it', recalled a researcher at the Western Electric Engineering Research Center, 'that you were not going to be allowed to eat in an area where there was a laser for fear of radiation contamination' (Bromberg 1991: 202). Military chiefs, too, were explicit in their comparisons of the laser with the atomic bomb, and not simply in terms of advanced technology, but as weapons of raw power: 'as an anti-personnel or anti-tank weapon the device would be useful', *Aviation Week* reported in 1962, 'but, some industry sources speculate, is roughly like shooting pheasants with an elephant gun' (Miller 1962b: 45). In a similar vein, the Head of Army Ordnance Missile Command wrote: 'I feel as others do here that the laser may be the biggest breakthrough in the weapons since the atomic bomb' (Seidel 1988: 37). Indeed, *Aviation Week* announced in January 1962 that

> military enthusiasm . . . has reached such a peak that there is scarcely an Air Force, Army, and to a lesser degree, Navy agency that does not now support, or talk of supporting in the near future, some type of basic or applied research or experimental development with optical masers.
>
> (Miller 1962a: 92)

Townes himself joked that the acronym maser actually meant 'means for acquiring support for expensive research' (Seidel 1987: 113)!

The fact that the laser was hailed as 'something out of science fiction' does not in itself mean that science fiction was instrumental. However, whilst we may expect public hype to surround a new invention with its potential to solve old problems, it is remarkable just how vigorously the laser was pursued by the military. The key question is: what generated such optimism, and was it justified? There were obvious advantages that a laser weapon would possess: travelling at the speed of light would mean that it would not have to be aimed ahead of a target like a bullet, require its own tracking system like a missile or be affected by wind and gravity. Yet the excitement generated by the laser in the few years before and after its arrival was of an intensity probably only rivalled by that of the Manhattan Project. Although research was progressing quickly, by the time of the 1962 comments above, there was *no* laser which could have been used as a directed-energy weapon. At that time, the only devices available were masers, ruby-rod lasers, helium-neon and helium-xenon gas lasers; the 'death rays' were in reality little more powerful than a light bulb; the military's 'elephant gun' hardly even a popgun. Neither carbon dioxide nor hydrogen-chloride lasing was demonstrated until about 1965 (such lasers were the first to be of energies suitable for actually destroying a target through thermal damage), and even then it was rumoured that demonstrations of their destructive capability were staged by employing deliberately weakened targets.

Yet despite the repeated failure of high-energy weapons to live up to expectations in tests, the unanimous attitude seems to have been that it was only a matter of time before a suitably powerful laser would be found: the Air Force even set up a programme named *Project 1559* to facilitate the rapid transition from laboratory to battlefield of the promising new lasers that it anticipated would be discovered. As late as 1980, DARPA was still proclaiming that 'there is a . . . big gap between what has been demonstrated and what is believed possible' (Klass and Robinson 1980a: 55), whilst the trade press warned that 'industry is already complaining about continuing technology for technology's sake' (Klass and Robinson 1980b: 48). As with Reagan's vision for SDI, this was clearly not a case of applying a new invention, but of forcibly driving an accelerated research programme towards the desired goal of a beam weapon, in the firm – even obstinate – belief that it would ultimately prove effective.

Conclusions

The laser, like the maser, was emphatically not a product of pure research, a fortuitous discovery that led to a multitude of technological applications. In 1980, the military was still the largest consumer of lasers by far, with approximately 60 per cent of the market. Driven since conception by the military, the laser only became a chiefly civilian tool following the development of bar-codes, compact discs and the laser printer in the mid-eighties. Though the military's interest in and development of low-power laser applications is understandable, their interest in high-power laser weapons was obsessive, driven not by economic or strategic sense but by fantasy. As Seidel puts it,

> the laser . . . promised to realise an ancient dream epitomised in Archimedes' idea to attack the Roman fleet at Syracuse by using mirrors and lenses to focus burning solar rays on ships at sea. Science fiction's preoccupation with burning 'death rays' added modern sanction to the ancient dream.
>
> (Seidel 1988: 37)

The post-war, space-age climate made the fiction seem all the more feasible, as did the rate of discovery within the field of opto-electronics: each time new laser materials were discovered, research found new reason to continue. Confidence in technology was at a high during this initial period of discovery: the phenomenal impact of the transistor, for instance, was still being felt. Anything seemed possible. Science had successfully developed the first 'raw power' weapon of science fiction – the atomic bomb – so why not try for the second? It will also be recalled that politically this was a time of extreme tension: the Berlin Wall had just been erected, and the Cuban missile crisis was as its height. Technology offered to redress the imbalance of numbers: though the Soviets had more soldiers, the West could compensate with greater weaponry.

With contemporary sociology and philosophy of science arguing that extra-scientific ideas are an unavoidable, indeed necessary, part of the scientific enterprise, these conclusions should perhaps not surprise us. Researchers are increasingly acknowledging the role of science fiction in their work: SF authors were consulted over whether or not to sterilize the early Viking probes to Mars, for instance; the US Army Armament Research Development and Engineering

Center invited 'futurists and science fiction writers' to contribute to its *Force XXI* future weaponry programme (Steadman 1996: 20); and DARPA has held work-shops to 'bring together leading scientists, technologists and futurists' to promote cross-fertilization and novel ideas (DARPA 2000). Similarly in the field of non-lethal weaponry, the US government has enlisted SF writers as advisors, and both the US and the UK are now experimenting with long-used ideas like the 'Riot Foam' featuring in the comic *2000AD*. It is also interesting to note the role which fiction is beginning to play in the teaching of science – hence a recent NASA issue: 'Science Fiction Space Technology: A Tool for Learning' (NASA 1989). Conscious acknowledgement of this kind shows that there is more to the SF/ military connection than simply a common pool of ideas in the collective consciousness.

Yet the aim of this essay is *not* to claim that science fiction is a good predictor of future technology. Indeed, the lesson from the development of the laser is possibly the opposite – that despite the predictions, a feasible laser weapon has yet to appear. Rather than simply looking to science fiction as an indicator of material production, then, we would do better to consider it as an influence of scientific *practice*. But we need also to recognize the permeability of the boundary between work and play: insofar as it exists, the demarcation between science and fantasy is *produced* by the failure or success of projects like the laser and the Strategic Defence Initiative. On a micro-level, science fiction plays a significant part of what the philosopher Karl Popper might have called the 'illogic of scientific discovery'. On a macro-level, the military-industrial complex which has domin-ated post-war science has itself been disposed towards dreams of futuristic high-tech: 'cutting-edge' has, consciously or unconsciously, become equivalent to the realization of science fiction. Even in a technocracy, one can only reify that which the culture thinks a plausible fiction. Science fiction is that which provides our culture with potential futures from which to choose.

Notes

1 Ben-Tov also notes that SDI included an experimental rail gun code-named *Gedi*.
2 E.g. *New York Times* 21 May 1924 p. 1, 25 May 1924 p. 1, 28 May 1924 p. 25, 2 March 1925 p. 4, 30 January 1933 p. 1, 11 July 1934 p. 18, 15 March 1935 p. 1, 2 May 1935 p. 22, 18 October 1935 p. 17, 22 September 1940 p. D7 and *The London Times* 23 May 1924 p. 9, 26 May 1924 p. 16, 27 May 1924 p. 13, 28 May 1924 p. 14, 29 May 1924 p. 8, 29 May 1924 p. 13, 3 June 1924 p. 11, 6 June 1924 p. 11, 17 June 1924 p. 13, 19 August 1924 p. 11.
3 ARPA has changed its name several times, adding and dropping the prefix 'Defense'. It is currently known as DARPA.

References

Aldiss, B. (1973) *Billion Year Spree*, London: Weidenfeld & Nicolson.
Bartter, M. (1988) *The Way to Ground Zero*, Westport, Connecticut: Greenwood Press.
Baucom, D.R. (1992) *The Origins of SDI, 1944–1983*, Lawrence, Kansas: University of Kansas Press.

Ben-Tov, S. (1995) *The American Paradise*, Ann Arbor: University of Michigan Press.

Bertolotti, M. (1983) *Masers and Lasers*, Bristol: Adam Hilger.

Broad, W.J. (1986) *Star Warriors*, London: Faber & Faber.

Bromberg, J.L. (1991) *The Laser in America, 1950–1970*, London: MIT Press.

Brown, R.G.W. and Pike, E.R. (1995) 'A History of Optical and Opto-electronic Physics in the Twentieth Century', in Brown, L. M., Pais, A. and Pippard, B. (eds) *Twentieth Century Physics*, vol. 3, Bristol: Institute of Physics Publishing.

Cantril, H. (1940) *The Invasion from Mars: A Study in the Psychology of Panic*, Princeton: Princeton University Press.

Clarke, I.F. (1992) *Voices Prophesying War*, Oxford: Oxford University Press

DARPA (2000) *DARPA Over The Years*. Online. Available HTTP: http://www.darpa.mil/body/overtheyears.html (22 August 2000).

Forman, P. (1992) 'Inventing the Maser in Postwar America', *Osiris* 7, 105–34.

Hunter, K.L. (1992) 'The Reign of Fantasy: The Political Roots of Reagan's Star Wars Policy', *American University Studies* x, 34.

Klass, P.J. (1961) 'US Increases Radiation Weapons Studies', *Aviation Week* 75, 23 (4 December 1961) 52–67.

Klass, P.J. and Robinson, C.A. (1980a) *Aviation Week* 113, 4 (28 July 1980) 33–66.

Klass, P.J. and Robinson, C. A. (1980b) *Aviation Week* 113, 5 (4 August 1980) 44–68.

Manchester, H. (1963) 'Light of Hope – or Ray of Death?', *Readers Digest* 82, 491 (March 1963, UK edition), 138–43.

Miller, B. (1959) 'Optical Signals Have Space Potential', *Aviation Week* 71, 24 (14 December 1959) 87–91.

Miller, B. (1962a) 'Services to Push Optical Maser Effort', *Aviation Week* 76, 3 (16 January 1962) 92–115.

Miller, B. (1962b) 'US Begins Laser Weapons Programs', *Aviation Week* 76, 13 (26 March 1962) 41–5.

Moylan, T. (1986) *Demand the Impossible: Science Fiction and the Utopian Imagination*, London: Methuen.

Myers, R.E. (1983) *The Intersection of Science Fiction and Philosophy: Critical Studies*, London: Greenwood Press.

NASA (1989) 'Science Fiction Space Technology : A Tool for Learning', in *Space Educators Handbook*, Report Number OMB/NASA S677.

Robinson, C.A. (1981a) 'Laser Technology Demonstration Proposed', *Aviation Week* 114, 7 (16 February 1981) 16–19.

Robinson, C.A. (1981b) 'Advance Made on High Energy Laser', *Aviation Week* 114, 8 (23 February 1981) 25–7.

Robinson, C.A. (1981c) 'Beam Weapons: Technical Survey', *Aviation Week* 114, 21 (25 May 1981) 40–70.

Seidel, R.W. (1987) 'From Glow to Flow: A History of Military Laser Research and Development', *Historical Studies in the Physical and Biological Sciences* 18, 111–47.

Seidel, R.W. (1988) 'How the Military Responded to the Laser', *Physics Today*, 41, 10 (October 1988) 36–43.

Steadman, N. (1996) 'Ghost of H.G. Wells Calls the Shots in Future Weapons Plans', *Target Gun* (November 1996) 20.

Suvin, D. (1988) *Positions and Presuppositions in Science Fiction*, Basingstoke: Macmillan.

US News (1962) 'Light Ray – Fantastic Weapon of the Future' (2 April 1962) 47–50.

Vaughn, S. (1994) *Ronald Reagan in Hollywood*, Cambridge: Cambridge University Press.

Part II
Mirror, mirror

3   Metropolis, Maslow and the Axis Mundi

James M. Tolliver and Daniel F. Coleman

The stories we tell each other define our place in the world and some of these stories, such as those which tell us what structure *really* is, follow themes used for hundreds, or perhaps thousands, of years. Now this may seem to be an extravagant claim, but if we are correct we should see such stories in our concepts of structure and even in our science fiction. In the paper that follows we hope to build a case for this viewpoint by examining one such story-line in two different forms: Maslow's Need Hierarchy (e.g., 1943), and a story of the silent picture era, *Metropolis*. We'll discuss what elements *Metropolis* has in common with our thinking about organizations, then follow this discussion with an in-depth analysis. Later we'll discuss Maslow's theory using these same elements. It promises to be an interesting journey, so let's start with a trip to the movies, in the year 1927.

Metropolis

Before *Blade Runner*, *Dark City* or *Total Recall* there was *Metropolis* (1927).[1] Metropolis is a huge city surrounded by fields and forests. But it is more. It is also a huge machine of different levels and classes, and at the top is John Masterman, a machine of a man, to rule a machine of a city. Masterman is

> nothing but work, despising sleep, eating and drinking mechanically, press[ing] his fingers on the blue metal plate, which apart from himself, no man had ever touched, so long as the voice of the machine-city of Metropolis roar[ed] for food, for food, for food.
>
> (von Harbou 1927: 23)

And the 'food' the machine–city craves is workers. Dressed from throat to ankle in dark blue, men walk to their shifts with hanging fists and hanging heads. Row upon row, they shuffle in lockstep into elevators taking them into the city's machine rooms. These machine rooms are places of roaring furnaces, heat-spitting walls, the odour of oil, and dark machines like crouching animals, far below the streets. There workers a few hours into their shift both pray to the machines and curse them as 'the great wheels which break the limbs of thy creatures' (von Harbou 1927: 42–3). Those who finish their ten-hour shift look to be a thousand years old (von Harbou 1927).

Metropolis, you see, is also a city of contrasts. Above ground Metropolis is a place of exotic clubs, of gardens and a life of ease for the rich. It is a place of endless roadways, of flying machines and boundless pleasures. It is a place for the few, provided by the many. But below ground are the machine rooms, the railways and the workers' city. Lower still are the thousand-year-old catacombs and below this dank and frightful place is a huge river, kept from flooding the workers' underground city only by massive pumps. So Metropolis is a city of haves and have-nots, ordered from the most to the least, from the pinnacle of power in the city's tallest and most central building, to underground hovels barely above the raging flood.

And there is little understanding from the master of Metropolis concerning the least of his charges who work and live in the depths. The men who tend his machines

> have eyes, but they are blind but for one thing, the scale of the manometer. They have ears, but they are deaf but for one thing, the hiss of their machine. They watch and watch having no thought but for one thing: should their watchfulness waver, then the machine awakens from its feigned sleep and begins to race, racing itself to pieces.
>
> (von Harbou 1927: 34–5)

And this watchfulness in the depths takes a frightful toll. Masterman, however, believes 'That men are used up so rapidly at the machines, . . . is no proof of the greed of the machine [sic], but of the deficiency of the human material' (von Harbou 1927: 35).

This is the setting in which Fred,[2] John Masterman's son, finds himself. But Fred's life is changed when Maria, one of the workers, enters his club leading a group of children. She brings them to see the pleasure gardens of the rich, and before Maria and her charges are unceremoniously expelled, she tells the children, and the rich in the garden too, that they are 'brothers' – all part of the human race. Her statement moves Fred to find out more about the workers' lives and, not incidentally, to discover who Maria might be. So he follows the workers underground and takes the place of one of them, experiencing the torment of being a slave to the machine. But while there he also discovers that Maria is the workers' spiritual leader. She holds meetings promising hope in the form of a mediator between the hands (the workers) and the brain (the master of Metropolis), a mediator who must above all have compassion, that is be the city's 'heart'. This is the central theme of *Metropolis* that without compassion, and the understanding compassion brings between those who do the work and those who plan it, failure will result. This theme, in fact, is also central to the 'Tower of Babel' parable which Maria relates to the workers at one of her secret meetings. According to Maria, as the work on the Tower of Babel grew the workers and the planners became enemies; 'The hymn of praise of one became the other's curse.' 'Babel' meant 'Divinity, Coronation, Eternal, Triumph!' for the planners while it meant 'Hell, Slavery, Eternal, Damnation!' for the workers. 'Babel' had different meanings such that 'The same word was [both] prayer and blasphemy' (von Harbou 1927: 76). So Maria's biblical parable reflects the conflict between John Masterman and the workers, and is, at its core, the very structure of *Metropolis*.

Well, not only does Fred find Maria, but John Masterman does too, through the efforts of Rotwang, John's chief scientist. Now John Masterman does not take secret meetings lightly, especially where his leadership is criticized, if only by implication. Consequently, Rotwang and John Masterman plan to kidnap Maria and put in her place a robot that will encourage open revolt rather than patience, provide a pretext to punish the workers and discredit the real Maria. It is well suited for this work. A prototype for machines to replace the workers, and provide Masterman even more control, it is unbearably cold and 'made of crystal, through which bones shone silver' (von Harbou 1927: 61).

Maria is kidnapped, the robot is reconfigured to resemble her, and it leads a revolt. But the robot succeeds too well, for the ensuing worker mob storms the central power supply for the controls of Metropolis. The workers destroy this machine and in doing so they also stop the pumps keeping their underground city from flooding. It is left to Fred and Maria to save the workers' children from this new danger (she having escaped Rotwang's clutches). Eventually the children are saved, the workers burn the false Maria, Fred triumphs over Rotwang in a protracted fight and serves as the promised mediator, the 'heart', between his father and the workers.

The film's reviews were mixed. For example, H. G. Wells (1927: 15) hated it, but recognized the central theme as 'all the air and happiness are above and the workers live, as the servile toilers . . . down, down, down below'. Others (e.g., Vreeland 1927: 7), believed the film had something to offer and recognized that the film's 'main drift is that the standardizing efficiency of our age, stressing material advancement rather than spiritual progress, carries the seeds of its own destruction in its metallic bosom'. Yet, as Organ says, reviewers of the time generally derided the idea that machines and technology could give rise to worker enslavement, rather than empowerment, and rejected 'the idea that the "heart" is needed to facilitate cooperation between capital and class, and thereby minimise exploitation' (Organ 1999: 1).

Metropolis, then, is a film concerned with the relationship between capital and labour, the results of mechanization and the flaw of emphasizing material advancement. But we can also use what the film tells us to test our understanding of *why* we think and feel the way we do when we talk about organizational structure. First, however, we need additional information about how we think about structures and more information about the film itself.

Thought and organizational structure

One of the keys to *Metropolis* is the use of height in its presentation of power and class; the other key is the film's disdained call for mediation of 'hands' and 'brain' by the 'heart'. In fact equating height with increased status and power is a common structural theme which has been noted before (e.g., Miller 1964); the call for spiritual progress recognized above (Vreeland 1927) and Maria's calls for compassion are also heard in the work of management scholars (e.g., Maslow 1964; 1987). These themes, however, are seldom related to each other or to more general themes – those stories we referred to above. Yet we believe that the theme of height as power or class and the theme of the 'high' and the 'low' being bridged by the 'heart' or compassion is an enduring story that has its origins in metaphor.

Consequently, on one level our claim will be that structural thinking is informed by equating power and status with height and perceived inferiority with the depths, while recognizing the need for a mediator to bridge these 'highs' and 'lows' through compassion. But on another level we'll argue that these stories are real in their *effects* since the myth and its root metaphor determines how we behave in organizations, constructing much of what we call reality. We can establish these points with some plausibility, but first we have to tell you more about organizational theory and theories of myth and metaphor.

Thinking about organizations

Any basic text (e.g., Gibson *et al.*. 1982) says that structure refers to a relatively fixed set of job relationships based on decisions concerning division of labour, departmentalization, delegation of authority and span of control. It's accepted dogma that these decisions are made rationally, considering the composition of the organization's environment and technology (e.g., Thompson 1967). But some writers such as Bobbitt and Ford (1980) don't see a direct connection between environments, technologies and structures. They argue that structure results from managerial *choice* which is coloured by managers' cognitive and motivational orientations. Simply put, different managers respond to the same environmental or technological demands in different ways, and these different responses result in structural variations. So far, so good, but some people aren't sure that organizations are rationally structured entities at all. Further afield, Mintzberg (1979) argues that organizational structures are not always rational responses to environmental or technological demands but often result from fashion or fad. This means that managers are bound less by considerations of effectiveness and efficiency than by style, politics and a desire to have an organization structured like everyone else. Later writers, such as Weick (1987), argue that managerial actions (influenced by mental models) *create* external environments. In this view when a manager acts *as if* external events are tied together they *become* more orderly and more constraining. Environmental order is created by managerial behaviour, and this order subsequently validates the managers' initial mental models as a type of self-fulfilling prophecy. Management–worker relationships are just as tricky, since the basis for managerial action is the 'double interact' (that is the actions of person A with regard to person B and then B's response) and it is the *consequences* of this double interact, also based on perceptions, which determines the organizational reality ultimately called structure (Weick 1987).

This view is somewhat unique, but it is supported by other work. Even technology, which traditionalists (e.g., Thompson 1967; Woodward 1965) treat as objective, has been argued to be a reality constructed by managerial choice. Glisson, for example, suggests that technology is really the way managers have chosen to order the workflow and, since managers try to reduce uncertainties faced by lower level workers, the technology that most workers perceive is likely to be quite routine (Glisson 1978). Real technology, therefore, matters little, if at all (though some writers disagree, e.g., Fry 1982).

To put these points more directly, organizational structure results from how we feel about organizations, what we believe about them, and the actions we take – actions which may confirm our beliefs and our feelings. In this context the fitting of structure to technology or environment is a form of self-fulfilling prophecy. This leads, of course, to the question of what determines our less than rational thoughts and feelings about organizations. One answer to this question is provided by Morgan (1997).

Morgan argues that how we read organizational life, and so a key to how we act, is the metaphor. Simply put 'all theories of organization and management are based on implicit images or metaphors that lead us to see, understand, and manage organizations in distinctive yet partial ways' (Morgan 1997: 4). In Morgan's approach metaphor doesn't simply embellish discourse, but provides a way of thinking and seeing that highlights particular features of reality while disguising others. In short we 'attempt to understand one element of experience in terms of another' (Morgan 1997: 4) and metaphors, partially false, yet useful and inescapable, are the foundation for all organizational theory. Starting with this premise, Morgan analyses a number of organizational metaphors noting the strengths and weaknesses of each. We'll return to metaphors below, but for now we want to clearly state the points we hope we've established, specifically that metaphors are the stuff of theory, implicitly or explicitly held, which determines how we think about organizations and how we *see* them. Further, if our seeing and thinking control how we act, that is to the degree that what we do in organizations is theory based, metaphors also control our cycle of interactions with others and so the organizational reality we may create. In short, much of what happens in organizations may be self-fulfilling prophecy founded on metaphor.

Now approaching organizational structure as an application of metaphor raises three interrelated questions: first, is there a series of basic or root metaphors that are constantly repeated in our theories and in complex stories such as *Metropolis*? Some authors (e.g., Lakoff and Johnson 1980) believe the answer to this question is 'yes', they believe, like Morgan, that most of our thoughts and acts are fundamentally metaphorical in nature. Second, are complex stories, called *myths*, related to metaphors? If so, are myths reflected in how we conceive structure, or to turn the question on its head, are structures more reflective of deeply held, inexpressible emotions (a component part of myths) than of rational thought? It turns out that myths and metaphors are intertwined (Campbell 1986) and are reflected in our thinking about structure, as we'll discuss below. Third, and finally, is it plausible that organizational structures are not only metaphorically based but replicate fundamental myths that have been entwined with such metaphors? In other words, is it possible that what we call 'organizational structure' is, in part, a story we tell ourselves, a story containing a series of inescapable root metaphors, expressing a collection of emotions that are best expressed through myth?

Root metaphors

Lakoff and Johnson (1980: 6) arguing that 'the human conceptual system is metaphorically structured and defined' classify metaphors into a number of basic categories including Ontological (e.g., 'The mind is a machine'); Personification (e.g., 'Inflation as an adversary'); Structural (e.g., 'Time is a resource') (all examples from Lakoff and Johnson 1980); and Orientational metaphors which 'have to do with spatial orientation: up–down, in–out, front–back, on–off, deep–shallow, central–peripheral' (Lakoff and Johnson 1980: 14). They go on to say that *up–down* metaphors are tied directly to our physical and cultural environments (Lakoff and Johnson1980: 119) such that happy, consciousness, health, life, having more, good, virtue, rationality and having control or status is *up*, while sadness, unconsciousness, a lack of status, irrationality and being subject to control is *down* (Lakoff and Johnson 1980: 14–19). These metaphors, grounded in our experience (e.g., well people usually stand *up* while ill people are usually *down*), enable us to describe vague concepts in terms that are concrete and clearly delineated.

But these authors go further. When we structure vague concepts in concrete, but metaphorical terms, 'there is a similarity induced by the metaphor that goes beyond the mere similarities between the two ranges of experience. The additional similarity is a *structural* similarity' (Lakoff and Johnson 1980: 150). This is to say that the least concrete part of the metaphor has a psychological structure *only* because we metaphorically tie it to something that is more concrete. For instance the Ontological metaphor, 'the organization is a machine' (discussed by Morgan 1997) would result in the organization being experienced as a coherent whole – simply put, no metaphor, no coherent experience. Further, an objective state may be true only in reference to the metaphor that has created that particular social reality (Lakoff and Johnson 1980: 150–5), so the metaphor not only constructs the experience but serves as a comparison standard. To extend their point slightly, it is a metaphor such as the 'organization is a machine', not simply managerial action, which orders Weick's 'real world' of management, a world loaded with confusion, stress, politics, emotional disturbances, disappointments, trial and error (Weick 1987, citing Mali 1981) and it is against such *metaphors* that organizations are judged.

One central metaphor in *Metropolis* is an Orientational (*up–down*) metaphor described earlier. It is clear in *Metropolis* that *up* is equated with happy, consciousness, health, life, having more, good, virtue and rationality, as well as having control and status. *Down* is equated to sadness, unconsciousness, a lack of status, a lack of rationality (being fooled into flooding your own homes and your own children is hardly rational) and being subject to control. But thinkers from Weber to Mayo have used this *up–down* metaphor to describe the relationship of capital to labour. For example, Weber (e.g., 1946) thought the most competent workers in his rational legal system were *up*, while others thought workers used a 'logic of sentiment' but management (*up*) functioned 'rationally' (e.g., Hawthorne studies, Wren 1994).

Even now we talk about going 'up' the organization, going 'straight to the top' or even an organization's 'head'. Organizations are seen as being 'tall' or 'flat' (that is less *up*), having a 'bottom', a 'middle' and a 'top', each with an appropriate status (from low to high), a distribution of implied rationality (also from low to high), and a distribution of talent (from less to more). But if organizations are simply cycles of interactions they do *not* take up space. They most assuredly take time, but only in the most convoluted argument do the interactions have an *up* or *down* component (and in discussing space in an organization don't confuse the person with an *interaction episode* between two or more people or a person and a machine). Organizations don't have an *up–down* orientation, but due to the metaphor in use we think and talk about the relation between workers and management, or capital and labour if you prefer, in just this way. Capital is *up*, equated unjustly with good, virtue, happiness, or rationality while labour is *down*, in a realm of dark, steam, oil, irrationality, unhappiness and a lack of virtue. Further, this metaphor is a comparative standard (Lakoff and Johnson 1980) for what 'should be' (as a quick test imagine a company where the cleaning staff occupied the corporate penthouse and the company president had a closet in the basement!).

Now this is quite a conceptual load for metaphor to carry (to indulge in some metaphorical language ourselves) but the Orientational metaphor is entangled with an equally important myth. So our next chore is to look at the linkage between myth and metaphor in general terms, and to outline the myth that expressly uses this *up–down* metaphor. This mythic framework is called the 'Axis Mundi', but before we discuss the Axis Mundi we have to clear up a misconception or two about myths and mythical thinking.

Myth and the axis mundi

It's unfortunate in Western society that 'myth' has become synonymous with 'a lie'. Nothing, in fact, is further from the truth. Rather than being a lie a myth serves four, very emotional, functions (Campbell 1988). First, myth sensitizes us to the mystery of our lives. Second, myth describes, in psychological terms, the universe we live in. Third, myth often validates a particular social order. Finally myth teaches us how to 'live a human lifetime under any circumstances' (Campbell 1988: 31–2). In short myth deals with the content of a human lifetime, describing how to emotionally relate to society, how society relates to the world and how the world is related to the cosmos at large. So rather than a lie, myth teaches us emotionally who we are, our place in the world, how we should behave, and how we should feel about this behaviour. Myth is also a guide to life's stages conducting us through the transformations of 'birth, childhood and adolescence, age, old age and the release of death' (Campbell 1986: 20), trans-formations that are highly emotional. Fundamentally, then, myths are universal stories connected to common experiences and common emotional truths, made tangible in reference to the materials, people and geography of the myth maker and his/her audience, that serve common pedagogical ends (e.g., Campbell 1986). But even when grounded in the material world, and in what people already know, these common stories function by way of metaphor. As Campbell puts it '. . . a mythology is metaphorical of the psychological posture of the people to whom it pertains' (Campbell 1986: 12).

Even if we know what myth is, it may seem odd to link myth and organizational structure, but this link is not new. Bowles (1989), for instance,[3] argues that 'Organ-izations . . . sometimes create images of quest and trial, struggling, like the hero, for survival against life-destroying forces' (Bowles 1989: 413) in an attempt to foster team spirit, to direct employees' emotional lives and to provide a justifica-tion for organizational actions. But while Bowles' (1989) paper shows how and why executives stage-manage myths, it overlooks the point that myths are not so easily stage-managed, and may actually inform much of what we do in organiza-tions, intentional or not. To put it another way, myth, and its root metaphor(s), could be reflected in our thinking and feeling about organizational structures whether we will it or not. Our challenge, then, is to find a plausible, universal, myth in *Metropolis* and our thinking about organizations, one that both informs our thinking about organizational structure and uses the *up–down* root metaphor. The myth we have in mind for this task is the universal Axis Mundi myth.

The Axis Mundi

What is the Axis Mundi? According to Campbell (1968b: 40) it is the symbolic centre of the universe, around which the world revolves. It is the point where, from 'above' (*up*), comes the 'Grace, food substance, energy' of the world, while beneath this world spot (*down*) is the 'abyss', the 'flood', the 'serpent' or the 'dark'. The Axis Mundi is the point from which the 'tree of life' grows, 'rooted in the supporting darkness' with a spring or inexhaustible well at its foot (Campbell 1968b: 41). It is the centre line that joins the ultimate *up* with the ultimate *down*, represented in different societies by a tree or a cross (e.g., Norse, Christian myths), a mountain with the city of the gods at the top or the local temple altar (or hearth) with the smoke representing the *up* axis that links the earthly to the 'celestial wheel' (Campbell 1968b: 40–3). Being linked to both places of light (above) and dark (below) the Axis Mundi 'yields the world's plentitude of both good and evil. Ugliness and beauty, sin and virtue, pleasure and pain are equally its production' (Campbell 1968b: 44).

One classic example of the Axis Mundi is 'Yggdrasil', a mythical ash that linked the three levels of the nine worlds, including Hel (sic) at the bottom-most level, the world of mortals in the middle and the world of the gods above (Grant 1990; Campbell 1986). Further examples such as chakras, trees in the garden of Eden myth, or the Blue Corn Silk (all from Campbell 1986: 104) exist but we think the point is clear: the Axis Mundi is the tree, mountain, pillar of smoke or what have you that links the higher 'good' world of the gods (however conceived) and the 'bad' world underground or, perhaps, life and death (Campbell 1976: 121) through the common world of society. *Up* (the condition of happy, consciousness, health, having more, good, virtue, and rationality, status, bliss and eternal life) is linked to *down* (the condition of sadness, unconsciousness, torment, a lack of status, a lack of rationality and damnation) through the normal world of experience by the tree, line, pillar, mountain or altar smoke. In this case the root Orientational metaphor (*up–down*) is clear.

Metropolis *and the Axis Mundi*

The Axis Mundi myth is clearly demonstrated by *Metropolis*. At the centre of the city is the tallest building, the 'New Tower of Babel', with John Masterman at the top. The elevators[4] which take the workers to the machine-filled depths are in its base. The above-ground city is the world of common experience linked to *up* by the tower of the god-king of Metropolis and to *down* by its elevators which ultimately descend to the world of the dead and the flood. Both the story of *Metropolis* and its story within the story – Maria's Tower of Babel parable – are exemplars of the Axis Mundi myth; Campbell, in fact, refers to ziggurats as 'those storied temple towers, symbolic of the *axis mundi*, which are caricatured in the Bible as the Tower of Babel' (Campbell 1986: 34).

This link between mythology and *Metropolis* is not surprising for several reasons: first, when von Harbou wrote *Metropolis* she 'indiscriminately passed on whatever happened to haunt her imagination. Metropolis was rich in subterranean content, that, like contraband, had crossed the borders of consciousness without being questioned' (Kracauer 1947: 162–3). Second, von Harbou's work is part of German Expressionism, a style dedicated to the portrayal of subjective emotions (Encyclopaedia Britannica 1999a). Third, this film is one of a set of films concerned with placing the laws of nature above the dictates of reason, and romanticizing the suffering that had taken place through Fordism and the streamlining of the workplace (Kracauer 1947). Consequently it would not be unusual to expect a film that was mythically, and so metaphorically, directed to this end.

But we are now left with two additional questions. First, is the major theme of the film the reconciliation of the head and hands (or capital and labour) by the 'heart' in accordance with the Axis Mundi myth? Second, is there anything comparable in our current literature that affects how we look at organizational structure? The answer to both questions is, we believe, 'yes'.

Reconciliation of the hands and the head by the heart

There is no doubt that reconciliation of the head and hands by the heart is *Metropolis*' central theme. Reviewers of the time clearly recognized this theme, as did Lang in a 1969 interview concerning *Metropolis*: 'after it was completed I said to myself, you can't change the social climate of a country with a message like

"The heart must be the go-between of the head (capital) and the hands (labor)" '
(cf. Jurkiewicz 1990: 50).

So reconciliation of *up* and *down* by compassion was central to *Metropolis*, but is
it also central to myth? It is. This theme is central in Indian myth where the first
three stages of a 'personal' Axis Mundi (chakras, see Campbell 1990) refer to
feeding, sexuality and power which in the negative form refers to 'an insatiable
will to conquer, plunder and subjugate, converting everything and everybody
within reach into one's own or one's like' (Campbell 1986: 63),[5] while the upper
levels of this Axis Mundi are directed toward spiritual effort. These '*up*' (spiritual)
concerns and '*down*' conditions (feeding, sex and the will to power) are linked by
'the heart', a link that enables transcendence of the 'bestial order of life' (that is
material and power concerns), and progress to 'self-development'. This is accomplished when the 'other', treated 'as an it', becomes a 'thou' (Campbell 1986: 63–
6). Thus, in this Axis Mundi myth the 'heart' is symbolic of relinquishing a strict
concern with the material conditions of life through first recognizing others'
humanity. The symbol for this particular link (Solomon's Seal[6]) consists of two
triangles, one pointed upwards to the 'spiritual' condition, while the other is
pointed down to the material concerns (Campbell 1986: 125). In short, the reconciliation of *up* and *down* in the Axis Mundi by compassion is a central theme in
Eastern mythology (and Western mythology as well, e.g., 'The Fisher King',
Campbell 1968a: 454, 503). Given the universality of this theme it is not surprising that von Harbou chose the 'heart' to reconcile John Masterman, who is flawed
by seeing every other person (even Fred[7]) as an 'it', with the workers and especially
Maria who begs that her charges be treated as 'thou'. Consequently a major sub-
text of *Metropolis* is that despite his lofty position (one that should have been
reached only by being compassionate) Masterman can't understand others'
suffering or even comprehend his son's pleas for their better treatment. It is this
flaw that sets the stage for Metropolis' destruction. Reconciliation comes when,
through fears for his son's life, Masterman develops enough compassion to listen
to Fred's pleas. This sub-text is in accord with Masterman as the rebuilder of
Metropolis and Fred, who suffers as a worker *and* has been a master, as the 'heart'
– a role that John Masterman can't play since he has never experienced both the
world of the masters (*up*) and the workers' struggle (*down*). Fred *has* experienced
both worlds and so answers the question posed by Lang, who in the interview
above, asked 'How can a man who has everything really understand a man who
has very little?' (cf. Jurkiewicz 1990: 50). The answer is that he can't. As Fred
observes 'There can be no mediator between heaven and hell who never was in
heaven and hell. . . . I never knew hell until yesterday' (von Harbou 1927: 79).
Fred becomes the logical candidate to link the *up* and *down* world of Metropolis
and to shift his father's perspective from the worker as an 'it' to the worker as a
'thou'.

We believe we have established *Metropolis* as a mythical movie, anchored in the
root metaphor of *up–down*, where the Axis Mundi's extreme positions are reconciled by the 'heart' or compassion. It is the Axis Mundi myth which serves as an
implicit ideology governing, in part, how we think, feel and behave in organiza-

tions. For example Salaman (1979) notes that the struggle for control takes place 'on a vertical organisational axis' and that status graduations disturb the solidarity between organizational groups and enable 'some employees to see themselves as holding superior positions' (Salaman 1979: 158). Similarly, Klein and Ritti (1984) view structure as 'a structure of opportunity' where success is defined by advancing more quickly than your reference group upwards through the structure while 'failure, like success, is evidenced by movement relative to that of others, in this case downward through the organization' (Klein and Ritti 1984: 297). They also note that 'we ascribe to lower participants characteristics that fit their position in the organization, further testifying to the equity of the assignment' (Klein and Ritti 1984: 302). What better 'justification' for such perceptions and 'equity' than if *up* is associated with good, virtue and rationality while *down* is the realm of the machine, irrationality and a lack of virtue? What better justification for differential treatment of others than believing those who are *down* are some-how further from perfection? What better way to reinforce that one's position in the structure is an investment, so a career[8] becomes a form of control (e.g., Salaman 1979)? What better justification for viewing the other, specifically labour, as an 'it'? From our review we would think none.

The humanists, structure and compassion

But what of *structural* reconciliation? Is there any attempt in traditional organizational literature to reconcile the *up–down* dichotomy similar to the reconciliation in the Axis Mundi myth? Once again we believe there is, but this reconciliation is not obvious in the current literature. Traditional reconciliation efforts that come to mind are arguments for job enrichment (e.g., Hackman and Oldham 1976, 1980) that form the basis for the current empowerment craze, Senge's (1990) notion that visionary leaders are concerned with subordinate welfare and Transformational Leadership (Bass and Avolio 1990), which asks leaders to inspire self-actualization and the need to work for the collective good in their followers. These are laudable efforts, but it seems this literature argues not for reconciliation of the *up–down* dichotomy but its elimination – if all have an equal voice, if power is delegated, if decisions are shared or if the leader has our best interests at heart aren't the effects of the *up–down* dichotomy eliminated? Well, perhaps, but we still believe that it is not so easy to eliminate the effects of this metaphor or to control the influence of the myth (a point raised earlier when discussing Bowles 1989) especially when it becomes a self-fulfilling prophecy connected to vested interests (e.g., Klein and Ritti 1984). A number of writers, in fact, have similar concerns and are dissatisfied with empowerment and job redesign efforts although they express their concerns differently.

Some writers doubt if the best interests of those who are *down* are really being served by empowerment or job redesign. It is also clear that recommendations concerning 'enrichment' always come with modifiers attached (e.g., 'growth need strength', Hackman and Oldham 1976, 1980). Additionally some writers such as Dickson (1981) argue that participation is a method of control favouring management (which we would see as buttressing the *up–down* dichotomy). From Dickson's viewpoint participation is a form of control because management decides what issues can be raised by those who are *down* – the result is that only trivial, non-threatening things are discussed. McKendall (1993) is of a similar mind concerning the power-sharing offered by organizational development consultants. For McKendall participation is a means of control and change is directed toward the ends of management, rather than the good of all. She notes that while commonly espoused organizational development values include mutual influence, individual freedom and self-esteem, organizational change agents concentrate on goals such as efficiency which incorporate the values of the powerful, instead of the values of 'freedom, dignity, autonomy or self reliance' (McKendall 1993: 95). In fact McKendall forcibly argues that organizational change *increases* management power by reaffirming managements' rights and position (McKendall 1993: 98–9).

Practice substantiates such concerns. When discussing service worker empowerment Bowen and Lawler (1992: Table 1), for example, tell us that empowerment should *not* be used and jobs should *not* be enriched when an organization has limited customer ties, routine technology, a predictable business environment or employs the wrong 'types of people'. These decisions, of course, are made by management in a self-fulfilling prophecy framework (see Weick 1987) perhaps informed both by the *up–down* dichotomy and the Axis Mundi myth. Curiously then, job design and empowerment work seems at odds with itself – presenting solutions that continue to embody the *up–down* dichotomy while seeking to eliminate it (perhaps an impossible task if the metaphor is useful and if the Axis Mundi myth fulfils a number of important functions as Campbell contends).

But humanist writers aren't oblivious to the *up–down* metaphor, in fact attempts at reconciling this dichotomy exist in the thinking of the humanists for at least the last fifty years. Bowles, for example, proposes a new organizational mythology to legitimize individual expression and experience. He traces this call to the writings of Maslow but laments that much of Maslow's work has been misrepresented by theorists and practitioners (Bowles 1989: 416–18). We agree, but would carry the argument a step further. We believe that many of the current solutions to the problem of how to encourage individual expression and legitimize individual experience in organizations, solutions such as job redesign and empowerment, really founder when they attempt to provide a scientific solution to what is essentially a *mythical* problem. Many of these scientific solutions are some attempted levelling of the organization, based on appeals to materialism (higher productivity, less cost) rather than *emotional* arguments for compassion. They are unsatisfactory since, at an emotional level, they attempt to reconcile the *up–down* dichotomy through a denial of its implications including the Axis Mundi myth. We believe, however, the traditional method of reconciliation – the argument for compassion – while perhaps unintentionally dropped from much job redesign and empowerment work is present in the work of some humanists. To establish this case we'll use the work of Maslow, arguing that Maslow gives a *mythical* solution to the *mythical* problem of reconciliation both on an individual and a collective level. We'll then conclude this paper by arguing that Maslow's work has endured, despite criticism, because his 'solution' to the mythical problem of reconciliation of opposites is the same one proposed by von Harbou in *Metropolis*, specifically, compassion.

Maslow's theory

Maslow's theory is seen as a theory passed its time, lacking empirical support (e.g., Lawler and Suttle 1972; Wahba and Bridwell 1976; Miner 1980), and containing logical inconsistencies (e.g., Neher 1991). But the theory is still taught, usually with the comment that it is in accord with the 'intuition' of both researchers and managers. Now part of this intuition may be that Maslow's hierarchy both follows the Axis Mundi myth and has at its core the *up–down* metaphor. Briefly, Maslow proposes five needs arranged in an order of importance: physical needs, safety needs, belongingness needs and esteem needs (these four are called Deficiency Needs) and finally self-actualization (the only Being Need) (Neher 1991; Maslow 1987). Maslow argues these natural and innate needs exist as three 'motivational levels': the materialistic level, the social level and the transcendent or metamotivational level (Maslow 1987: xxi). We all pursue the transcendent needs or attempt to 'become fully human' if left to our own devices (Maslow 1964, 1987). This progress from one level to the next

> amounts to the subjective discovery of the objective, that is, the species-specific characteristics of humanness. It amounts to the individual discovery of the general and the universal, a personal discovery of the impersonal or the transpersonal (and even the transhuman).
>
> (Maslow 1987: 55)

In summary, as Neher notes (1991), Maslow believes we are endowed at birth, with a complete need complement that, if allowed expression, enables us to grow in a healthy direction. Deficiency Needs should be satisfied so we are 'free' to pursue self-actualization, a need that is 'already in the organism, or more accurately of what *is* the organism itself' (Maslow 1987: 66). Now this pursuit is laudable, since according to Maslow self-actualizers have: a superior ability to perceive truth; complete self-acceptance; humility and respect for all; love others most; and are the most developed idiosyncratically (Maslow 1987). Not inconsequentially, to be stuck at a 'lower level' is to be stuck in a region of ill health or incompleteness. Maslow (1964), in fact, contends that self-actualization, 'built-in' as a drive for transcendent or 'peak' experiences, is at the core of every religious revelation: 'it has recently begun to appear that these "revelations" or mystical illuminations can be subsumed under the head of the "peak-experiences" or "ecstasies" or "transcendent" experiences' (Maslow 1964: 19–20). In fact, peak experiences and self-actualization are seen to vary only in duration:

> peak experiences can be considered as transient self-actualization of the person. It can therefore be understood as lifting him 'higher,' making him 'taller,' etc., so that he becomes 'deserving' of more difficult truths, e.g., only

integration can perceive integration, only the one who is capable of love can cognize love, etc.

(Maslow 1964: 80)

This way to health for Maslow, unfortunately, can be blocked by any of the forces that 'diminish us' such as 'ignorance, pain, illness, fear, "forgetting", dissociation' or an obsessive focus on the rational, mechanistic or the material side of life to the exclusion of all other considerations (Maslow 1964: especially 32).

From this description it is clear that Maslow's theory follows the traditional root metaphor, from *down* (material needs) to *up*[9] (transcendental or self-actualization); *down* (Deficiency Needs) are seen as subservient to the *up* (Being Need) and inferior to it. Further, Maslow's argument parallels the Axis Mundi myth, where material concerns (e.g., physical, safety) are *down*, while spiritual concerns (transcendental experiences) are *up*. These opposites are again bridged by the transpersonal concerns of the giving and receiving of love and concern with the opinions of others (e.g., ego needs).

But Maslow goes beyond the simple recountal of an Axis Mundi myth and the argument that obstacles supposedly standing in the way of individual transcendent experience should be removed. He also argues that the factors blocking such 'growth' in *society* should be removed, or, as Maslow would have it, *society* triumphs when the transcendental experiences of self-actualizers become part of ideal art, ideal science, ideal knowledge and ideal education. Maslow's work is consequently both an argument that society benefits and an argument that 'higher level needs' are desirable in themselves.

On the organizational level those arguing for more humanistic *structures* (e.g., group centred leadership, high perceived contribution opportunity and high interaction opportunity; Miner 1980: 26, citing Clark 1960) do hold that lower level needs should be met to encourage growth, but often ignore the fact that such growth, as seen by Maslow, is predominately spiritual (in our terms progression up an Axis Mundi). Further, the encouragement of growth demands recognition of Maslow's contention that the capability for self-actualization exists in *everyone*. More germane to organizations, this position requires recognizing Maslow's *prescriptive* demand that we set aside the focus on the completely rational, our obsession with the 'mechanistic' side of life and strict material concerns (such as efficiency). It also denies that the only source of individual development is found in the *up–down* dichotomy of the organization (such as career progress) and argues, instead, that each person is capable (if only given the chance) of transcendence, that is of finding their way *up* to conditions previously described as 'happy, consciousness, health, life, having more, good and virtue'. Simply put, if the 'other' is capable of transcendental experience it becomes increasingly difficult to maintain on the basis of a 'structure' that superiors are somehow superior, to ascribe to 'lower level' participants only 'lower level' characteristics (e.g., Theory X, McGregor 1960), or to delude ourselves that the unfortunate lot of those who work 'below' us is somehow equitable (Klein and Ritti 1984).

Now this recognition does not require that each person truly *be* capable of self-actualization, a claim that is both empirically and conceptually in doubt (e.g., Neher 1991; Wahba and Bridwell 1976) but it does require that humanists must argue *as if*[10] each individual is so capable – and deserves to be so treated. It also does not deny the *up–down* dichotomy, but addresses the metaphor's emotional connotations by the argument that within *each* individual is a path to transcend this dichotomy, and so to grace. In fact Maslow himself when discussing 'The Resolution of Dichotomies in Self-Actualization' argues

> it was concluded that what had been considered in the past to be polarities or opposites or dichotomies were so *only in less healthy people*. In healthy people, these dichotomies were resolved, the polarities disappeared, and many oppositions thought to be intrinsic merged and coalesced with each other to form unities.

And further, 'The higher and the lower are not in opposition but in agreement, and a thousand serious philosophical dilemmas are discovered to have more than two horns, or paradoxically, no horns at all' (Maslow 1970: 178–9).

Again we have to emphasize that while Maslow's arguments are both metaphorical and structured along the Axis Mundi this does not mean that they are not real in their effects. Another way to put this same point is from Emery and Trist (1965) who, when discussing turbulent fields, argue that such fields are stabilized only by value prescriptions that structure reality. In our context compassion is a value prescription which structures those managerial 'turbulent fields' noted by Weick (1987). It is also the hallmark of humanitarianism which, 'strictly defined, is the institutionalization of compassion' (Encyclopaedia Britannica 1999b: 2).

Summary

If we argue for compassion we create one type of world, if we are blind to compassion we create another. It is the demand that others be seen as fully capable of transcendent experience, in conflict with John Masterman's blindness, that leads Maria to tell the rich in the garden and the children too that they are 'brothers'. It is the demand for compassion which, while inadvertently minimized, also informs the work of humanists who have an interest in organizational structure, and those who doubt that a reconciliation between the head and the hands can ever be achieved, believing that without the necessary experience, those at the 'top' of an organization can never fully comprehend the results of being on the 'bottom' and never truly believe that the 'other' is capable of transcendence.

If our analysis is correct, organizational structures can be seen as patterned on the root metaphor of *up–down*, with the ensuing impression that those who are *down* are creatures not capable of transcendence. And if we are correct, the counter to this error is a *mythical* argument, also based on the root metaphor and the Axis Mundi, but individualized. It is the argument that the potential for both development and darkness lies not in the one's organizational *position* but in one's *self*. It is the mythic argument that the individual, not the organization, should be the focus of the root metaphor that is symbolic of the internal and individual struggle for reconciliation between material and spiritual concerns and so self-development. It is also an argument that this potential is not only in each of us but is what we *are*. This realization, consequently, becomes an argument for compassion and for a recognition of the capacity for transcendental experiences in all. It is this mythic realization which serves as a partial antidote to the great philosophical mistake in Metropolis, the approach to other human beings as an 'it'.

Notes

1 Fritz Lang usually receives credit for *Metropolis*, but the film script and the novel can more reasonably be credited to Thea von Harbou.
2 In the novel 'Freder'. In the review by Sime (1927) 'Eric'. 'John Masterman' is 'Joh Fredersen' in the original.
3 Lightfoot (2000) notes that Roland Barthes discusses how mythologizing makes capitalist relations seem natural and right.
4 In the novel 'gates and stairs' (von Harbou 1927: 23, 41) but also see the 'Pater-noster lift' (von Harbou 1927: 39).
5 Compare to 'socialized' and 'personal' power needs (e.g., Yukl 1998: 238–9).
6 Solomon's Seal is on Rotwang's door. This is how John Masterman finds his way to the catacombs. Fred's mother was in love with Rotwang but chose John Masterman, choosing power and material comfort (lower order concerns) over love (higher level concerns). She dies when Fred is born, but 'She really died on the day upon which she went from Rotwang to John [Masterman] wondering that her feet left no bloody traces behind on the way' (von Harbou 1927: 58–9). Fred rights this wrong by following the path of his heart to Maria.
7 Fred is only an 'it' to his father, so much so he contemplates leaving earth .
8 Lightfoot (2000) says that the *up–down* metaphor is often seen in writings about strategy; additionally those who are promoted (making the journey part-way *up*) are often seen as more worthy of future development.
9 *Motivation and Personality* was originally to be called *Higher Ceilings for Human Nature* and directed toward 'reaching into the "higher" levels of human nature' (Maslow 1970: ix).
10 Paradoxically, Maslow is not highly in favour of *as if* arguments (e.g., Maslow, 1970: 325–6). Also see Campbell (e.g., 1986).

References

Bass, B. M. and Avolio, B. J. (1990) 'Developing transformational leadership: 1992 and beyond', *Journal of European Industrial Training* 14, 21–7.

Bobbitt, Jr, H. R. and Ford, J. D. (1980) 'Decision-maker choice as a determinant of organizational structure', *Academy of Management Review* 5, 1: 13–23.

Bowen, D. E. and Lawler, III, E. E. (1992) 'The empowerment of service workers; what, why, how and when', *Sloan Management Review* 33, 3: 31–9.

Bowles, M. L. (1989) 'Myth, meaning and work organization', *Organization Studies* 10, 3: 405–21.

Campbell, J. (1968a) *Creative Mythology: The Masks of God*, New York: Penguin Books.

—— (1968b) *The Hero with a Thousand Faces* (2nd edn), Princeton, N. J.: Princeton University Press.

—— (1976) *Primitive Mythology: The Masks of God*, New York: Penguin Books.

—— (1986) *The Inner Reaches of Outer Space: Metaphor as Myth and as Religion*, New York: HarperCollins.

—— (1988) *The Power of Myth with Bill Moyers*, ed. by B. S. Flowers, New York: Doubleday.

—— 1990 *Transformations of Myth Through Time*, New York: Harper & Row.

Clark, J. V. (1960) 'Motivation in work groups: a tentative view', *Human Organizations* 13, 199–208.

Dickson, J. W. (1981) 'Participation as a means of organizational control', *Journal of Management Studies* 18, 2: 159–76.

Encyclopaedia Britannica (1999a) 'Expressionism', online. Available HTTP: http://www.ed.com:180/bol/topic?eu = 34042&sctn = 1 (June 28, 1999).

—— (1999b) 'Social science: new intellectual and philosophical tendencies', online. Available HTTP: http://www.ed.com:180/bol/topic?eu = 117534&sctn = 8 (April 3, 2000).

Emery, F. E. and Trist, E. L. (1965) 'The causal texture of organizational environments', *Human Relations* 18, 1: 21–32.

Fry, L. W. (1982) 'Technology–structure research: three critical issues', *Academy of Management Journal* 25, 3: 532–52.

Gibson, J. L., Ivancevich, J. M. and Donnelly Jr, J. H. (1982) *Organizations: Behavior, Structure, Processes*, Plano, Texas: Business Publications.

Glisson, C. A. (1978) 'Dependence of technological routinization on structural variables in human service organizations', *Administrative Science Quarterly* 23, 383–95.

Grant, J. (1990) *An Introduction to Viking Mythology*, London: New Burlington Books.

Hackman, J. R. and Oldham G. R. (1976) 'Motivation through the design of work: test of a theory', *Organizational Behavior and Human Performance* 16, 259–79.

—— (1980) *Work Redesign*, Reading, Mass.: Addison-Wesley.

Jurkiewicz, K. (1990) 'Using film in the humanities classroom: the case of *Metropolis*', *English Journal* 79, 3: 47–50.

Klein, S. M. and Ritti, R. R. (1984) *Understanding Organizational Behavior* (2nd edn), Boston, Mass.: Kent Publishing.

Kracauer, S. (1947) *From Caligari to Hitler: A Psychological History of the German Film*, Princeton, N.J.: Princeton University Press.

Lakoff G. and Johnson, M. (1980) *Metaphors We Live By*, Chicago: University of Chicago Press.

Lawler, III, E. E. and Suttle, J. L. (1972) 'A causal correlational test of the need hierarchy concept', *Organizational Behavior and Human Performance* 7, 265–87.

Lightfoot, G. (2000) '*Metropolis*, Maslow and the Axis Mundi', personal communication by e-mail from 'Geoff Lightfoot' <swedging@sword-of-truth.fsnet.co.uk> (March 27, 2000).

McGregor, D. (1960) *The Human Side of Enterprise*, New York: McGraw-Hill.

McKendall, M. (1993) 'The tyranny of change: organizational development revisited', *Journal of Business Ethics* 12, 93–104.

Mali, P. (1981) *Management Handbook*, New York: Wiley.

Maslow, H. A. (1943) 'A theory of human motivation', *Psychological Review* 50, 370–96.

—— (1964) *Religions, Values, and Peak-Experiences*, Columbus, Ohio: Ohio State University Press.

—— (1970) *Motivation and Personality* (2nd edn), New York: Harper & Row.

—— (1987) *Motivation and Personality* (3rd edn), revised by R. Frager, J. Fadiman, C. McReynolds and R. Cox, New York: Harper & Row.

Miller, W. B. (1964) 'Two concepts of authority', in H. J. Leavitt and L. R. Pondy (eds) *Readings in Managerial Psychology*, Chicago: University of Chicago Press.

Miner, J. B. (1980) *Theories of Organizational Behavior*, Hinsdale, Ill.: Dryden Press.

Mintzberg, H. (1979) *The Structuring of Organizations: A Synthesis of the Research*, Englewood Cliffs, N. J.: Prentice-Hall.

Morgan, G. (1997) *Images of Organization*, Thousand Oaks, California: Sage.

Neher, A. (1991) 'Maslow's theory of motivation: a critique', *Journal of Humanistic Psychology* 31, 3: 89–112.

Organ, M. (1999) '*Metropolis*, section 7: contemporary reviews', online. Available HTTP: http://www.uow.edu.au/~morgan/Metroh.html (June 29, 1999).

Salaman, G. (1979) *Work Organizations: Resistance and Control*, London: Longman.

Senge, P. M. (1990) 'The leader's new work: building learning organizations', *Sloan Management Review* 32, 1: 7–23.

Sime (1927) '*Metropolis*', *Variety*, March 16, 1927, in M. Organ (1999) '*Metropolis*, section 7: contemporary reviews', online. Available HTTP: http://www.uow.edu.au/~morgan/Metroh.html (June 29, 1999).

Thompson, J. D. (1967) *Organizations in Action*, New York: McGraw-Hill.

von Harbou, T. (1927) *Metropolis*, Boston, Mass.: Gregg Press (first British publication 1929, 1975 reissue).

Vreeland, F. (1927) '*Metropolis*', *The New York Telegram*, March 7, 1927, in M. Organ (1999) '*Metropolis*, section 7: contemporary reviews', online. Available HTTP: http://www.uow.edu.au/~morgan/Metroh.html (June 29, 1999).

Wahba, M. A. and Bridwell, L. G. (1976) 'Maslow reconsidered: a review of research on the need hierarchy theory', *Organizational Behavior and Human Performance* 15, 212–40.

Weber, M. (1946) 'Bureaucracy', in H. H. Gerth and C. W. Mills (eds) *From Max Weber: Essays in Sociology*, New York: Oxford University Press.

Weick, K. E. (1987) 'Perspectives on action in organizations', in J. W. Lorsch (ed.) *Handbook of Organizational Behavior*, Englewood Cliffs, N. J.: Prentice-Hall.

Wells, H. G. '*Metropolis*', *The New York Times*, April 17, 1927, in M. Organ (1999) '*Metropolis*, section 7: contemporary reviews', online. Available HTTP: http://www.uow.edu.au/~morgan/Metroh.html (June 29, 1999).

Woodward, J. (1965) *Industrial Organization: Theory and Practice*, London: Oxford University Press.

Wren, D. A. (1994) *The Evolution of Management Thought* (4th edn), New York: Wiley

Yukl, G. (1998) *Leadership in Organizations* (4th edn), Upper Saddle River, N.J.: Prentice Hall.

4 The rape of the machine metaphor

Nanette Monin and John Monin

Introduction

In this paper we intend to play with metaphor. And we are aware that while our playing is utterly serious, it may yet, like that of the child whose sandpit play is intensely real and deeply formative to the playing child, be somewhat amusing to the adult onlooker. But because metaphors are complex, because they are infinitely dynamic and elusive of meaning capture, we think that it is only by exploring, experimenting and playing with them that we grow to understand their potential effects within organizations.

Learning through playing begins with enactment, so seeking out evidence of the machine metaphor in action, we have chosen to look first at a particular short story. In our paper we share our reconstruction of this story and then build it into a theoretical commentary. We assume that if Gareth Morgan spoke for the research community when he posited the negatory question 'Is there anything more to be said about metaphor?' (Morgan 1996), then most of our readers are familiar with metaphorical theorizing in organization studies to date; and we fully concur with Morgan's 'postmodern' (Morgan 1996: 236) ontological positioning of metaphor in organizational theory. On the other hand we intend to demonstrate that we think there is still much 'more to be said' about the role of this ancient trope in contemporary organizations.

At the outset we aim to *shock* readers into reassessing the potential of metaphors to further illuminate organization studies, and we have elected to use a short story as a 'case study' of what we are calling a 'dramatized metaphor' for two reasons. First, short stories are often structured so as to make a resounding impact in a succinct and entertaining narrative – hence the element of surprise. Second, authors of literature are both seers and participant observers who imaginatively create innovative worldviews. We think that the 'reality' they recount is as reliable and valuable as that of any actor within an organization or of any observer from without.

We begin, in a moment, with the story, because now that we have said that we intend to shock, we do not want to prolong reader suspense – by explaining at this point and at length, what we mean by 'metaphor'. Simply, our concern is not with the classical, macro-level machine metaphor, but with the metaphor's influence on the construction of the worldviews of individuals within an organization. The story we tell is a story of the enactment of the dreams of human persons, as technologists, and their reconstruction of themselves in the image of deities, as they attempt to make human-like machines and machine-like humans.

We begin, at the end, with the story's 'climax'.

A kind of climax

The Tinkerer is in love with an ancient computer. It is about to be junked, but before he leaves it for the last time 'he turns and looks at the monitor and the 360 looks back at him . . . there is a flicker on the computer monitor like the batting of an eyelid' (Taylor 1995: 40) for the computer has seemed to the Tinkerer, to know, to understand exactly that the red-haired Lara must be reprogrammed. 'The 360 is like a human being. Spread out under glass', while Lara 'lies on the floor making strange noises in her throat.' It is the Tinkerer who, not understanding at first, 'then realizes what it must be: the noises are whirrs and clicks, like the machines. Lara he tells himself is being overwritten' (ibid.).

Computer and user, 360 and his lover, have just committed a horrendous assault on the woman who had threatened their relationship, and in a story which moves relentlessly and unnervingly from insecurity and inadequacy to obscenity, one of the accomplices to the crime seems to be the metaphor of the dramatized narrative. It is a story from which the reader may pull away with distaste, but at the same time, as was our experience, may unwillingly suspend disbelief. Taylor's language is also our language, his metaphors, the familiars of popular techno-logical discourse, are the taken-for-granted, ordinary citizens of our everyday culture so they belong to all of us, and perhaps if, as in this story, they are pathologically interpreted and enacted, then the responsibility for awful outcomes is a collective responsibility.

For this is a story of obsession, rape and insanity – yet we will suggest that it is also a story that points to metaphor's complicity in the crimes of the Tinkerer.

The story: an introduction

The scenes on which we drew back the curtain above are played out in the conclusion to Chad Taylor's short story 'The Man Who Wasn't Feeling Himself' (1995), but the whole story can be read as dramatized root metaphor: one that demonstrates a pathological transference of perceptions of people, of computers and of the person–computer relationship leading to monstrous behaviour.

It is also a story that takes its place in a developing body of literature, known as cyberpunk or postmodern science fiction (McCaffery 1991; Tabbi 1995), which portrays people as intimately identified with electronic robots: human characters who act, think and emote as if they are mechanical creations; and technology created entities which take on human attributes, the cyborgs (Haraway 1991; Morse 1994), and the sentient computers (Gibson 1986). A central technological theme in the cyberpunk novel is the removal of the distinction between animate and inanimate in respect of body parts: prosthetic limbs, implanted circuitry (Gibson 1994 and 1996), brain–computer interfaces, and genetic re-engineering. Dale Spender (1995) has said of Marge Piercy's *He, She, or It* (1991) that 'when she portrays human beings with extensive computerized parts, and robots with soft-ware that has been programmed to make them the most understanding of human beings' she 'blurs the boundaries' (p. 256). But Spender then asks: 'So what's human and what's a machine – and does it matter?'

A reading of Taylor's short story shows that it matters very much indeed. His horrifying narrative, which illustrates a pathological response to the computer as person and person as computer metaphor, centres on the protagonist's romance with a computer, and rape of a woman. In New Zealand, where Taylor's work has been admitted into established literary circles it has been welcomed by some, yet he has also been accused of peddling pornography (Ferrall 1996). It seems to us that at one level 'The Man Who Wasn't Feeling Himself' can be read as a timeless tale of courtly love: rejection, perilous journey and a final return home to find true love. But in this story the adored other is a computer, and the pathological love relationship threatened by a rival – a woman on whom terrible vengeance is wreaked – turns the protagonist into a robotic invention calmly clicking to a binary rhythm.

Taylor presents us with a two-way mirror: we are privy to the mind and actions of an anti-hero with a pathological perception of the person/machine metaphor; and simultaneously, as readers, we see a reflection of our own collective guilt. Our society has spawned a nameless protagonist who thinks and behaves as if programmed by a computer, attributes human feelings and vitality to a computer, and assumes that his violation of a woman will 're-program' her into an accept-able machine mode.

We first meet this man in the bathroom. He is wet-shaving in a meticulous routine. We only see him alone with his reflected mirror image, but discover as he ruminates, that his early attempts to live comfortably in a human world ended in misery and in mockery. His careful travel plans were shambolized by people and the elements, at work he is censured for his technical expertise and women laugh at him.

When not mocking, the other characters in the story, all females, have 'related' to him in perfunctory, mechanical 'interfaces'. While he was still at high school a fellow art student symbolically walked away with his manhood (in the form of a plaster cast of his erect penis), and then long after he had swapped art for math-ematics, a mechanical sex act with an anonymous crone simply made him 'warm, then wet, then cold once more' – like a machine being switched on and off.

Thus far there is nothing particularly distinctive about this robotic creation. Even his burning emotional attachment to the old IBM360 computer which, as a contemporary knight gallant, he rescues from oblivion, seems relatively normal: 'It was sorrow. And rage. And loss. And desperation. It was love.'

It is only when his attempt to reincarnate the antiquated 360 is threatened by a female colleague, Lara, that the horror of his pathological understanding and relationships emerges. 'As the screen chatted away to him' she (Lara) moved closer, 'much too close', and when the 'screen asks: 360 CONFIRM? Y/N', and 'looks up at him helplessly', he perceives in Lara 'someone about to take the 360 away for the second time'. He stops her, and while she lies coughing on the ground, the computer (he has pressed Y) hums. The 'monitor flickers. Black, white, black, white,' he feels a surge of power and 'surprised at the firmness of his grip on her thighs, he pushes her down again', and 'tears away her clothes':

> numbly searches for her keyboard. She struggles, but he finds it. He finds the interface. It is hidden in her mouth. . . . Calmly he reaches for the disk. . . . Seeing it Lara's eyes widen. . . . with a force that surprises them both, he inserts the disk. Before he leaves he turns and looks at the monitor and the 360 looks back at him. The 360 is like a human being. . . . Lara lies on the floor making strange noises in her throat. He does not understand at first but then realizes what it must be: the noises are whirrs and clicks, like the machines. Lara he tells himself, is being overwritten. She will go cold, then warm, then cold again . . . . He is reassured by the thought.
>
> (p. 40)

At home, safely back into the meticulous routine of his wet-shave, Taylor's anti-hero is tranquil, repeating to himself the 010101010101 rhythm of his first computer program, a practical joke. Back in the laboratory the computer monitor seems to wink.

Should metaphors be blamed for all, or even some, of the inversions and perversions of the roles played out in this story?

Our answer is quite simply 'We don't know'. But we do know that while our intellects concede justice, emotionally we rebel, outraged. While we fervently wish to dissolve Taylor's image, its power is inescapable. It is etched into memory, its connections indelibly forged, and our only defence is to recognize it for what it is: a dramatized metaphor.

Metaphor as a cyborgian construct

In the popular discourse of computing the personification of computers is all-pervasive. In the language of architects and marketers, journalists and end-users, metaphors that ascribe human attributes to computers (personifications) endlessly elaborate and extend the links between human attributes and electronic machines. Comment on this particular rhetorical construct has, to date, tended to focus on end-user relationships with the anthropomorphized machine. Karlqvist and Svedin (1993), Marakas (1994) and Prasad (1995) have all highlighted the role of this root metaphor in the discourses of the workplace, pointing out the impact that such discourse may have on behaviours in the social environment of the organization. Moving a step beyond these concerns and, picking up on a theme that we first addressed at an ACM conference (Monin and Monin 1994), we will propose that this is a root metaphor that is sometimes pathologically enacted.

In organization studies, a mechanistic root metaphor has long been recognized and debated (Morgan 1996). It is an old familiar in the history of theory, where, in industrial imagery, people are likened to machines, mechanical entities – anonymous, predictable, cogs in the turning wheels of the industrial world (Solomon 1992). Business organizations that expect people to perform like the 'inanimate cogs and wheels' of an anonymous machine, make 'the workers servants or adjuncts to machines that are in control of the organization and place of work' (Morgan 1986: 29–31).

In the ready application of computer terminology to human activity and identity this same machine metaphor lives on. Solomon (1992) concludes that in the contemporary world new grafts onto the mechanistic root metaphor portray every 'human relation [as] an "interface," and we begin to describe the workings of our own minds in the computer language of memory banks, downtime, glitches, data searches and so on' (p. 29).

Solomon's moral unease is not generally shared by leading academics researching the social effects of electronic technologies. Allucquère Stone, intimately involved in cyberspace as both inhabitant and anthropologist, seems to welcome the imminent advent of the person/machine. Describing an image of her 2-year-old daughter, hands on keyboard and her grin illuminated by 'the brilliant yellow glow' of a computer screen, she says:

> She seems to evince a generous permeability, an electronic porosity that is pathognomonic of the close of the mechanical age . . . I see the machine doing it too, as they hover on the brink of collapsing into each other . . . neurology and electronics, musculature and hydraulics, biology and technology, all hover on the edge of a stunning and irrecuperable mutual annihilation. She will survive that implosion and emerge as what the New Testament called in its efficient business Greek, *kaine ktisis*. New creature.
>
> (Stone 1995: 166–7)

But in this paper we suggest that if such a 'hybridization' is emerging, and if it is possible that the discourse of computer users is playing a part in this cataclysmic evolution, then as researchers we should engage in further exploration of computer language. We begin our exploration of this territory with reminders of a significant development of the machine metaphor: an inversion of the primary and secondary domains of the metaphor, so that where we have been used to finding mechanized people, we now find personified computers. Not so long ago, in the days of the main-frame computers, the era of the IBM360, British Computers Ltd (BCL) gave their computers female names. *Sallies* were quickly superseded by *Susies* and *Susies* were then replaced by *Sadies*. These 'ladies' who were said to rely on their *housekeeping* software, could *read* and *write*, *access*, *search* and *sort*, but were often *incompatible* and unable to *talk* to each other unless a communication *protocol* was well defined.

Times and technology have changed. Today a computer without software is a *naked* machine, and will accept the *insertion* of almost any *floppy*, even while supported by a *hard* disk. Such *user-friendly* behaviour exposes it to *bugs* and *viruses*, which if they *infect memory*, may necessitate *antiviral* procedures. *Aborting* may be necessary, and perhaps a *resident disk doctor* will be installed. But if, after its owner has *corrupted* it anyway, the computer should *die*, and refuse to be *booted* back into action, it will be *flushed*, and its *black box* immediately switched off. With *motherboards* connected to *daughtercards* to boost performance, *client servers* are now more responsive – and users can choose the control of a *thrustmaster* in place of a *mouse*.

Meanwhile computer users joke about *Aids*, recommend *condoms* for their disks, and advocate *safe sex methods on Marijuana Friday* (Monin and Monin 1994).

At one level, attempts to portray computers as mechanical entities that have some attributes in common with people – in so far as they are 'intelligent', 'expert' and 'friendly', but subject to 'bugs' and 'viruses' – may simply be a convenient communication device: metaphor performing a customary role by introducing new ideas and abstract notions, through relating the unfamiliar to the familiar. But at another level such personification can be viewed as influencing future action. As a consequence of our response to this metaphor, our expectations of computer performance and end-user relationship to the computer may be modified; and, even if we are unaware of the subliminal yet persuasive power of the metaphor, its seductions, as described below, because they are bedded in and grow from a timeless and universalized fantasy, may easily assume control of our emotional responses to computer technology.

It is far below the excavated roots of this metaphor that a mythic saga lives on in which humankind, specifically mankind, dreams of creating a being more obedient, more aesthetic, more intelligent, in short more perfect, than ourselves. Tellings and retellings of this ambitious fantasy reveal a universal pathos and catastrophe from which we do not learn.

One of the most dominant myths of today (Warner 1994) finds its most powerful expression in Mary Shelley's 1818 *Frankenstein* which has 'become *the* contemporary parable of perverted science' (p. 20). 'Hubris' (insolent pride) and the desperate urge to exercise control are suggested as driving this need to move beyond natural order:

> Frankenstein offers a dazzling allegory of monsters' double presence: at one level they're emanations of ourselves, but at another, they're perceived as alien, abominable and separate so that we can deny them, and zap them into oblivion at the touch of a button.
>
> (Warner 1994: 21)

Karlqvist and Svedin describe attempts to 'transform man's technical creations into something similar to life' as the 'ultimate hubris': an attempt to establish Man on a par with the Creator (1993: 1). In support of their claim that this is impossible, and paves the way for disaster, they remind us of the ballet, *Coppelia* in which an old doll maker works unsuccessfully to give life to the doll that he has elaborately created. They suggest that we look for a pathology in the ambition of both doll-maker and computer architects (and in the present context, users).

The lesson is that the aspiration of transcending the borderline from man-made artifacts to living things is not only pathological but also futile. . . . Life is seen as a qualitatively different type of phenomenon from artifacts [such as] self-instructing programming machines.

(Karlqvist and Svedin 1993: 2)

The cyberspace equivalent of the doll-maker is the software creator of an interactive fantasy/virtual reality game played over the Internet (Dibbell 1993). A fictional character invents a voodoo doll and uses its magical powers to 'rape' and 'stab' a female character. There is once again, because of the 'reality' of the technology, a blurring of the distinction between real life (RL) and virtual reality (VR).

This then may be the source of a pathology embedded in computing discourse: it may be the source of a worldview that initiates action consequent to the metaphorical construction of a pathological 'reality'. And it is in the realms of that 'reality' that we find the anthropomorphized computer. Mythic ambition and social outcome, pathological 'relationship' between person and computer, all are constantly reinforced and renewed in the continuing elaboration and evolution, and we suggest hubris, of the root metaphor.

Metaphor and action

That there is an intimate link between the language that expresses the way we perceive our world, and the actions which reflect that language, is a view that is widely endorsed (Lacan 1977; Lakoff and Johnson 1980; Morgan 1986; Eccles *et al.*. 1992; Kendall and Kendall 1993; Prasad 1995). But the suggestion that the action that is inspired by metaphorical understandings may, in extreme interpretations, be pathological (Richards 1936) has not been explored in organizational theory. If for example, it can be demonstrated that metaphors popular with computer users are sexist personifications, then it may be that an end-user who develops a pathological interpretation of the metaphor is persuaded to relate to computers as if they have human attributes of an inferior female order.

Intimate and influential, the metaphor–action link is also very distinctively individualistic. One of the extraordinary powers of metaphorical communication is that it is infinitely ambiguous. It is open to as many interpretations as there are interpreters. The distinctive demand that it makes of its interpreters is that although one subject is being spoken of in terms of another, only *some* attributes of the first subject (or domain) are expected to be linked with *some* attributes of the second subject (domain) (Richards 1936; Black 1962; Indurkhya 1988). Thus when we describe the hand-held device that controls a computer as a mouse, we link the attributes that both the device and a mouse have in common: both are small, round and slip easily across the desk surface sporting a long tail. We do not need to be told that we should not think of the mechanical object as furry, verminous or pink-nosed! The mind that assumes so literal an interpretation of the word 'mouse' would be 'diagnosed as being in a pathological state' (Monin and Monin 1994).

But could it be that such a pathological transference of meaning might be encouraged by the pervasiveness of the root metaphor of computer as person? We have already suggested that the metaphor taps into a fantasy with a mythic history and now suggest that part of the answer can be found in theoretical explanations of the metaphorical process.

In our everyday communications we interpret aspects of what we do and who we are, by making connections between one activity and another or one entity and another: we describe one activity or entity in terms of another (Lakoff and Johnson 1980; Black 1962; Morgan 1986; Tsoukas 1991). Thus just as a person may be described as a machine, a computer may be described as if it has human attributes such as intellect or memory, and a body (prone to disease!). The more deeply embedded these concepts become in our conceptual thinking, the more they are popularized in everyday speech, the more they may possibly influence action.

Over time, as the original subject or activity, the 'tenor', is gradually subsumed into the 'vehicle' (Richards 1936), the process of transfer advances to a point at which the entity or action imaged in the vehicle becomes exclusively identified with its analogous partner. Both tenor and vehicle become 'transformed'. Instead of the vehicle illuminating attributes of the tenor, each domain becomes a reflection of aspects of the other.

Another dimension of this process is supported by recalling the very broad division that Richards made 'between metaphors which work through some direct resemblance between two things, the tenor and the vehicle, and those which work *through some common attitude* [my italics] which we may (often through accidental and extraneous reasons) take up towards them both' (p. 118). Thus when working with a piece of hardware that has no physical, intellectual or emotional resemblance to a human person, we may yet recognize that we have an intimate involvement with it: physically through the sense of touch; intellectually through data input and manipulation; and consequently also relate to it emotionally. It is this last link that may lead to pathological interpretation of the metaphor – a vulnerable individual may so identify with the analogously linked vehicle that a total transference of meaning takes place across domains.

Lakoff and Johnson maintain that their evidence demonstrates that 'metaphor pervades our normal conceptual system' (1980: 115), that not only do metaphors 'make coherent certain aspects of our experience', they may also

> create realities for us, especially social realities. A metaphor may thus be a guide for future action. Such actions will, of course, fit the metaphor. This will, in turn, reinforce the power of the metaphor to make experience coherent. It is in this sense that metaphors can be self-fulfilling prophecies.
>
> (p. 156)

It is in this sense then that although metaphors contribute endlessly to elusive *différance* (meaning which is infinitely beyond the play of signification and therefore beyond definition (Derrida 1993)) they can also, ironically, bring about closure: conceptual thinking may be trapped within the classifications and connections structured by a popular root metaphor.

Metaphors have a social impact of consequence when they are taken up into popular usage, influence common perceptions and thereby contribute to the so-called social construction of reality. And when this happens, the more adventurous the initial surprise, then the more indelibly the connection is forged into a 'worldview'. Over time, with continued popular use, the image of the vehicle becomes the accepted, the 'normal' view of the tenor or subject. It is a dialectical process which transforms the vehicle into a new tenor (Pepper 1942 and 1972; Turner 1974; Ricoeur 1978; Lakoff and Johnson 1980).

So it has been with the history of the personification of the computer. Early computers, with their languages, housekeeping software and nakedness, were originally depicted in exciting metaphors. Decades later these metaphors are dead. They have become clichés. Images of a machine which 'aborts', is 'booted' into action or smokes pot (the Marijuana virus) may well have seemed outrageous initially, but are now inconspicuous jargon. Users simply accept that this is the discourse of the PC user. But a social issue lives on, for whereas the original disparity was dramatic and exciting, if a pathological transference is effected through popular use, then a dramatization of the metaphor may be extreme. Pathological interpretation may lead to pathological action.

Richards explained that where metaphor commands the person, rather than the person commanding the metaphor, it is psychologists who have pointed out that the mind so commanded is in a pathological state:

> The psycho-analysts have shown us with their discussions of 'transference' – in this context another name for metaphor – how constantly modes of regarding, of loving, of acting, that have developed with one set of things of people, are shifted to another. They have shown us chiefly the pathology of these transferences, cases where the vehicle – the borrowed attitude, the parental fixation, say – tyrannizes over the new situation, the tenor, and behavior is inappropriate. The victim is unable to see the new person except in terms of the old passion and its accidents. He reads the situation only in terms of the figure, the archetypal image, the vehicle.
>
> (Richards 1936: 135)

It is from psychology, where this notion of cross-imaging has been fully explored, that Lakoff and Johnson draw some of their conclusions as to popular effects of metaphors upon action. Used to explain associations that indicate psychotic conditions, cross-imaging (Lacan 1977), or pathological transfer of the vehicle, also demonstrates the danger of accepting the unique perception as being appropriate to all.

It is this kind of danger, the danger that metaphors will inspire madness, that sparked Plato's distrust of the charm, the potential seductiveness, of poetry. And if personification of the computer is indeed inspiring a kind of 'madness' then this in our time should be a cause of deep concern. What we have seen described in the work of Karlqvist and Svedin as the 'ultimate hubris' of ascribing to machines human attributes which they do not have is simply denoted 'madness' by Burke: 'One uses metaphor without madness insofar as one spontaneously knows that the literal implication of the figure is not true . . .' and yet:

> despite the freedom of the rational discount, there may be sheer necessity in the trend of the images as such . . . they may compel us despite our genius for the negative; that is, we may not 'discount' them enough, not fully recognizing how imaginally positive they are.
>
> (Burke 1950: 463)

Computers are tools, albeit very sophisticated tools, which can neither think nor feel. Their every function is dependent upon the human technician, programmer and user. But, such is the power of the negative in metaphor's creation of meaning, the metaphors in which they are popularly described tend to distort this reality. If we have already become so accustomed to the idea that a machine can become infected, think, and relate that we no longer even notice such usage, then much of the personification of the computer is already a dead metaphor. But as vital metaphors evolve into dead metaphors, they yet continue to direct the subconscious into channelled modes of thinking and experiencing. Dead metaphors, particularly where they have become root metaphors, work at a subconscious level, and in so doing may incite emotions which the rational, conscious mind would repudiate (Wheelwright 1962). Although our rational faculties may have confidently rejected a complete synthesis of primary and secondary subjects, the emotional differentiation may not have been so successful. It is in the context of this understanding that the root metaphor of the personified computer may be a cause for concern.

Conclusions

In our reconstruction of Chad Taylor's story, the anti-hero dramatizes the chaotic madness into which those gripped by the imaginary may be plunged. Floating about in this shambles, probing this depiction of a monstrous attempt to control women and emote with a computer, we have found that metaphor theory suggests a world that can best be understood as the construct of a pathological symbolic ordering.

Our interpretation suggests that anthropomorphous and cyborgian metaphors in popular use in the language of technology may sometimes initiate pathological perceptions. It seems that when these metaphors migrate into popular usage, they may both influence perception in such a way as to contribute to a shared socially constructed reality; and, in the imagination of a vulnerable individual, if a metaphor suggests links between radically disparate subjects, may also lead to confusions of identity. When it is the technological and the human that are intimately metaphorically and emotively linked, a transfer of identity may pave a route to pathological confusion.

Taylor's cyberpunk narrative is built around a dramatization of the anti-hero's relationship to a personified computer. Its horrifying catastrophe, the violation of a woman with a computer disk, suggests that popular identification with the metaphor may be instrumental in initiating grotesque individual perception and action: it enables a pathological real life (RL) and virtual reality (VR) transfer in a world where a man emotes with an electronic machine, and a woman is abused because she is perceived as a mechanical entity.

Metaphor theory suggests then, that in metaphorical sense-making the yoking of two disparate spheres of meaning in the imagination may initiate inappropriate transference.

References

Black, M. (1962) *Models and Metaphors: Studies in Language and Philosophy*, Ithaca, New York: Cornell University Press.

Burke, K. (1950) *A Rhetoric of Motive*, Englewood Cliffs, N.J.: Prentice-Hall.

Derrida, J. (1993) *Speech and Phenomena and Other Essays on Husserl's Theory of Signs*, trans. D.B. Allison, Evanston: Northwestern University Press.

Dibbell, J. (1993) 'A rape in cyberspace, or how an evil clown, a Haitian Trickster spirit, two wizards, and a cast of dozens turned a database into a society', *Village Voice*, 21 December.

Eccles, R.G. and Nohria, N. with Berkley, J.D. (1992) *Beyond the Hype: Rediscovering the Essence of Management*, Boston: Harvard Business School Press.

Ferrall, C. (1996) '"The man who wasn't feeling himself", Chad Taylor', *Landfall: New Zealand Arts and Letters*, vol. 4, 1 March.

Gibson, W. (1984) *Neuromancer*, New York: Berkley.

Gibson, W. (1986) *Count Zero*, New York: Arbor House.

Haraway, D. J. (1991) *Simians, Cyborgs, and Women: The Reinvention of Nature*, New York: Routledge.

Indurkhya, B. (1988) 'Constrained semantic transference: a formal theory of metaphors', in A. Prieditis (ed.) *Analogica*, London: Pitman.

Karlqvist, A. and Svedin, U. (1993) 'Introduction', in H. Haken, A. Karlqvist and U. Svedin (eds) *The Machine as Metaphor and Tool*, Berlin: Springer-Verlag, pp. 1–8.

Kendall, J.E. and Kendall, K.E. (1993) 'Metaphors and methodologies: living beyond the systems machine', *MIS Quarterly*, June, pp. 149–71.

Lacan, J. (1977) *Ecrits*, trans. A. Sheridan, London: Tavistock.

Lakoff, G. and Johnson, M. (1980) *Metaphors We Live By*, Chicago and London: University of Chicago Press.

McCaffery, L. (1991) *Storming the Reality Studio: A Casebook of Cyberpunk and Postmodern Science Fiction*, Durham and London: Duke University Press.

Marakas, G. M. (1994) 'Anthropromorphic behaviour and information technology: when the metaphor becomes the model', in *Proceedings of the Association for Computer Machinery, Special Interest Group Computer Personnel (ACM SIGCPR) Conference*, March 24–26, 1994.

Monin, N., and Monin, D.J. (1994) 'Personification of the computer: a pathological metaphor in information systems', in *Proceedings of the Association for Computer Machinery, Special Interest Group Computer Personnel (ACM SIGCPR) Conference*, March 24–26, 1994.

Morgan, G. (1986) *Images of Organizations*, Beverly Hills, CA: Sage.

—— (1996) 'An afterword: is there anything more to be said about metaphor?', in D. Grant and C. Oswick (eds) *Metaphor and Organizations*, London: Sage.

Morse, M. (1994) 'What do cyborgs eat? Oral logic in an information society', in G. Bender and T. Druckrey (eds) *Culture on the Brink: Ideologies of Technology*, Seattle: Bay Press, pp. 157–90.

Pepper, S.C. (1942) *World Hypotheses: A Study in Evidence*, Berkley and Los Angeles: University of California Press.

Pepper, S.C. (1972) 'The root metaphor theory of metaphysics'. in W. Shibbles (ed.) *Essays on Metaphor*, Wisconsin: The Language Press.

Piercy, M. (1991) *He, She, or It*, New York: Knopf.

Prasad, P. (1995) 'Working with the "smart" machine: computerization and the discourse of anthropomorphism in organizations', *Studies in Culture, Organizations and Society*, vol. 1, pp. 253–6.

Richards, I. A. (1936) *The Philosophy of Rhetoric*, Oxford: Oxford University Press.

Ricoeur, P. (1978) *The Rule of Metaphor: Multi-Disciplinary Studies of the Creation of Meaning in Language*, trans. R. Czerny, K. McLaughlin and S.J. Costello, London: Routledge.

Shelley, M.W. (1989) [1818] *Frankenstein*, New York: Penguin.

Solomon, R. C. (1992) *Ethics and Excellence: Co-operation and Integrity in Business*, New York: Oxford University Press.

Spender, D. (1995) *Nattering on the Net: Women, Power and Cyberspace*, Melbourne: Spinifex Press.

Stone, A. R. (1995) *The War of Desire and Technology at the Close of the Mechanical Age*, Cambridge, Mass: MIT Press.

Tabbi, J. (1995) *Postmodern Sublime: Technology and American Writing from Mailer to Cyberpunk*, Ithaca, New York: Cornell University Press.

Taylor, C. (1995) *The Man Who Wasn't Feeling Himself: Short Stories by Chad Taylor*, Auckland: David Ling.

Tsoukas, H. (1991) 'The missing link: a transformational view of metaphors in organizational science', *Academy of Management Review*, vol. 16, pp. 566–85.

Turner, Victor (1974) *Dramas, Fields and Metaphors: Symbolic Action in Human Society*, Ithaca, New York: Cornell University Press.

Warner, M. (1994) *Managing Monsters: Six Myths of Our Time: The 1994 Reith Lectures*, London: Vintage.

Wheelwright, P. (1962) *Metaphor and Reality*, Bloomington: Indiana University Press.

5 Organizing men out in Joanna Russ's *The Female Man* and Fay Weldon's *The Cloning of Joanna May*

Maria Aline Ferreira

A recurring trope in science fiction narratives has been an intense concern for environmental issues, anxieties about which have been translated into a vast number of post-apocalyptic narratives[1] and fictional accounts of alternative worlds where one of the reigning preoccupations is the ecological balance between eco-systems. The urgent need to introduce ecological principles in the running of organizations and industries in order to minimize planetary pollution as well as the development of new conceptual models of organizational structures have played a fundamental role in the management and containment of the ecological crisis which has set in. Here I will be focusing upon the intersections of ecofeminism and organizational theory and practice as they appear dramatized in Joanna Russ's *The Female Man* (1975) and Fay Weldon's *The Cloning of Joanna May* (1989), two texts which, as I will be arguing, share many feminist concerns and offer apposite instances of science fiction's engagement with gender.

Especially since the 1970s, when a spate of feminist science fiction novels were published,[2] this genre's involvement with issues of gender has demonstrated a growing concern and preoccupation. Many authors have found the freedom to speculate granted them by science fiction an ideal medium through which to outline the contours of future, alternative worlds where women would have greater independence and the autonomy to shape them according to their own personal as well as sociopolitical agendas.

The science fiction and utopian societies[3] I will be analysing here are centrally concerned with issues of organization, with institutional arrangements and how they will in very practical terms affect people's daily lives and improve them.

The ideals of competitiveness advocated by capitalist society have come under severe criticism on the part of individuals, communities and organizations concerned with environmental welfare. As Carolyn Merchant pointedly remarks:

> Theories about nature and theories about society have a history of interconnections . . . as the ecology and economy of farm, forest, and fen were altered by new forms of human interaction with nature, traditional models of organic society and modes of social organization were likewise being undermined and transformed.

(1990: 69)

Market-oriented values coupled with capitalist modes of production spelt the destruction of great portions of fertile land, while nuclear energy further threatened already endangered, fragile ecosystems. The long history of human domination of the natural world, traditionally gendered as female, has as a close counterpart male exploitation of women and their reproductive capacities. These are precisely two of the most important thematic concerns in *The Female Man* and *The Cloning of Joanna May*, two novels which further engage with some of the intersections of the problems outlined above. Indeed, male imperialism of individuals and organizations over the female domain of procreation and the 'feminized' natural world are the central thematic issues of Russ's and Weldon's books. Both novels thus dramatize some of the potential evils perpetrated by societal organizations and human agency on the environment and women's bodies, and suggest possible solutions to deal with these problems.

The Cloning of Joanna May

In *The Cloning of Joanna May* the threat to the natural environment and to people is centred around the Chernobyl nuclear disaster and the role of the protagonist, Carl May, in the supervision of that crisis, addressing the question of potential ecological calamities and their repercussions. The action of the novel takes place in London against the background of the Chernobyl disaster, in 1986. Weldon explicitly links male power over women's bodies and their reproductive functions with domination over the natural world, suggesting that male exploitation is responsible for the subjugation of both women and nature. Carl May, the husband of the novel's protagonist, Joanna May, is the Chairman of British Nuclear Agents, Britnuc for short. He embodies the dangers of a monopoly of power in organizational life, of decision-making as a hazardous power game when concentrated in a single person.[4] Britnuc, with its two nuclear reactors, has a particular responsibility in keeping the environment uncontaminated. Carl May's nods to public pressure and the incorporation of ecocentric values in his business enterprises are basically reduced to cosmetic gardening around the nuclear power stations to maintain the illusion of healthy, clean air and verdant pastures. Weldon's novel dramatizes a widely held assumption on the public part that, as Carolyn P. Egri and Lawrence T. Pinfield note,

> governmental and business organizations are judged not to take the interests, aspirations and needs of their citizenry into account in their pursuit of organizational goals and objectives. . . . The 'environmental problem' is a consequence of how society is structured, for as multiple organizations pursue their self-interests, the interstices of society become an increasingly degraded residual.
>
> (1999: 209)

If 'organizations . . . are the fundamental building blocks of modern societies' as Aldrich and Marsden maintain (1988), measures geared towards a greater respect for the environment and less polluting emissions have to come from inside the organizations themselves, less from an orgocentric perspective and more with an outlook towards the greater good of all. Carl May is the epitome of the self-centred, selfish individual, bent on the pursuit of personal and financial success and the commercial and financial prosperity of his business, Britnuc, without any concern for the damaging consequences the practices condoned by him can have on people and the environment. This is significantly an area which is addressed by Egri and Pinfield in their reflections on organizations and the biosphere: the warring impulses of self-interest are contextualized and examined in different situations, the authors concluding that 'a shared appreciation of environmental issues is critical as resolution of environmental threats invariably requires inter-dependent collective action' (1999: 225), a line of action Carl May consistently and irresponsibly veers away from.

In his study of the 'culture of narcissism' (1983: 89) which, according to Christopher Lasch, characterizes our contemporary world, Lasch comments that the narcissistic organizational culture produces the kind of leader who 'sees the world as a mirror of himself and has no interest in external events except as they throw back a reflection of his own image' (ibid.: 96), words that fittingly apply to Carl May's prepotent behaviour. As Albert J. Mills in related vein remarks, 'such leaders are often more concerned with image than substance – advancing through the corporate ranks not by serving the organization but by convincing his associates that he possesses the attributes of a "winner"' (1994: 140), a perception that can be said to correspond to May's professional trajectory. As Lasch further contends, 'for all his inner suffering, the narcissist has many traits that make for success in bureaucratic institutions, which put a premium on the manipulation of inter-personal relations, discourage the formation of deep personal attachments, and at the same time provide the narcissist with the approval he needs to validate his self-esteem' (ibid.: 91–2), an insight which is pertinent to the analysis of Carl May's authoritarian conduct and its pernicious repercussions.

Intricately connected with the question of narcissism and the exercise of power within organizations is the issue of the gendering of authority in business enter-prises. Organizational culture, traditionally dominated by men, is heavily gen-dered, as many commentators have noted.[5] Sylvia Gherardi, for instance, observes that 'culture, gender and power are . . . intimately bound up with each other in organizations as well as in society' (1995: 17). However, as she remarks, 'organizational theories . . . claim to be gender neutral' (ibid.: 17), even though, as she observes, 'there is an implicit subtext to this literature which assumes that workers are male, that managers are men with virile characteristics, and that organizations are the symbolic locus of production just as the home is the locus of reproduction' (ibid.: 17). In related fashion, Rosemary Pringle, in her examination of the working relations between male bosses and female secretaries, came to the conclusion that 'male managers use sexuality and family relations to establish their control over secretaries', treating them '"narcissistically" as an extension of themselves' (1989: 173), just as May behaves towards his secretary, Bethany. It is precisely this kind of organizational culture, which to a great extent mirrors male-dominated societal patterns of organization, that comes under incisive scru-tiny in *The Cloning of Joanna May*.

The other fundamental theme in Weldon's novel is human cloning, science fiction becoming (almost) science fact. As she herself explains: 'In *The Cloning of Joanna May* I take birth away from women, and hand it over to men: as they are of course busy doing for themselves in the real world' (1994: 206). Our contemporary world is fascinated with the idea of human cloning, which makes true the fantasy of creating life on one's own, without the help of the opposite sex, a dream which has been a long-standing ambition of humankind, nurtured by both women and men. Together with Dr Holly, who works for Martins Pharmaceuticals, of which Carl May is meaningfully a director, Carl May manages to remove an egg from his wife's anaesthetized body and have four cloned embryos of Joanna May implanted in four healthy wombs and subsequently born. Carl May's action may be inscribed in his overarching dream of domination over both women and the natural world. He fantasizes about creating the perfect woman but, like Frankenstein, neglects to take responsibility for his creations, in what can be regarded as a parallel neglecting of implementation of strict security measures in the nuclear power stations belonging to Britnuc. In her 'Egg Farming and Women's Future', philosopher Julie Murphy addresses the complex issue of reproductive technologies and rights in words that pertinently fit Joanna May's situation. According to Murphy, women 'are defined in patriarchy as "reproductive bodies". . . . We are constantly discouraged, forbidden to use our bodies for ourselves. Reproductive technology, in the service of patriarchy, assumes that women's bodies are fertile lands to be farmed. Women are regarded as commodities with vital products to harvest: eggs' (1984: 68–9), just as Joanna May's body is harvested for her ripe eggs, a body which Carl May wishes to have full control over as he would of a fertile plot of land to be exploited for one of his business enterprises.

Science historian Donna Haraway's vision of nature is relevant here, providing a critical counterpart to Carl May's imperialist views of control and exploitation of the natural world. She considers that

> nature is not a physical place to which one can go, nor a treasure to fence in or bank, nor as essence to be saved or violated. Nature is not hidden and so does not need to be unveiled. Nature is not a text to be read in the codes of mathematics and biomedecine. It is not the 'other' who offers origin, replenishment, and service. Neither mother, nurse, nor slave, nature is not matrix, resource, or tool for the reproduction of man.
>
> (1992: 296)

As Haraway goes on to assert, 'we must find another relationship to nature besides reification and possession' (ibid.).

Donna Haraway also significantly stresses the links between the politics of reproduction in late capitalism and the effective exercise of power in society and organizations. As she notes:

> Reproductive politics provide the figure for the possibility and nature of a future in multinational capitalist and nuclear society. Production is conflated with reproduction. Reproduction has become the prime strategic question, a privileged trope for logics of investment and expansion in late capitalism, and the site of discourse about the limits and promises of the self as individual.

Reproductive 'strategy' has become the figure for reason itself – the logic of late capitalist survival and expansion, of how to stay in the game in post-modern conditions. Simultaneously, reproductive biotechnology is developed and contested within the large symbolic web of the story of the final removal of making babies from women's bodies, the final appropriation of nature by culture, of woman by man.

(1989: 352)

Carl May's act of playing God, of taking into his hands decisions about his wife's procreative rights and considering only his own best interests, namely the possibility of having at his disposal in the near future younger copies of his Joanna May who might take her place, are on a par with his exercise of power games in the organizations in which he is Chairman. Being at the top of the organization hierarchy, he has been able to delegate and concentrate his energies in higher 'ministerial dealings' (Weldon 1993: 76). Carl May is considered as a 'monster' (ibid.: 58) by one of his colleagues, who acknowledges that 'our organization is a little sketchy . . . and I am not getting much cooperation where I had hoped to find it' (ibid.: 58), since May's managerial skills tend to obliterate hard realities and potentially hazardous situations to the public, such as, in this case, the threats that the Chernobyl disaster might entail to the British population, as well as the conceivable dangers posed by a similar malfunction in the nuclear power stations owned by Britnuc.

A related theme which comes in for severe criticism in Weldon's novel is the fetishization of youth and the concomitant misogynistic discourse that considers older women as dispensable, almost as inconsequential non-entities, as Carl May insinuates when he declares to his 60-year-old ex-wife, Joanna: 'You should have died twenty years ago, what use to the world are you? A woman without youth, without children, without interest, a woman without a husband' (ibid.: 106). Indeed, Carl May's interconnected dream of creating a 'perfect woman' (ibid.: 78), who according to him would be one 'who looked, listened, understood and was faithful' (ibid.: 78) is also inextricably linked with his fantasy of an ideal of womanhood, youthful, passive and compliant, existing only to fulfil his wishes, growing progressively worthless with age. This egocentric daydream is closely intertwined with Carl May's illusory hope that by creating four younger versions of his wife he would be able to recover her youth and benefit again from the favours of those youthful copies of Joanna May, a totally fallacious expectation, as he comes to realize. His anticipation that they would 'love him as Joanna had', since 'they were Joanna' (ibid.: 241) is proven false, as well as his assertion that when 'he multiplied her he had not so much tried to multiply perfection . . . he had done it to multiply her love for him, . . . multiply it fourfold' (ibid.: 241). As Lana Faulks observes, in relation to Carl May's actions: 'Control and power are the objectives of those who try to create a world of sameness: identical beliefs and behavior sell commodities fueling the marketplace. Corporations feast on feeble minds that digest the carefully crafted ideology of progress and production' (1998: 61), words that aptly synthesize Carl May's motives and corporate behaviour.

The rigidly stratified and hierarchical organizational system epitomized by Carl

May's leadership is a concrete example of the types of society that come in for criticism from Luce Irigaray:

> all the systems of exchange that organize patriarchal societies and all the modalities of productive work that are recognized, valued, and rewarded in these society's are men's business. The production of women, signs, and commodities is always referred back to men.
>
> (1985: 170)

In related vein, Irigaray forcefully notes, again in words that are particularly relevant to Weldon's novel, that '*the feminine occurs only within models and laws devised by male subjects*. Which implies that there are not really two sexes, but only one. A single practice and representation of the sexual. . . . This model, a *phallic* one, shares the values promulgated by patriarchal society and culture, values inscribed in the philosophical corpus: property, production, order, form, unity, visibility . . . and erection' (ibid.: 86), insights that can be usefully extrapolated to offer a pertinent comment on the relative positions of Carl May, his wife and her clones.

Metaphors of phallic mastery over the surrounding world and other people are recurrently attached to Carl May. The building where his office is situated, in a tower block, 'had been designed to dominate the city skyscape' (Weldon 1993: 75), even though no sooner was it finished than 'all around arose the thrusting towers of usurping empires – leaner, taller, glassier' (ibid.: 75). He is variously described as a 'vampire' (ibid.: 38) and a wolf whose 'teeth were fangs and growing as long as the wolf's were in "Red Riding Hood"' (ibid.: 108). With his selfish dreams of being 'master of mortality' (ibid.: 109), Carl May, with the help of the scientific expertise of Dr Holly, epitomizes the paradigmatic 'mad male cloning scientist' (ibid.: 109), another 'Frankenstein' (ibid.: 109) with powers over life and death, the 'devil' (ibid.: 109), as Joanna May also calls him.

All these images of exploitation of others conspire to emphasize Carl May's omnipotence in the realm of work and the personal sphere. He considers himself invincible, God-like. As he explains to Joanna May:

> I can make a thousand thousand of you if I choose, fragment all living things and re-create them. I can splice a gene or two, can make you walk with a monkey's head or run on a bitch's legs or see through the eyes of a newt: I can entertain myself by making you whatever I feel like, and as I feel like so shall I do.
>
> (ibid.: 109)

He implicitly brings nature and woman together in his manicheistic discourse about good and evil: both woman and nature need to be controlled and manipulated, since both are found faulty. He further elucidates his grand designs:

> I would perfect nature's universe, because nature is blind, and obsessive, and absurd . . . and has no judgement, only insists on our survival, somehow, any

old how: nature is only chance, not good or bad. All I want is the any old how properly under control, directed. . . . I, man, want to teach nature a thing or two, in particular the difference between good and bad; for who else is there to do it? But how can I, because woman makes man bad.

(ibid.: 111)

The text suggests that one of the principal factors that led to Carl May's becoming this monstrous other may be rooted in his childhood, in the lack of parental care, a situation which also links him with Frankenstein's monstrous creature. Indeed, we learn that

Carl's mother had kept him much of the time, when he was little and hungry and stole, chained up in the dog's kennel in the yard, to teach him a lesson. His father was a dead dog; his mother was a bitch.

(ibid.: 14)

It is thus pertinent to conjecture, from a psychoanalytic point of view, that Carl May's treatment of women as objects may betray his repressed wish to punish his mother for the heartless way she behaved towards him.

Carl May's close connections with the discourse and politics of biopower are severely condemned in the book and his arrogance will be heavily punished in the end. Not only do Joanna May's clones band together against himself, finding strength in their very close bond, but his policies of lack of transparency and monopoly in decision-making in Britnuc, as far as the Chernobyl crisis is concerned, also bring about his downfall. In order to prove to the public how safe the cooling ponds in the nuclear power stations that belonged to Britnuc are, whose PR team assures the media that Chernobyl could not possibly happen there, Carl May decides to call the press to witness him swimming in one of them, Britnuc B, in the Welsh hill country, whose wild beauty as well as 'the overwhelming presence of nature unorganized and unconfirmed' (ibid.: 257) poses a sharp contrast to the Ukrainian incident. At the end of the book Carl May is dying from the consequences of this fatal swim. After he had come out of the supposedly non-radioactive cooling pond, 'the meters – the ones put in to reassure the visitors – had started to chatter' (ibid.: 261).

The final twist, however, is that Carl May will leave his own progeny, in spite of having had a vasectomy when he was 18. Just before dying, he pleaded with Joanna May to 'remake him' (ibid.: 262), to which she acceded. Alice, one of her clones, gives birth to a clone of Carl May, a baby ironically brought up by Joanna May herself who, in her function as substitute mother and educator has now full power over him, although presumably she will use that power to make a better human being of him and possibly at the same stroke providing ammunition to the nature versus nurture debate, this time on the nurture side. A caring environment and family education will, the novel suggests, go a long way towards at least partially reversing the influence of genes.

Carl May's whole attitude towards life reveals the at times dangerous consequences of too great a concentration of power in individuals inside organizations, while the novel as a whole questions the pitfalls of institutionalized networks of power enmeshed in political power games whose practices may lead to abuses of authority and, potentially, public disasters. Weldon's novel also implicitly engages with the conventional view that links masculinity with individualization, an assumption taken to extremes in Carl May's character, as compared with a femininity that equals collectivism, a notion that is given fictional representation in the strength found by Joanna May and her clones in their coming together and joining forces against Carl May. These conjectures are problematized in the novel, whose narrative drive implicitly suggests that the preponderant embeddedness of masculinity within bureaucracy should be offset by a greater presence of women within organizations, which would provide for a more collective form of decision-making, which in turn would create a more eco-amiable organization. In *The Cloning of Joanna May* woman is depicted, from Carl May's perspective, as still very much the Other of the Same, to use Luce Irigaray's terminology, that is, woman in a patriarchal world, conceived in terms of a male normative logic, reduced to '*the economy of the Same*' (1985: 74). Her 'otherness', then, becomes to a great extent dissolved in order to be incorporated and regulated to the familiar standard of masculinity, a standpoint the novel goes a long way towards subverting, proposing a more egalitarian perspective, where the otherness of the other, man or woman, would be partially included in the other sex, taking into account differences in order to bring about a more balanced organizational order.

Kathy Ferguson offers a critique of contemporary bureaucracy and argues that women can provide an alternative perspective on organizational structures, characterized by non-hierarchical and non-bureaucratic arrangements. Ferguson argues for a greater integration of the public sphere, where men have been the principal actors, with the private one, the domestic one, which women have considered as one of the chief areas of their subordination, a policy which would pave the way for a less aggressive and more co-operative organizational life. As Ferguson remarks: 'In their role as subordinates, women's experience sheds considerable light on the nature of bureaucratic domination; in their role as caretakers, women's experience offers grounds for envisioning a nonbureaucratic collective life' (1984: 26). This is the plea that both Fay Weldon's *The Cloning of Joanna May* and Joanna Russ's *The Female Man* implicitly articulate.

The Female Man

Joanna Russ's *The Female Man* radically calls into question the patriarchal and hierarchical functioning of Western society, dismantling the cultural structures that regulate the construction of genders and gender-related functions. As in *The Cloning of Joanna May*, in *The Female Man* some male stereotypes and masculinist representational structures similarly come under heavy scrutiny and satire.

I see the two novels as engaged in a critical dialogue with each other and would like to suggest here that *The Cloning of Joanna May* can be read as in part a response to *The Female Man*, in their acute sardonic criticism of patriarchy and in their invocation of the power of close female bonds to change society's mostly male organizations and their practices. Indeed, Jane, Julia, Gina and Alice, the clones of Joanna May, are almost the equivalent of Joanna Russ's four J's, Joanna, Janet, Jeannine and Jael, who is also called Alice Reasoner (maybe in a veiled reference to Alice, one of Joanna May's clones). In addition, both novels' protagonists share the same name: Joanna.[6]

Donna Haraway considers Joanna Russ's *The Female Man* 'the founding text in anglophone feminist SF' (1997: 75). Russ's novel deals with the intersections and meetings of four genetically identical women, Joanna, Jeaninne, Janet and Jael, who live in alternate worlds and come together in a time warp in Joanna's time, the 1970s, in New York. The four clone sisters,[7] who inhabit different chronotopes, share the same genotype and are described as four versions of the same woman, like the four clones of Joanna May.

Joanna, a radical feminist, is a contemporary version of and spokesperson for Russ herself, while Jeaninne works as a librarian in New York City in 1969. In Jeannine's world, however, the Second World War never took place and the Great Depression still shapes quotidian life. Jael, a cyborg warrior woman, named after the biblical Jael in The Book of Judges, lives in Womanland, a radical version of Janet's Whileaway, a utopian country where only women reside. In Jael's world, the men inhabit Manland and the women Womanland; the former are the 'Haves' and the latter the 'Have-nots', an asymmetrical pattern that has led to a war which has been raging for forty years between Manlanders and Womanlanders. Indeed, characterized by a warring mood between men and women, the state of affairs in Jael's country can be seen as a more radical version of Joanna May's world, where women are victims and prey in Carl May's hands and are often depicted in a rebellious mood against the 'Haves', that is, the likes of Joanna's husband. In *The Female Man* men come in for relentless criticism and satire, depicted as arrogant, violent, mindless of women's feelings and aspirations, in many ways like Dr Holly and Carl May in Weldon's novel.

Here I wish to concentrate on Whileaway, an all-female society, another alternative world where Janet, who comes from the far future, 'but not my future or yours' (Russ 1986: 161), lives. The societal and institutional organizations in Whileaway differ considerably from Western models and are depicted not as straightforward examples to be followed but as a tongue-in-cheek, satirical vision of a speculative world made up only of women who nevertheless do not exhibit so-called 'feminine' traits and have developed along lines that deviate from the characteristics a Western observer would expect from an all-female society. In other examples of women-only worlds, such as Mary E. Bradley Lane's *Mizora* (1890) and Charlotte Perkins Gilman's *Herland* (1915), the societal organization conforms to conventional expectations of a pastoral, profoundly ecologically-minded, peaceful and fulfilling world. While some of these traits apply to Russ's utopian society, there is a certain amount of violence, which undermines such essentialist notions as that of women's supposedly inherently peaceful propensities, which would make for a totally placid and unruffled world.

The male population in Whileaway was all wiped out by a plague which came in P.C. 17 (Preceding Catastrophe) and ended in A.C. 03 (After Catastrophe). In the third century A.C. genetic engineering became widely available, although the merging of ova had been used much earlier. In Whileaway women have their children around the age of 30, 'singletons or twins as the demographic pressures require. These children have as one genotypic parent the biological mother (the "body mother") while the non-bearing parent contributes the other ovum ("other mother")' (Russ 1986: 49), a process similar to that used by Dr Holly to create the clones of Joanna May, who coincidentally was also 30 when she had her mock pregnancy and her eggs were taken from her body without her knowledge. Reproductive technology in Whileaway stands in stark contrast to the violations of the protagonist's bodily integrity in *The Cloning of Joanna May*. Indeed, women in Whileaway have total control over their reproductive system and their own bodies. They choose when to have their children, usually at 30, and do not have to depend on sperm to produce their offspring. Having a child is considered as 'a vacation' (Russ 1986: 14), a time when the women can 'pursue whatever interests [they] have been forced to neglect previously, and the only leisure they have ever had – or will have again until old age' (ibid: 49). Indeed, the description of a mother in Whileaway, as 'someone on vacation, someone with leisure, someone who's close to the information network and full of intellectual curiosity' (ibid.: 23) also presents a sharp contrast to the conventional image of mothers in traditional Western societies, overworked and overburdened, with no leisure time to devote to intellectual or other pleasurable activities, totally absorbed in the raising of their children. Unlike this prevailing representation of mothers in the Western world, mothers in Whileaway would constitute a 'top class' (ibid.: 23), if there was one in this non-hierarchical society. While Joanna May finds her justification and fulfil-ment as a woman in being Carl May's wife, in making him feel good as well as in her desire to be a mother, women in Whileaway do not have to hold up a mirror to men, to borrow Virginia Woolf's resonant expression, being thus able to con-centrate on their own and the community's development and well-being. As Woolf puts it, in satiric vein:

> Women have served all these centuries as looking glasses possessing the magic and delicious power of reflecting the figure of man at twice its natural size. . . . How is he to go on giving judgments, civilizing natives, making laws, writing books, dressing up and speechifying at banquets, unless he can see himself at breakfast and dinner at least the size he really is?
>
> (1928; 1967, 37–8)

This insight aptly defines Carl May's behaviour and often appears dramatized in *The Female Man*. As the narrator puts it, carrying out a deconstruction of the clichés of a characteristically 'romantic' situation which portrays Jeannine in a pleasure boat with a suitor: 'from shore it must really look quite good, the canoe, the pretty girl, the puffy summer clouds, Jeannine's sun-shade. . . . His contribu-tion is *Make me feel good*; her contribution is *Make me exist*' (Russ 1986: 120).

In Whileaway there are no true cities and social life is based on a complex clan organizational structure, whose core consists of families of thirty to thirty-five persons, the farms being the only family units. As Janet explains, there is no government in Whileaway in the traditional sense and in addition 'there is no one place from which to control the entire activity of Whileaway, that is, the economy' (ibid.: 91). Whileawayans have consistently striven to achieve a non-hierarchical, egalitarian society, a model which *The Cloning of Joanna May* similarly endorses, in its severe criticism of institutionalized hierarchical practices. Bringing feminist and organizational theory into productive conjunction, Kathleen P. Ianello considers the possibility of alternative models that privilege non-hierarchical, more participatory forms of organization, like the one put forward in Whileaway,[8] where society is communal, children move at ease all over the planet past puberty and 'the kinship web . . . is world-wide' (ibid.: 81).

The invention of the induction helmet, which 'makes it possible for one work-woman to have not only the brute force but also the flexibility and control of thousands' (ibid.: 14) brings about a radical transformation in Whileawayan industry, turning it 'upside down' (ibid.: 14). Indeed, Whileaway is 'engaged in the reorganization of industry consequent to the discovery of the induction principle' (ibid.: 56), an event which made it possible to introduce a drastically reduced work-week of sixteen hours.

Ecological concerns are of momentous significance to Whileawayans, who are farmers, scientists, police officers, artists and so on. Whileaway is 'so pastoral that at times one wonders whether the ultimate sophistication may not take us all back to a kind of Pre-Paleolithic dawn age, a garden without any artifacts. . . . Meanwhile, the ecological housekeeping is enormous' (ibid.: 14). Waste is a taboo in Whileaway, which is 'inhabited by the pervasive spirit of underpopulation' (ibid.: 100). Whileawayans are characterized by 'the cast of mind that makes industrial area into gardens and ha-has, that supports wells of wilderness where nobody ever lives for long, that strews across a planet sceneries, mountains, glider preserves' (ibid.: 54) and so on. By means of a self-consciously satirical discourse which subverts what are often considered typical and unchanging feminine distinguishing attributes, Whileaway, although clearly not a serious utopian blueprint for a realistic future society, nevertheless provides an effective criticism of patriarchal institutions through parodical revision of some of its organizations, such as the army and institutionalized industry.

While *The Cloning of Joanna May* does not advocate such a radical scenario as the abolition of men, the narrative drive strongly suggests the urgent need to rethink hierarchical practices in organizations in order to minimize gender inequalities, as well as a pressing need to protect the environment, so powerfully expressed in *The Female Man*.

Towards the end of both novels family reunions which bring together the four J's and Joanna May's four clones are staged. In *The Female Man* the narrator declares very early on that 'eventually we will all come together' (ibid.: 18), Jael later deciding to find 'her other selves' (ibid.: 160), whereas in *The Cloning of Joanna May* Joanna takes the initiative to look for her clones, whom she calls 'my sisters, my twins, my clones, my children' (Weldon 1993: 246), her 'sisters and daughters both' (ibid.: 127). In both cases, the experience is an empowering one, producing a feeling of strength deriving from the emotional network of support provided by Joanna's clones,[9] while a similar sentiment of reliance on the sisterhood of the four J's applies. In Joanna's case, she finds that 'all of a sudden there was more of me left . . . reinforcements came racing over the hill; Joanna May was now Alice,

Julie, Gina, Jane as well. Absurd but wonderful!' (ibid.: 247). Indeed, the family reunions in both books suggest a gathering of forces on the women's side to fight against the abusive authority of the 'Manlanders', the 'Haves', in Russ's case, and the ruthless domination exerted by Carl May in his managerial and personal affairs.

Jael's description of the origin of the four J's is strikingly reminiscent of the creation of Joanna May's four clones, both narratives actively participating in the debate which pits against each other the theories of biological determinism versus social constructionism, nature versus nurture. As Jael explains, musing about her 'other selves' (Russ 1986: 160), in spite of all the differences amongst the four of them,

> we started the same. . . . If you discount the wombs that bore us, our pre-natal nourishment, and our deliveries (none of which differ essentially) we ought to have started out with the same autonomic nervous system, the same adrenals, the same hair and teeth and eyes, the same circulatory system, and the same innocence. We ought to think alike and feel alike and act alike, but of course we don't. . . . I can hardly believe that I am looking at three other myselves.
>
> (ibid.: 162)

Jael further remarks, prompting Joanna, Jeannine and Janet to observe themselves: 'Look in each other's faces. What you see is essentially the same genotype, modified by age, by circumstances, by education, by diet, by learning' (ibid.: 161), an insight which is repeated in *The Cloning of Joanna May*. Indeed, in the case of Joanna May's clones, when they first come together without knowing each other, Dr Holly's secretary assesses them in a detached way: 'Reared separately, no doubt, though they'd end up much the same in the end. The impact of the rearing environment wore away with time' (Weldon 1993: 225–6). Like the four J's in *The Female Man*, who, as Jael explains, 'started the same' (Russ 1986: 162), the four clones of Joanna May also look different, although they can be recognized as belonging to the same genotype. The underlying implication, in both cases, suggests that in spite of their superficial differences, due to their distinct upbringing, the empathy experienced by the cloned women and the strength they derive from that feeling is a feature they have in common and which cannot be easily erased. The reunion of the cloned women brought about by Jael and Joanna May thus turned out to be a site of empowerment for each of them individually and as a group, providing added impetus to their future lines of action against patriarchy, as well as stressing the intensity of the biological link that unites them.

When Joanna May eventually acknowledges her clones, she realizes that 'when I stood out against Carl May, I found myself. . . . He thought he would diminish me: he couldn't: he made me' (Weldon 1993: 246). Indeed, the endings of the two novels also bear some similarities. While Jael's purpose is to enlist the other J's help in the war being waged between the Manlanders and the Womanlanders, Joanna May and her four clones unite against Carl May and Dr Holly's tyrannical, manipulative and secretive ways within May's institutional empire.

Cyborg monsters and inappropriate/d others

Donna Haraway has often acknowledged her debt to writers of 'science fiction', namely Joanna Russ, considering that 'the cyborgs populating feminist science fiction make very problematic the statuses of man or woman, human, artefact, member of a race, individual entity, or body' (1991: 178). Haraway located in science fiction texts some of the sources of her socialist-feminist ironic cyborg myth, a political manifesto that fits particularly well Russ's characters in *The Female Man*. As Haraway asserts: 'Cyborg monsters in feminist science fiction define quite different political possibilities and limits from those proposed by the mundane fiction of Man and Woman' (ibid.: 180), a description that seems tailor-made for defining Joanna, Janet and Jael in *The Female Man*. Indeed, these 'cyborg monsters' in Russ's conception might become fundamental actors in the kind of 'regenerative politics' Haraway envisions as essential grounding for the concretization of her dream of a future socialist-feminist structure where these 'inappropriate/d' others will play a fitting and active role (1992: 300). Characters like the four J's in *The Female Man*, who refuse to be classified according to the prevalent masculinist norm and less radically but none the less in an effective way Joanna May and her four clones, who gravitate away from the centripetal pull of Carl May's empire, whose tentacles extend in many directions, constitute apt examples of 'others' who have not been appropriated and shaped by restrictive patriarchal rules. As Haraway pertinently comments:

> Science fiction is generically concerned with the interpenetration of boundaries between problematic selves and unexpected others and with the exploration of possible worlds in a context structured by transnational technoscience. The emerging social subjects called 'inappropriate/d others' inhabit such worlds. SF – science fiction, speculative futures, science fantasy, speculative fiction – is an especially apt sign under which to conduct an inquiry into the artifactual as a reproductive technology that might issue in something other than the sacred image of the same, something inappropriate, unfitting, and so, maybe, inappropriated.

> (ibid.: 300)

This 'cyborg subject position' (ibid.: 300) constitutes indeed a powerful strategic stance from which to argue an effective dis-connection from the 'sacred image of the same', that is, the masculinist norm enforced on the women characters in *The Female Man* and *The Cloning of Joanna May*. The female characters in these novels and, by extension, women in general, might then, in Haraway's terms, become 'inappropriated', their own selves, not mirror images of male narcissistic will-to-power.[10]

Conclusion

The many convergences between *The Female Man* and *The Cloning of Joanna May* help to shed light on the various intersecting thematic concerns that the two novels have in common. Both works can be described as 'reactive' in the sense described by Joanna Russ, that is, 'they supply in fiction what their authors believe society . . . and/or women, lack in the here-and-now' (1981: 81).

In its extremely satirical portrayal of Carl May, *The Cloning of Joanna May* thematizes the old stereotype of a greater masculine distancing from and control over feminized nature, as well as interference in the female reproductive sphere. Carl May's ultimate punishment and fate forcefully suggest that a new model of organizational theory and practice, based on ecologically grounded procedures, is urgently needed.

Val Plumwood concisely sums up an ecofeminist position which 'accepts the undesirability of the domination of nature associated with the masculine' (1988: 22) without falling into the traps of essentializing the supposed closer connnection of the (biological) feminine with nature or unproblematically associating the masculine with aggression and violence towards the natural world. Plumwood believes that only a degendered model, one that transcends the masculine and the feminine 'could provide some sort of basis on which to mount a revised ecofeminist argument' (ibid.: 24).

One of the principal thrusts of Weldon's book is an exhortation for women to become intervening organizational agents at all levels of societal and governmental structuration, especially as far as reproductive technologies and environmental issues are concerned, to become actively implicated in decision criteria within organizations. As Haraway maintains: 'If we learn how to read these webs of power and social life, we might learn new couplings, new coalitions' (1991: 170). Traditionally perceived as passive and susceptible to exploitation and subjugation, both women and nature have to become intervening actors in the struggle for juster organizational structures, more interactive and earth- and women-friendly, but also more politically engaged in the defence and promotion of women's rights as well as the preservation and improvement of the environment.

The Female Man, similarly, constitutes an eloquent plea for a peaceful world where women are granted due respect and ecological values are implemented, where 'women in the integrated circuit' (Haraway 1991: 170), at all institutional levels, are the rule and not the exception. Haraway's appeal for strategic alterations, for women to become dynamic agents within organizations, can be seen as an integral part of the process of trying to change existing legislation and widely accepted practices in organizational management. As Egri and Pinfield conclude: 'While the dominant social paradigm emphasizes humans' dominionistic and utilitarian relations with nature, the radical environmentalism perspective emphasizes humans' emotional, aesthetic and spiritual connections with the natural environment' (1999: 227). They suggest, in words that aptly describe Carl May's actions, that 'focusing solely on the material value and benefits to be derived from the natural environment . . . informs environmentally unsustainable actions' (ibid.: 227). On the other hand, preserving the natural environment purely for its aesthetic value . . . to the exclusion of other relations with the natural environment denies the development of material relations necessary for human physical existence. In the end, there is a need for a balance among these disparate and sometimes conflicting relationships with the natural environment – not a static final balance, but a dynamic balancing between evolving human and natural systems of existence.

(ibid.: 227)

While Egri and Pinfield do not address the question of sexual politics within organizational dynamics, I want to suggest here that *The Cloning of Joanna May* plays an intervening role in introducing the question of gender into the whole larger subject of the running of organizations and institutional life, a debate in which Donna Haraway's cyborg politics participates in a fundamental way. In this essay I have tried to bring into political play and productive convergence the intersections and contributions of these various discourses which can be seen fictionally engaged in a dialectical struggle in both Russ's and Weldon's novels. In the disentangling of these variegated webs of power, with the help of organizational theory, several strands of environmental discourses as well as gender politics suggest potentially productive new directions to integrate the aspirations for change implicit in *The Female Man* and *The Cloning of Joanna May*. These texts thus become political manifestoes for action along the lines put forward by Donna Haraway and her ironic cyborg myth, as well as exhortations for a development of a discourse of organization theory and practice which are both environmentally responsible and respectful of gender asymmetries.

Notes

1 Such novels as Naomi Mitchison's *Solution Three* (1975) and Kate Wilhelm's *Where Late the Sweet Birds Sang* (1976) take place in a post-apocalyptic world, ravaged by cataclysmic ecological disasters which have destroyed the planetary eco-systems and decimated most of the population.
2 Examples of these novels include: Joanna Russ's *The Female Man* (1975), Naomi Mitchison's *Solution Three* (1975), Pamela Sargent's *Cloned Lives* (1976), Kate Wilhelm's *Where Late the Sweet Birds Sang* (1976), Marge Piercy's *Woman on the Edge of Time* (1976), Sally Miller Gearhart's *The Wanderground* (1978) and Suzy MacKee Charnas's *Motherlines* (1978), to cite only some of the most representative.
3 The boundaries between the genres of science fiction and utopias have become increasingly blurred and indeed often intersect.
4 As Miller, Hickson and Wilson maintain, 'the lone decision-maker making choices about his or her own interests might be thought to act rationally (although psychologists may argue the evidence here) but the complexities of managerial decision-making in concert with others have been well documented' (1999: 45).
5 See for instance Hearn and Parkin 1983; Ferguson 1984; Hearn *et al.*. 1989; Mills and Murgatroyd 1991; Mills and Tancred 1992; Savage and Witz 1992; Albert J. Mills 1994; Sylvia Gherardi 1995.
6 In an e-mail message to the author, Fay Weldon confirmed that it was quite probable that she had read *The Female Man* 'and then forgot it, consciously but not unconsciously'.
7 I have always thought about the four J's as clones, contrary to the opinion of some

critics. I was therefore pleased to find that Haraway also calls them the 'four clone sisters' (1997: 69).

8 Having studied three different forms of feminist organizations, Ianello identifies the 'modified consensual model' as an organizational structure that closely corresponds to a more co-operative, less hierarchical organizational form that 'needs to be tested in large-scale organizations' (1992: 122).

9 This leads to a related question. Will the cloned person feel threatened by the know-ledge that he/she will have exactly the same genetic make-up as his/her parent and might thus grow up to be an almost exact copy of that person? Will there be room for individual growth, recreation, self-building? The biological determinism versus social constructionism argument suggests that in spite of the same genetic material two or more people sharing that same biological origins will nevertheless grow up with a different psychological make-up on account of distinct environmental factors and par-enting. Fay Weldon's *The Cloning of Joanna May* actively participates in this debate, showing how the four clones of Joanna May turn out very different.

A related issue has to do with the fundamental problem of the genetic make-up of the cloned person, who will have 'only' the genetic material of one progenitor, mother or father. Will that 'lack' of DNA from the second progenitor be perceived as a disadvantage, as a serious 'loss', potentially conducive to psychological dilemmas and inbalances? That question is left unanswered in Weldon's novel, since the clones only find out about their origins towards the end of the book, and that issue never surfaces.

10 While we have to be cautious of considering the cyborg figure as unproblematically liberatory for women characters, since science fiction works are crowded with female cyborgs that have been configured as fantasy figures, playing the role of objects of pleasure for the voyeuristic male gaze, there are other elements to the cyborg woman that help break down deeply entrenched dichotomies that have contributed to the stratification of women's position in society. It is these transgressive characteristics that I am interested in here, traits that Joanna, Janet and Jael strongly evince.

References

Aldrich, H. E. and Marsden, P. V. (1988) 'Environments and Organizations', in N. J. Smelser (ed.), *The Handbook of Sociology*, Newbury Park, CA: Sage.

Charnas, Suzy MacKee (1989) *Walk to the End of the World and Motherlines*, London: The Women's Press.

Clegg, Stewart R., Hardy, Cynthia and Nord, Walter R. (eds) (1999) *Managing Organizations: Current Issues*, London: Sage.

Egri, Carolyn P. and Pinfield, T. Lawrence (1999) 'Organizations and the Biosphere: Ecol-ogies and Environments', in Stewart R. Clegg, Cynthia Hardy and Walter R. Nord (eds), *Managing Organizations: Current Issues*, London: Sage, 208–33.

Faulks, Lana (1998) *Fay Weldon*, New York: Twayne Publishers.

Ferguson, K. E. (1984) *The Feminist Case Against Bureaucracy*, Philadelphia, PA: Temple Uni-versity Press.

Gearhart, Sally Miller (1984) *The Wanderground*, London: The Women's Press.

Gherardi, Sylvia (1995) *Gender, Symbolism and Organizational Cultures*, London: Sage.

Gilman, Charlotte Perkins (1979) *Herland*, Int. Ann J. Lane. New York: Pantheon Books.

Haraway, Donna (1989) *Primate Visions: Gender, Race, and Nature in the World of Modern Science*, New York and London: Routledge.

—— (1991) 'A Cyborg Manifesto: Science, Technology, and Socialist-Feminism in the Late Twentieth Century', in *Simians, Cyborgs, and Women: The Reinvention of Nature*, London: Free Association Books.

—— (1992) 'The Promises of Monsters: A Regenerative Politics for Inappropriate/d Others', in Lawrence Grossberg, Cary Nelson and Paula A. Treichler (eds), *Cultural Studies*, New York: Routledge, 295–337.

—— (1997) *Modest Witness @ Second_Millenium.Female Man©_Meets_Oncomouse ™: Feminism and Technoscience*, New York and London: Routledge.

Hearn, J. and Parkin, W. (1983) 'Gender and Organizations: A Selected Review and Critique of a Neglected Area', *Organisation Studies* 4(3): 219–42.

Hearn, J., Sheppard, D. L., Tancred-Sheriff, P. and Burrell, G. (eds) (1989) *The Sexuality of Organization*, London: Sage.

Iannello, Kathleen P. (1992) *Decisions Without Hierarchy: Feminist Interventions in Organization Theory and Practice*, New York and London: Routledge.

Irigaray, Luce (1985) *This Sex Which is Not One*, trans. Catherine Porter with Carolyn Burke, Ithaca, New York: Cornell University Press.

Lane, Mary E. Bradley (1999) *Mizora*, Int. Joan Saberhagen. Lincoln and London: University of Nebraska Press.

Lasch, Christopher (1983) *The Culture of Narcissism*, New York: Warner Books.

Merchant, Carolyn (1990) *The Death of Nature: Women, Ecology and the Scientific Revolution*, San Francisco: HarperSanFrancisco.

Miller, Susan J., Hickson, David J. and Wilson, David C. (1999) 'Decision-Making in Organizations', in Stewart Clegg, Cynthia Hardy and Walker R. Nord (eds), *Managing Organizations: Current Issues*, London: Sage, 43–62.

Mills, Albert J. (1994) 'Organizational Discourse and the Gendering of Identity', in John Hassard and Martin Parker (eds), *Postmodernism and Organizations*, London: Sage, 132–47.

Mills, A. J. and Murgatroyd, S. J. (1991) *Organizational Rules: A Framework for Understanding Organizations*, Milton Keynes: Open University Press.

Mills, A. J. and Tancred, P. (eds) (1992) *Gendering Organizational Analysis*, Newbury Park, CA: Sage.

Mitchison, Naomi (1995) *Solution Three*, Afterword by Susan M. Squier. New York: The Feminist Press at the City University of New York.

Murphy, Julie (1984) 'Egg Farming and Women's Future', in Rita Arditti, Renate Duelli Klein and Shelley Minden (eds), *Test-Tube Women: What Future for Motherhood?*, London: Routledge & Kegan Paul.

Piercy, Marge (1979) *Woman on the Edge of Time*, London: The Women's Press.

Plumwood, Val (1988) 'Women, Humanity and Nature', *Radical Philosophy* 48 (Spring): 16–24.

Pringle, Rosemary (1989) 'Bureaucracy, Rationality and Sexuality: The Case of Secretaries', in J. Hearn *et al.*. (eds), *The Sexuality of Organization*, London: Sage, 158–77.

Russ, Joanna (1986) *The Female Man*, Boston: Beacon Press.

—— (1981) 'Recent Feminist Utopias', in Marleen S. Barr (ed.), *Future Females: A Critical Anthology*, Bowling Green, Ohio: Bowling Green State University Popular Press, 71–84.

Sargent, Pamela (1976) *Cloned Lives*, Greenwich, Connecticut: Fawcett.

Savage, M. and Witz, A. (1992) *Gender and Bureaucracy*, Oxford: Blackwell.

Weldon, Fay (1993) *The Cloning of Joanna May*, London: Flamingo.

—— (1994) 'Of Birth and Fiction', in Regina Barreca (ed.), *Fay Weldon's Wicked Fictions*, Hanover and London: University Press of New England.

Wilhelm, Kate (1977) *Where Late the Sweet Birds Sang*, New York: Pocket Books.

Woolf, Virginia (1928; 1967) *A Room of One's Own*, Harmondsworth: Penguin.

6   Drowned giants

Science fiction and consumption
utopias

James A. Fitchett and David A. Fitchett

Through SF we have become accustomed to seeing in science, and particularly
machine technology, some of our greatest and most powerful aspirations and fears.

(Corbett 1998: 249)

Science fiction and mass consumer culture

Representations of progress have played a central role in the aspirations of most
consumer cultures. New products (and new uses for existing products) are, after
all, marketed to the mass consuming public in terms of enhanced performance,
lifestyle improvement, increased efficiency and other themes similarly suggestive
of progress. It is, therefore, necessary for all consumer cultures to incorporate
visions of a better tomorrow and to make these visions appear achievable and
attainable through specific types of consumer behaviour. Whilst pervasive conceptions of the future invariably mirror the concerns and apparent deficiencies
and inadequacies of an ever-changing and evolving present, the existence of a
progressive ideal future in consumer culture has itself remained constant. During
the mid-nineteenth century for instance, the consumer culture of the newly emerging bourgeois leisure classes placed considerable emphasis on ideals of refine-
ment and social improvement (Veblen 1899/1995). Style, taste and fashion
enacted through specific types and knowledge of consumption practices offered a
mechanism through which class and status could be emulated and achieved by
those with access to the necessary cultural and economic capital. As Corrigan
(1997) remarks, the 'better tomorrow' that characterizes this period was clearly
underpinned by broader modern aspirations of the times relating to a very
European vision of civilization and progress.

During the inter- and post-war years when mass consumer culture developed
first in North America and then in Europe, new progressive visions emerged that
mirrored the social and cultural ideologies of the period. The developing mass
consumer culture was far less exclusive in that greater numbers of people from a
wider social strata could for the first time engage in consumption related pursuits
and behaviours (Bocock 1993; Lee 1993). In order for consumer culture to
embrace this new social diversity it inevitably evoked ideas of progress and
advancement in a form consistent with the hopes and dreams of western society

at this time. Science fiction (SF), a genre that began to enjoy its 'golden age' and increasing mass popularity throughout the 1930s, 1940s and 1950s was central in the creation of the dream of a 'better tomorrow'. Pulp novels, comic books and mass cinema entertainment sketched out, in colourful and strikingly concrete terms, a blueprint for a brighter future that could be bought into and believed in the present. Whilst the visions supplied by popular science fiction retained the hallmark characteristic of all utopian visions, i.e. that the ills of today will be overcome in the future, the discourses it employed had some singular aspects. A generally positive belief in the merits of technology and technological progress, which could be achieved through consumption, became a dominant theme.

> Did [the future] arrive too soon, some time during the mid-century, the greatest era of modern science fiction . . . when even static objects like teapots were streamlined and much of the furniture and kitchen equipment around me seemed to be forever moving past at 100 m.p.h.
>
> (Ballard 1993/1996: 192)

> The Thirties had seen the first generation of American industrial designers; until the Thirties, all pencil sharpeners had looked like pencil sharpeners – your basic Victorian mechanism, perhaps with a curlicue of decorative trim. After the advent of designers, some pencil sharpeners looked as though they'd been put together in wind tunnels. For the most part, the change was only skin deep; under the streamlined chromium shell, you'd find the same Victorian mechanism. Which made a certain kind of sense, because the most successful American designers had been recruited from the ranks of Broadway theater designers. It was all a stage set, a series of elaborate props for playing at living in the future.
>
> (Gibson 1981/1986: 39)

Whilst SF can be read as fuelling the ever-increasing application of technology in consumer markets, both these statements demonstrate that it tended to emphasize the importance of aesthetic appearance over any functional improvements or refinements. SF was not important in consumer culture as a source of new product ideas but rather because it positioned consumption as the primary practice by which technology and utopian ideals could be attained.

The theme of technological utopia has its roots in SF prior to this period. For example Hugo Gernsback's pulp novel *Ralph 124C41 +* (1925), unambiguously sub-titled as 'A Romance of the year 2660' (Gernsback 1925/2000), and the Earl of Birkenhead's *The World in 2030 AD* (1930) provided speculative accounts of a future in which technological progress is seen to overcome current social and economic ills. Such visions dominate the popular view of SF but they are not the only ones. There has, of course, always existed a different SF tradition that peddles a wholly opposing set of beliefs and ideas. From Mary Shelley's *Frankenstein* (1817) to H.G. Wells' *The Time Machine* (1895/1995) in nineteenth-century literary fiction, and from Fritz Lang's *Metropolis* (1926) to Ridley Scott's *Blade Runner* (1982) in twentieth-century film, science fiction has also had the capacity to identify the potentially harmful effects of technology.

Although these two opposing agendas have always been present, an optimistic strand in SF became especially popular and mainstream from the 1930s to the 1960s. This period was the 'golden age' of SF, giving rise to the pulps. *Amazing*, edited by Hugo Gernsback as a 'magazine of scientification' was the first of the modern pulps started in 1926. Featuring *Buck Rogers* and abridged classics from Verne and Wells its layout set the standard for a plethora of derivative magazines whose titles blatantly reflect the optimism of the age. *Tales of Wonder* (1937–42), *Astounding Science Fiction* (1938–60), *Astounding Stories* (1930–8). *Air Wonder Stories* (1929–30), *Galaxy Science Fiction* (1950–80). and *Fantastic Universe* (1953–60), unambiguously denote this spirit (Clute 1995).

For SF to present these visions of technological advance as plausible it was essential to identify the economic and social mechanisms that would be expected to support it. For the fictional narratives of domestic robots and domed residences to seem credible and 'realistic' it was necessary to incorporate not only technological development into the genre but also the development of the ideologies and institutions that would facilitate this progress – namely the free market and the (American) corporation: 'Gernsback's vision was of an SF that would make readers *learn and earn* their way to the future, and when he founded his first SF magazine, *Amazing*, he intended it to teach' (Clute 1995: 119, italics added).

Golden age science fiction visualized and described technological utopian ideals and incorporated a model of the American commercial organization to illustrate how they would be organized and achieved. Consequently, consumption is legitimized as a practice by which utopian lifestyles will be one day obtained and maintained. A good example of this can be found in Stanley Kubrik's film *2001: A Space Odyssey*. The movie opens with a depiction of the technological progression of humanity (from ape to astronaut), culminating in a vision of the near future where space travel and moon vacations have become possible. The film visualizes the expectations and hopes that the audience has for the future. Technological progress promised affordable space travel and corporations (such as PAN-AM and Hilton Hotels) were seen to apply the technology and produce the necessary products and services (passenger shuttles, space stations and lunar resorts). This enabled the experience of space flight and vacations on the moon to appear attainable through consumption.

The ideological marriage between consumer culture and science fiction throughout the golden age, however, began to fracture. Realization of the negative and calamitous effects of technological development throughout the Cold War era and the emergent threat of ecological catastrophe undermined the naive optimism of popular SF: 'The Thirties dreamed white marble and slipstream chrome, immortal crystal and burnished bronze, but the rockets on the covers of the Gernsback pulps had fallen on London in the dead of night, screaming' (Gibson 1981/1986: 41).

Fears about the potential apocalyptic consequences of technology included insecurities generated by the threat of nuclear war and a general increase in suspicion regarding the benefits of consumption-focused lifestyles. Ralph Nader (self-styled champion of the American consumer in the late 1960s and early 1970s) with his campaign against dangerous automobile design was tapping into a general cultural angst about modern technology (Ballard 1971/1996: 260). Whilst corporate interests and most western governments continued to maintain the popular and conventional view that capitalism offered the most beneficial and constructive mechanism to achieve technological and social progress, science fiction gradually abandoned the vision it once so vigorously advanced. From the 1960s onwards some SF writers have adopted a more critical position not only towards the potential consequences of the continued application of technology but also towards the impact of organizational practices in terms of social costs. The shift from a position of cultural endorsement to one of critique can be seen in the SF of this period. Ballard is an author who typifies this shift. Better known for his controversial novel *Crash* (1973/1993) and the later *Empire of the Sun* (1984) made famous by Spielberg's 1987 film adaptation, Ballard is a science fiction author with an extensive and critically acclaimed *œuvre* that can be traced back to the early sixties. As part of that decade's subversive and experimental New Wave movement, his novels and short stories display a penchant for identifying the collapse in the viability of utopian visions that once dominated science fiction's traditional pro-technological and pro-organizational outlook. Ballard's writing ignores the staple diet of American science fiction, choosing as it themes not utopian visions of exploration in outer space or the amazing technological developments that would one day supposedly help to realize them, but rather the metalanguage of science fiction itself and its recourse to the terminology of advertising and technological jargon:

> When I began as a science fiction writer, I felt that science fiction wasn't making the most of its own possibilities. It had become fantasy; its two main preoccupations were outer space and the far future, whereas in its best days it had been a literature of commitment. I wanted to write a science fiction about the present day.
>
> (Ballard 1981/1984: 158)

Ballard focuses upon what he has coined 'inner space' – the over-lit realms of lifestyle advertising and mass-merchandising that has saturated the western collective consciousness with a plethora of myths about technological advances. He offers no moral stance on technology but instead examines the way its relentless promotion as a vehicle to obtain ideal lifestyles has shaped our relationship to, and understanding of, the world exterior to our central nervous systems. Undoubtedly his writing is suggestive of all kinds of areas relating to science and technology, not least their potential apocalyptic consequences. Here we want to focus specifically on how it raises important questions regarding the prospects of organized technological futures in relationship to the cultural climate that they are currently being cultivated in.

Ballard's critical science fiction can be read as a metaphorical expression of the demise in the surety of traditional science fictional visions of the future. As an example we have chosen to look at his 1964 short story 'The Drowned Giant'. Whilst on the surface this story seems to have little to do with the themes of science, technology or corporate organization, we suggest that it is a crucial parable in demonstrating the observations we have made thus far.

The drowned giant: an anatomy of apathy

Ballard has argued that a speculative and self-conscious SF can uncouple itself from the kinds of *a priori* logic inherent to so much science fiction writing only when it becomes 'abstract and "cool", inventing fresh situations and contexts that illustrate its theme[s] obliquely' (Ballard 1962/1996:198). This ideal is mastered in Ballard's thought-provoking short story 'The Drowned Giant' (Ballard 1964/1993, hereafter DG). This is a beautifully concise piece of under-statement and melancholy that implicitly exposes the relentless recourse to scien-tific rationalism in contemporary consumer-orientated capitalist society. The unnamed first-person narrator of the story, a research librarian living in an unspecified modern coastal city relates how the body of a giant man with 'magnificent Homeric stature' (DG: 46) is suddenly found one morning washed up on the local beach. In the eyes of the narrator the giant is a truly wondrous sight, a gargantuan of perfect human form, 'the authentic image of one of the drowned Argonauts or heroes of the Odyssey' (DG: 46). These references to the Greek classical epics emphasize the sheer grandeur of the giant's body. As the only person with any sustained interest in this amazing discovery, the narrator revisits the site of the giant body over a period of several weeks and systematic-ally describes the decomposition and eventual disintegration of the massive corpse.

It soon becomes clear that the narrator is the only person with any sustained interest in the wondrous occurrence. His library colleagues simply drift away unimpressed by the spectacle. After a brief flurry of mindless curiosity from other citizens, evidenced primarily by the marks of mutilation, graffiti and bruises on the giant's skin, collective interest in the giant corpse quickly dissipates. Even a party of local 'scientific experts – authorities on gross anatomy and marine biol-ogy' (DG: 43) show little more than a cursory interest in the stupendous specimen. When a police official offers to help this party to climb on to the massive frame, they hastily demur and leave the scene without comment. The narrator's repor-tage is delivered in a completely dispassionate tone that reinforces a pervading sense, for the reader, of the general lack of interest that the giant's body holds for the rest of the city's inhabitants. The violence that they perpetrate against the giant seems to indicate some deeply unconscious loathing of the penetration of the extraordinary into their safe and predictable lives and one can only assume that even the scientific authorities in this city have no interest in addressing the inexplicable.

After a few days the skeleton of the giant is revealed as the flesh decomposes. From this point onwards the narrator reports how it is methodically dismembered and disposed of piecemeal by various industrial and business organizations in the city:

> His right hand and foot had been removed, dragged up the slope and trundled away by a cart. After questioning the small group of people huddled by the breakwater, I gathered that a fertiliser company and a cattle food manufacturer were responsible.
>
> (DG: 47–8)

Eventually the thighbones end up in a wholesale meat market and the left humerus outside the entrance to a shipyard whilst the rest of the bones are crushed by the fertilizer and manufacturing companies.

The story concludes with the narrator visiting the beach after several months where he finds scant evidence of the giant's former existence. All that remains is part of the pelvis, now used merely as a perch by a flock of seagulls. The amazing event has been forgotten by all except the narrator and the giant's body has been erased from time, space and memory.

Significantly, the story does not conclude with any moral or philosophical observations on the narrator's part. He never directly induces the reader to perceive the sequence of events he describes as either wondrous or particularly saddening. That the reader is inclined to perceive the story as such is testimony to the critical perspective inherent to Ballard's speculative fiction. Contrast for example, Swift's famous novel, *Gulliver's Travels* (1726), concerning the marooning of a giant upon the shores of Lilliput. Whilst Swift clearly employs a sensationalist narrative style to convey a sense of wonder, the cool prose of 'The Drowned Giant' deliberately quashes such sensationalism. Ballard's story clearly evokes Swift's illustrious novel but the significance is surely that Ballard's giant is well and truly dead. That we notice the absence of wonder in Ballard's story is testimony to the effectiveness of his design. By forcing us to confront a scene in which the amazing has lost its power, he invites us to make comparisons with our own cultural condition and thereby provokes the reader to make his or her own conclusions regarding its allegorical message. The citizens, spectators and scientists in the story are inhabitants of Ballard's vision of our own near future. We, as readers, are astounded by their lack of interest in the beached leviathan, but such a response is a logical prediction from our own times in which a saturated consumer discourse has effectively rendered us immune to the idea of wonder. The message is unequivocal: there will be an inevitable death of affect in a society that bases itself upon technological progress accessed by the masses through consumption.

That the giant's body is actually *utilized* by industry is surely an allegory of the way in which consumer capitalist society envelops, processes and finally effaces that which was once *naturally* perceived to be amazing and incredible. The giant and its fate personifies the failure of golden age science fiction, a medium which was once capable of stimulating and astounding us and making us question the parameters and dimensions of the world we inhabit. In showing us the destruction of this capability 'The Drowned Giant' represents an allegorical attempt to actually rescue science fiction, to alert the reader to the way in which it has been incorporated into the totality of a rationalist outlook. From one perspective this is science fiction divorcing itself from the prevailing ideology of consumer capitalism. However, during both the 'golden age' and the 'new wave' period, it is important to recognize that science fiction is a part of consumer culture and is produced from within its bounds rather than from some imagined externally located cultural reference point. The new wave apathy towards consumption-orientated lifestyles and ambitions is indicative of the general disillusionment that has come to characterize the contemporary consumer experience for those brought up in a society saturated by consumption symbols, branding and advertising.

If the contemporary world were Lilliput, then we are the Lilliputians, only we show no awe at the giant. As the narrator remarks with a lack of conviction that defines his society, 'I had probably witnessed the approaching end of a magnificent illusion' (DG: 47).

Commodification and end of magnificent illusions

> The entertainment begins to pall after a while. It's like spending too long in a theme park, you begin to long to get out of it. And when you realise that there's nowhere to get out of, that it's all like this, that the theme park now circles the planet . . . that makes for desperation.
>
> (Ballard 1997: 51)

We read Ballard's 'Drowned Giant' as a parable of the disarming effects of commodification. The myths and optimistic visions of the future popularized in SF's golden age that provided such wonder and hope to consumers have gradually become distilled, dismembered and finally dismissed by the social action of capitalism and the offerings of the market.

The remains of the body of ideals that emerged from SF's brief union with corporate interests now exist only as a collection of largely fragmented and superficial signifiers for advertisers and marketers to exploit as part of their ongoing efforts to differentiate and add value to marginally related products and services (Goldman and Papson 1996). 'I could buy aliens, but not aliens that look like Fifties' comic art. They're semiotic phantoms, bits of deep cultural imagery that have split off and taken on a life of their own' (Gibson 1981/1986: 44).

Every now and again, for the vaguely interested, the increasingly decrepit Aldrin and Armstrong can be heard reminiscing about their brief lunar excursion in voice-overs for anything from new automobile designs to insurance, financial products and telecommunications services (Smith 1983). The recent marketing campaigns by Nestlé and Mars which parody Soviet space age achievements clearly illustrate how events once considered crucial for cold-war ideological supremacy are now useful only as background imagery for FMCG product advertising. So it is precisely when the 'wonder' of a utopian myth is subsumed by capitalist enterprise that its powers of inspiration and innovation are disarmed.

The death of affect that occurs when the market subsumes science fiction myth into a series of everyday commodities first weakens and then ultimately destroys the very futuristic discourses that established mass consumer culture.

Consumer culture must continually seek out and sponsor new myths and alternative 'better tomorrows' to ensure that consumer desire and demand for new types of products and services remains constant and unfulfilled. Concerns over potential future environmental problems and quality of life issues relating to pollution, food quality and health have become the main preoccupation of today's consumer culture myths. As a result, eco-utopian 'better tomorrows' have come to replace those that relied upon the imaginative application of machine technology as represented throughout golden age SF. Far from being a redundant genre, science fiction has reinvented its relationship with mainstream consumer culture and now relies upon being reflexive rather than collaborative with the ideologies of that culture. Science fiction has forged a critical space in which to illustrate various potential futures without necessarily having to author(iz)e and legitimize one particular 'better tomorrow'. J.G. Ballard's fiction is especially powerful in this regard and consequently can be read as a powerful source of ideas for those engaged in critical management research.

It would seem that SF adopting sceptical views towards technological and corporate progress has replaced utopian SF as the dominant type of narrative in the genre. Ballard's 'Subliminal Man' (1967) mirrors the sentiments of Pohl and Kornbluth's *The Space Merchants* (1953) with its description of a not so futuristic society in which covert commercial messages and corporate totalitarianism subject the population to an ever-worsening cycle of work and consumption. Corbett's (1998) analysis finds that only a fraction of futurist SF films show anything resembling the utopian vision of technological modernity characteristic of early SF. This suggests that it is becoming increasingly popular for contemporary SF writers and film makers to represent a high degree of paranoia towards organizations and the corporate elite (Parker and Cooper 1998). But SF can serve a much greater purpose than simply bringing to attention the potential dangers of technology in the hands of all-powerful market-driven interests. Once SF is divorced from its ideological marriage with capitalist interests it becomes possible to employ the genre in a critical assessment of the other visions of a better tomorrow.

Concerns regarding the ecological consequences of technological advances in capitalist society have given rise to a new set of myths of the near future in science fiction. As Corbett (1998: 254) remarks:

> Futuristic SF film-makers offer a simple choice: humanity must either accept ambivalent potentialities of technological 'progress' and develop new technologies to deal with problems created by other new technologies, or escape from the domination of technology by walking out into the wilderness, to return to a kind of lifestyle associated with times before the industrial revolution.

Yet even SF's post-industrial utopias are liable to a critical inspection by authors like Ballard. Take, for example, his lambasting of the eco-utopian ideal in his story 'The Ultimate City' (1976). In this story, a vast crumbling twentieth-century industrial metropolis lies abandoned in the desert, its former inhabitants having decamped to live in agrarian communities far away. One of these communities, suitably named Garden City, provides the backdrop for the story's opening. Here, only non-polluting technologies are used. Fossil fuels have been dispensed with in favour of environmentally friendly technologies of solar energy extraction. However, Ballard is keen to point out the extent to which the benefits of this mode of existence have their inevitable social disadvantages. The pedal-driven ambulances of Garden City are environmentally clean but inevitably they are not as fast as their petrol-run ancestors and when heart attacks or severe accidents occur, most victims tend to arrive at the hospital too late. Moreover, after twenty years of docile and peaceful existence, life in Garden City has become so mind-numbingly boring that it is not surprising when the story's teenage hero rebels and heads off in search of the Ultimate City with ambitions of 'kick-starting' its electrical and mechanical capacity back to life.

Satires at the expense of new utopian visions are perhaps predictable enough but critical SF in recent years has even developed the capacity to question its own pulp origins. Gibson's 'The Gernsback Continuum' (1981/1986) resurrects golden age SF to demonstrate the extent to which the dominant twentieth-century visions of the future are themselves now relics of the past. If Gernsback's clean and pure technocratic predictions of the future had been correct, asks Gibson, then what would living in the present be really like? If living at the end of the twentieth century meant giant propeller-driven airliners flying in ordered aerial traffic lanes above vast neo-classical spires and domes, we would clearly be living in the past. Gibson's conclusion, as he speculates upon the cape-wearing Aryan inhabitants of Gernsback's future cities who never materialized, is one of relief. Thank goodness the inhabitants of Gernsback's imagined future did not materialize from what were clearly imperialistic (if not outright fascistic) fantasies.

The future, as seen by authors like Ballard and Gibson is an out-of-date concept that reached its zenith in terms of cultural impact during the fifteen or so years that spanned the launch of Sputnik in 1957 to the last Apollo flights in the early seventies. This period is more popularly referred to as the Space Age and for Ballard its heroic phase is well and truly over. Here then, we have science fiction writers who historicize the future, who see it primarily as a seductive signifier used by, among others, corporate interests in the post-war era to uphold mass consumer culture ideology.

The future(s) of the future

The 'future', as a coherent, unified certainty upon which mass society can focus comfort and hope has been consistently eroded as a direct consequence of consumer culture itself. Optimistic and progressive mythological futures now compete with apocalyptic and uncertain visions which hold equal if not more potent cultural recognition. Similarly grand narrative 'futures' no longer retain any plausible or viable strategic value for organizational ideology which now prefers to court local and culturally specific market solutions. As a result alternative mythological 'certainties' are necessary to sustain and underpin contemporary consumer cultures. The 'future of the future' will perhaps become increasingly fractured and contradictory, juxtaposing myths from the past (those chrome technology futures of the past) with imagined futures (currently eco-topian) that are still able to exercise a favourable hold on the popular imagination. It is as if all these myths exist merely as commodity signs, detached from any temporal or spatially relative referent and can therefore be continually recycled, reinvented and ultimately dismissed – over and over again.

Perhaps a time is now upon us when consumer culture is becoming apathetic and dismissive towards the importance and desirability of the symbolic relevance of the future. It could be argued that provisional indicators, such as a general ambiguity towards the Enlightenment notion of progress and an accumulation of uncertainties about future social priorities, support this proposition. One day the advertiser's rhetoric, which uses promises of a bright future product or lifestyle as a primary sales drive, may well be greeted by consumers who feel that they have seen the future – many, many times.

References

Ballard, J.G. (1962/1996) 'Which Way to Inner Space?', in *A User's Guide to the Millennium*, London: Harper Collins, pp. 195–8.

Ballard, J.G. (1964/1993) 'The Drowned Giant', in *The Terminal Beach*, London: Phoenix.

Ballard, J.G. (1967/1992) 'The Subliminal Man', in *The Disaster Area*, London: Flamingo, pp. 55–76.

Ballard, J.G. (1971/1996) 'The Consumer Consumed', in *A User's Guide to the Millennium*, London: HarperCollins, pp. 259–61.

Ballard, J.G. (1973/1993) *Crash*, London: Flamingo.

Ballard, J.G. (1976/1993) 'The Ultimate City', in *Low-Flying Aircraft*, London: Flamingo, pp. 4–87.

Ballard, J.G. (1981/1984) 'An Interview with Alan Burn', in A. Juno and V. Vale (eds), *Re/Search: J.G. Ballard*, San Francisco: Re/Search Publications.

Ballard, J.G. (1984) *Empire of the Sun*, London: Triad Granada.

Ballard, J.G. (1993/1996) 'Back to the Heady Future', in *A User's Guide to the Millennium*, London: HarperCollins, pp. 192–4.

Ballard, J.G. (1997) 'An Interview with Ralph Rugoff', *Frieze*, 34 (May).

Bocock, R. (1993) *Consumption*, London: Routledge.

Clute, J. (1995) *The Illustrated Encyclopaedia of Science Fiction*, London: Dorling Kindersley.

Corbett, J.M. (1998) 'Sublime Technologies and Future Organization in Science Fiction Film, 1970–95', in J. Hassard and R. Holliday (eds), *Organization-Representation: Work and Organizations in Popular Culture*, London: Sage, pp. 245–58.

Corrigan, P. (1997) *The Sociology of Consumption*, London: Sage.

Earl of Birkenhead (1930) *The World in 2030 AD*, London: Hodder & Stoughton.

Gernsback, H. (1925/2000) *Ralpf 124C41 +: A Romance of the Year 2660*, Lincoln: University of Nebraska Press.

Gibson, W. (1981/1986) 'The Gernsback Continuum', in *Burning Chrome and Other Stories*, London: Voyager, pp. 37–50.

Goldman, R. and Papson, S. (1996) *Sign Wars: The Cluttered Landscape of Advertising*, New York and London: The Guilford Press.

Lee, M.J. (1993) *Consumer Culture Reborn: The Cultural Politics of Consumption*, London: Routledge.

Parker, M. and Cooper, R. (1998) 'Cyberorganization: Cinema as Nervous System', in J. Hassard and R. Holliday (eds.), *Organization-Representation: Work and Organizations in Popular Culture*, London: Sage, pp. 201–28.

Pohl, F. and Kornbluth, C.M. (1953) *The Space Merchants*, London: Ballantine.

Smith, M.L. (1983) 'Selling The Moon: The U.S. Manned Space Program and the Triumph of Commodity Scientism', in R.W. Fox and T.J.J. Lears (eds), *The Culture of Consumption: Critical Essays in American History 1880–1980*, New York: Pantheon Books.

Swift, J. (1726/1998) *Gulliver's Travels*, Oxford: Oxford University Press.

Veblen, T. (1899/1995) *The Theory of The Leisure Class: An Economic Study of Institutions*, Harmondsworth: Penguin.

Wells, H.G. (1895/1995) *The Time Machine*, London: Everyman.

7 Spectacle and inter-spectacle in *The Matrix* and organization theory

David Boje

> Have you ever had a dream, Neo, that you were so sure was real? What if you were unable to wake from that dream, Neo? How would you know the difference between the dream world and the real world?
>
> (extract from *The Matrix*)

We humans are the first species with the ability to perform directed genetic engineering on our ecology and ourselves. We create our own evolutionary successors while making a simple act of consumption. Corporations compete to patent plant, animal and human genomes. And with every new technology, there is an accompanying storyline (and ideology) to legitimate its production, distribution and consumption. This storyline is part of spectacle, the industry of media culture (film, television and radio as well as the theatrics of Disneyland and Las Vegas). Spectacles such as the utopian dreams of Tomorrowland (in Disney theme parks) and Paris, Paris (a Las Vegas casino and resort hotel) are totalizing self-portraits of power that mask the fragmentation and the human conditions of production as well as the ecological consequences of over-consumption. An apocalyptic example of spectacles of production, consumption, and distribution is the movie *The Matrix* where only a few awoke from the dream of virtual consumption and cyber-image to gaze the face of economic power and the eco-societal disaster. Do we already inhabit the Matrix with our images, heroes, work and consumption habits patterned by corporate-media we no longer control?

The technology and corporate changes we view in popular culture films include information technology (*Enemy of the State*), nanotechnology (*Johnny Mnemonic*), biotech genetic re-engineering (*Jurassic Park*), virtual technology (*eXistenZ*), high-speed transportation systems (*Star Trek*) and the science fiction of time/space travel (*Gateway*). The storyline of progress as our future legitimates the emergence of associated corporate governance, consumption and work-life patterns.

These science fiction genres are not only spectacles of particular forms of production and consumption, they are manifesting themselves even now in new forms of hybrid organization forms that Best and Kellner (1999b) and I (2000) call 'inter-spectacular'. Inter-spectacle refers to the sense that multiple spectacle genres crisscross, inscribing a future in which biotech and virtuality take over without even the Luddite resistance of the industrial revolution. The spectacle storylines and images of popular culture proscribe a philosophy of progressive life and work that makes the inter-spectacle organization forms seem 'common sense'. This is an effective camouflage against potential resisters making it almost invisible and inappropriate to resist.

Semiotician Julia Kristeva (1986: 36) argues that each text has an intertextual 'trajectory' of both 'historical' and 'social coordinates'. Just as the science fiction movie, future Organization Theory (hereafter OT) image and its corporate imitation constitute a reciprocally influenced intertextual trajectory. But, here the weave is constituted by many spectacle themes into an 'inter-spectacle network'. An inter-spectacle is a network of spectacles that constitute an 'intertextual system'. In terms of her work with novels, Kristeva notes 'it is a permutation of texts, an intertextuality: in the space of a given text, several utterances, taken from other texts, intersect and neutralize one another' (1986: 36–8). Inter-spectacle is an intertextual system written on a global stage. It is a perspective that has been under-applied to OT.

Disney, the resort casinos of Las Vegas, Monsanto and Nike (among many others) increasingly construct carnivalesque theatrical stages that enrol customers in inter-spectacular interpretations of corporately narrated identity. My thesis is that several spectacle sign systems are interlaced into one corporate inter-spectacle. There is a crowd of authors, actors and readers engaged in scenes of dynamic inter-spectacle production, distribution and consumption. The result is a smooth transition to global power with only infrequent protests like we saw in the Seattle World Trade Organization demonstrations. And this protest itself was a composite of so many interest groups from labour and ecology; inter-spectacle and networks of fragmented protest groups as the paradigmatic 'Matrix' theatre of global enterprise.

Before we can properly explore inter-spectacle, some basic spectacle theory is warranted. I will then work out the theory of 'inter-spectacle' and show how it differs from other spectacle genres. In the case of *The Matrix*, there are several spectacles in the intertext that for me constitute examples of the inter-spectacle ranging from biotech and virtuality to new forms of organizational community as well as new relationships to our global and cosmos ecology. Finally, I will draw some implications of inter-spectacle science fiction genres for organization theory. Specifically, I want to explore one question: do films such as *The Matrix* represent an interconnection between future organizational life spectacles and their science fiction equivalents?

Spectacle and inter-spectacle theory

Guy Debord (1967) defines spectacle in many ways. Here we will focus on spectacle as simply 'the existing order's uninterrupted discourse about itself, its laudatory monologue. It is the self-portrait of power' (Debord, 1967: #24). I assume each science fiction movie is a possible future portrait of power. And, 'in all its specific forms, as information or propaganda, as advertisement or direct entertainment consumption, the spectacle is the present model of socially dominant life' (Debord, 1967: #6). Horkheimer and Adorno (1972) argue that the kind of spectacle film I shall analyse is inherently dialectical. And some science fiction is a narrative in the service of mass culture control (Horkheimer and Adorno 1972: 121): 'Movies and radio need no longer pretend to be art. The Truth [is] that they are just businesses made into an ideology in order to justify the rubbish they deliberately produce.'

The media spectacle (including films) gives technology (and science) a rationale for domination itself in the culture industry (p. 121). 'Anyone who resists can only survive by fitting in' since 'not to conform means to be rendered powerless, economically and therefore spiritually – to be "self-employed"' (pp. 132–3). In a comment that speaks to Debord's theory of the spectacle, Horkheimer and Adorno (1972: 136) argue, 'the social power which the spectators worship shows itself more effectively in the omnipresence of the stereotype imposed by technical skill than in the stale ideologies for which the ephemeral contents stand in.' Below I will make the case, following Horkheimer and Adorno, that the film *The Matrix* is not only inter-spectacle, it is dialectic of science and myth.

We imitate the future portraits of power in the technology of our daily work and consumptive lifestyles. Debord attempted to extend Marx's focus on production (labour process theory) to consumption (fetish of over-consumption) theories of capitalism. Baudrillard built upon Debord's concept of spectacle and consumption to more radically theorize spectacle as the measure of authentic reality. And Best and Kellner (1997) also point to Debord's theory of spectacle as an archetype of critical postmodern theory. Debord posits two types of spectacle, concentrated and diffuse; each makes an important contribution to organization theory, which I intend to explore in this text.

Concentrated spectacle

'The concentrated spectacle' says Debord, 'belongs essentially to bureaucratic capitalism' (#64). The concentrated spectacle is where both production and consumption are constructed in a totalizing self-portrait of power that masks its fragmentation. An apocalyptic example is the movie *1984* and a more comic illustration is *Sleeper*. Spectacle 'concentrates all gazing and all consciousness' on particular cultural heroes that are legitimating of production and consumption practices (#3). Baudrillard (1992) describes the romantic sci-fi plot of Walt Disney: a refrigerated Disney suspended in liquid nitrogen reanimates after deep-freeze to the utopia of Future World in the Epcott Centre.

The concentrated form of the bureaucratic spectacle translates to: what is good for society (short-term employment) is what is officially and bureaucratically good for corporate power (i.e. downsizing and globalization). The gaze is concentrated onto the spectacle role models, those surrogate spectators constructed to channel our identification. These can be human-celebrities like Madonna, Spike Lee or Bill Clinton, or corporate-celebrities like McDonalds, Nike, Monsanto and Microsoft.

Despite their lack of study of the inter-spectacle world of organizations, I see several spectacles currently being interwoven into what will soon be commonplace

MBA education. The MBA is encouraged to join e-commerce, virtual team projects and embrace the new heroic forms of organization, the biotech and the virtual e-commerce firm. The inter-spectacle is already manifest in the MBA curriculum. *Wall Street Journal* and *Wired Magazine* announce the coming of the inter-spectacle form. What MBA student (or professor) resists inter-spectacle?

The American Dream is constructed and concentrated in the Business College with the CEO as hero (Bill Gates, Henry Ford and Michael Eisner), such that we can gaze and learn how to feel and behave towards others like heroic CEOs (what is your value added to my corporate wealth?). The utility of the concentrated spectacle to its producers is to keep 'spec-actors' (Augusto Boal's term for actors in the spectacle) from seeing how activities A, B and C are connected to X, Y and Z (e.g. how CEO pay is connected to keeping employees in part-time, no-benefit, minimum-wage employment). As workers are separated through division of labour from viewing the totality of 'the concentration of the production process . . . unity and communication become the exclusive attribute of the system's management' (#26).

In sum, the concentrated spectacle masks the material conditions of production and consumption from various disassociated stakeholders. Student consumers, for example, are protesting on college campuses demanding that administrations force vendors selling clothing on campus to disclose who is making the garments. But most consumers do not know who to confront to find out if the garment they are purchasing was made in an overseas or an inner-city sweatshop. For many ignorance is bliss.

Diffuse spectacle

The diffuse spectacle is one of fragmentation and specialization in the global economy, global marketplace and global division of labour. In the diffuse spectacle it is difficult to know who made what product and under what labour conditions. It is as if concentrated spectacle reverses to hidden background and all the messiness of fragmentation is now foreground. The 'diffuse spectacle' says Debord, 'accompanies the abundance of commodities, the undisturbed development of modern capitalism' as it reaches into every nook and cranny (#64). Late modern capitalism combines the massification of concentrated spectacle markets and production with the diffuse spectacle of fragmentation to penetrate and colonize differentiated tastes and lifestyles. Firat and Dholakia (1998: 160) speak of this diffuse political economy as our global 'theatres of consumption'. They contend we live in fragmented 'life mode communities' constructed into 'enclaves' that keep us physically separate from each other in what I will call 'tribal' communities.

In the postmodern condition people are navigating between and experimenting with multiple tribal communities to experience alternative life modes. Some are accountants and lawyers during the week and transform into temporary weekend warriors, Harley riders in heavy leather, or break from work here and there to go gender bending with alternative persona in chat rooms, and some are ballroom dancing in the evening in disguises in the clubs in Japan. Other life mode changes are more permanent as people redesign their body to look like celebrities such as Elvis or Barbie, or pierce and tattoo the body to be part of some trendy tribal community. Cyberpunk novelist William Gibson's book *Neuromancer* depicts a future world where cosmetic surgery will be not only affordable but also socially compulsory. Cindy Jackson, meanwhile, has had thirty surgical procedures in order to achieve what she claims is the Western ideal of beauty, a living approximation of a Barbie doll. Sacrificing natural to become the cultural icon of enlightened progress is the chief task of speculative production (Baudrillard, 1994). And the capitalist system of production and consumption is responding to the tribal life modes by allowing formerly passive spectator-consumers to become commodified designer-choices about life modes.

The new marketing challenge is more in the temporary than permanent life mode production, accommodating temporary players, who want to experience but not permanently inhabit a life mode. The diffuse spectacle is also colonizing the alternative life mode communities, privatizing every time and space, including mainstream and non-mainstream alternatives. Resistance points to predatory capitalism become commodified into eco-tourism and other temporary adventures. This means that the diffuse spectacle is no less hegemonic than the concentrated apparatus of power, and perhaps more so. But, as the diffuse spectacle engages in more flexible productions of theatre, it also produces new life modes, disaggregating its former concentrated spectacles into new modes that can be easily commodified. Yet even beneath the façade of diffuse consumption choices, there are material roots and the usual suspects are assembled in remote lands to sell out the production of the locals. And if we look critically, the spec-actors with the most dynamic involvement in self-designed role-playing are an elite consumer, far removed from the mass of passive spectators ensconced in more concentrated spectacle production and consumption. In its development 'irreconcilable claims crowd' the global stage as various products simultaneously evoke spectacle as an apologetic for their respective life mode projects, each claiming their product will make the individual, society and planet happy.

Both concentrated and diffuse spectacle has an impact on our biotic world. 'The spectacle of automobiles demands a perfect transport network which destroys old cities, while the spectacle of the city itself requires museum-areas' (#65). Postmodernists contend that the spectacle is made to appear more real than reality itself (Best and Kellner, 1997). And this legitimates despoiling the ecosystem by making happiness only attainable through accumulating more and more spectacles. I view organizations as concentrated/diffuse spectacles, not just evolutions of nature, not subjects of the laws of nature, but disrupters of nature through spectacle and part of the co-evolution of changes in technology, community and ecology. Reality is now a designer theory, a spectacle, instead of a fact of linear evolution. We are beginning to design our body and mind; we are already designing our environment so any pretension to 'natural' is illusory.

OT says Best and Kellner (1999a: 17), continues to endorse biological fallacy (i.e. environment as uncertainty, organic adaptiveness and turbulence), when our complexity, chaos and cyber-capitalism theorists 'wrongly dissolve the boundaries between natural and social systems'. Our preference is to look at the co-evolutionary reconstruction of 'nature' into spectacle. 'The theorization of society and the economy through biological metaphors such as self-organization is exceedingly risky, for one can easily lose sight of the enormous differences between biological and social systems' (p. 14).

Sci-fi films and OT

The four ideal type films in Table 7.1 are Biotech, Eco, Consumption and Tribal spectacles. I have organized the four spectacle genres of late capitalism along two dualistic dimensions: fragmentation/standardization and individual/community. Additional tables will move beyond the dualities.

These transformations of late global capitalism are beginning to interpenetrate one another in strange ways changes (fragmentation of technology, population and habitat).

Biotech spectacle

This spectacle is considered by Rifkin (1998) to be the launch of the Biotech Century, the Second Genesis of designer evolution. If we can play around with plants and animals, why not produce 'super humans' in this biotech century? With each wave of technology invention, its mechanical and social engineers are legitimated to re-engineer organizations and society based upon the latest idealized image mechanistic science.

The movies in Table 7.1 raise bio ethics issues that in all likelihood will face our society in the next decade with predictable consequences in employment patterns,

Table 7.1 Four ideal types of sci-fi movies reflecting global spectacles

		FRAGMENTATION		
		Biotech spectacle	**Eco spectacle**	
I		*Gattica*	*Armageddon*	**C**
N		*Twilight of the Gods*	*Deep Impact*	**O**
D		*Twins*		**M**
I		*Sleeper*		**M**
V		*Boys from Brazil*		**U**
I		**Consumption spectacle**	**Tribal spectacle**	**N**
D		*The Game*	*Star Wars*	**I**
U		*The 13th Floor*	*Star Trek*	**T**
A		*eXistenZ*	*Contact*	**Y**
L		STANDARDIZATION		

families and the global economy. In *Twins* Arnold Schwartzenegger and Danny Devito are cloned from genius sperm donors, but the twins end up with different physical, mental and moral qualities. The twins set out to find out the biological donors and to confront their genetic re-engineer who has played God with their genes and upbringing. In *Gattica*, an infant has escaped the DNA re-engineering protocol and now has to compete in a world of genetically engineered super humans. The hero confronts a society of DNA profile surveillance that disciplines a caste-society of DNA-spliced haves and DNA have-nots. Employment in professional occupations and out-world travel is restricted to DNA-superior humans. Others clean restrooms and wait on tables. Our anti-hero uses synthetic fingerprints, contacts and body scrubs to pass for a genetically perfected being. In *Twilight of the Gods* a mother learns, from her Genome project-engineer husband, that there is a 90 per cent probability that their son will be born gay. They now have the moral dilemma of having to choose to keep or to abort the foetus. The husband prefers to abort the foetus, and the mother eventually decides to give it birth. The couple separates and the husband moves out. In *Sleeper* and *Boys from Brazil*, more political issues of the Biotech Century are explored. These movies explore the idea of cloning Hitler or other fascist leaders form clone samples. The main character in *Sleeper* (Woody Allen) is thawed from cryogenics after 200 years in the freezer. The conspirators pursuing Woody Allen execute their social control by a new process of reprogramming people's brains through high-tech technology. As a result, there only remains a new society where people are controlled, manipulated and assimilated into the mainstream by the political interests of their governors who used (and took advantage of) technology as their main weapon. In the meantime, the leader of this government is killed in an explosion, but scientists are also able to turn him back to live by the process of cloning. And along the plot of this futuristic film, we can also see – as expected – the underground resistance army fighting back against the merciless government. (In the next table, we shall explore some of the cross-plots that make *Sleeper* and other movies Inter-spectacles.)

This next step forward for mechanistic science, the re-engineering of all life as complex machines is being marketed as a scientific and practical way to improve efficiency and reverse trends in ecological decay and world starvation. Instead of bland homogeneity the Biotech promise is one of untold variety through cloning and crossing genes of different species to yield new seeds, plants, animals and super humans. In the last decade the campaign is to adopt the biotech metaphor. With Biotech inventions, animals and plants became engineered machines of production and lucrative objects of consumption. In short, the proponents of Biotech distort its imagery through the theatrics of spectacle to make it appear as some sort of blessing from heaven.

Eco spectacle

Population changes are transforming the natural habitat. The Eco-habitat is fragmenting with more highways, development and deforestation, resulting in a decline in natural resources, increased global warming, a thinner ozone layer, poorer air and water quality, fewer rainforests, more desertification and spreading disease. There are a number of recent natural disaster movies in which Mother Nature threatens to get even with the human race. The disasters are larger than life disasters that can only be averted by a handful of daring people doing spectacle-things. *Armageddon* and *Deep Impact* threaten all human life on the planet. These are apocalyptic visions of natural destruction. For example, *Armageddon*'s plot is simple enough to define as Eco Spectacle because its premise is that a giant meteor is headed straight for the earth and when it hits, it will destroy the entire planet. Besides Eco spectacle, *Armageddon* has some subplots, some of which could be classified as Tribal spectacle (see below). For example, the movie has subplots that deal with different cultures and social classes having to come together to save the planet from this deadly meteor. Have you heard of all those racist web sites that promote ethnic cleansing? There are also examples of cyber-tribal spectacles that go beyond movies *per se*. We will look at inter-spectacle in movie genres in the next table.

Consumption spectacle

Consumption in Americana is a way of life that is rapidly colonizing the planet. Marx said: 'A commodity appears, at first sight, a very trivial thing, and easily understood. Its analysis shows that it is, in reality, a very queer thing, abounding in metaphysical subtleties and theological niceties' (Marx, 1867: 71). Marx argued that in the world of commodity production, there is a 'Fetishism which attaches itself to the products of labour, such that as soon as products are produced they become commodities' (p. 72). Did you hear about web sites that actually auction models' genes? The Fetish spectacle of consumption transmutes human-subject into human-object, many histories into one object-history, while endowing socially-produced-object into subjective-natural-living being. Consumers do not see the social or historical character of production ('material relations between persons', p. 73) and are therefore easily persuaded that commodities have meta-physical powers. Material commodities, not social relations, bring us happiness. Best and Kellner (1997: 86) summarize the temple of consumption:

> With cable and satellite TV, the spectacle is now so ubiquitous and access-ible that one need not even rise from the reclining chair to shop; only a telephone and credit card is required to purchase a vast array of products from TV home-shopping networks . . . creating new malls in cyberspace.

Consumption spectacles combine the construction of a fetishism with a new story (a grand narrative substituting for history) that can be consumed by indi-vidual spectators in ways that mask the social character of the production and the material conditions of the consumption process. In the movie *The Game*, actors use special effects to make Michael Douglas believe he must kill in order to survive. The Game turns out to be a prank played by his brother as a birthday present. The movie, *The 13th Floor* is a sci-fi thriller about using virtual reality so rich clients can possess the bodies of anyone they please. In the *eXistenZ* the spectacle is able to make virtual reality video games come to life. Again the Game becomes more real than real. We are given two choices: this is a virtual reality role-playing fantasy or the fantasy has turned real and the players keep playing the Game after their plug is pulled.

In each of these movies, we get a rare glimpse of the spectacle of production and consumption. We observe the spectacle of production interacting with consumption from the perspective of virtual game players. And we observe the class struggle of haves and have-nots. As Marx (1867: 80) puts it we get a rare glimpse behind the 'mystical veil'.

Tribal spectacle

There is accelerating bifurcation of societies into have-the-resources to survive, and have-nothing. *Star Wars*, *Star Trek* and *Contact* standardize man's quest to leave the planet in search of the interglobal community and interstellar civics, a United Nations of the worlds and a war of the worlds. *Star Wars* reveals a biomechanical world where Luke and his father Darth Vader are part human and part machine. It is also a world in which the rights of humans and the rights of machines (R2D2 and C3P0) have to be negotiated. In the old *Star Trek* movies man teletransports, rematerializes, in a new cyber-spectacle. We also see a new tribal civics among warring and peaceful worlds. The US Starship *Enterprise* is on a peacekeeping mission among the galaxies. This is analogous to the US role in safeguarding worldwide transnational production from any outside-tribal harm. The social commentary establishes a link to tribal spectacles – such as *Star Trek* – which reset current issues and moral dilemmas (e.g., cold war proxy conflicts, nuclear proliferation, race relations, exploitation of indigenous peoples) years into the future, after we have presumably gained the knowledge and understanding to resolve our most divisive social conflicts. In the new *Star Treks* (*Next Generation, Babylon 5*, etc.) we see more attempts to envision the civics of societies that are part robot and part human. The movie *Contact* presents a tamer spectacle in which, like *Star Trek*, more advanced worlds look after the nurture and development of less developed worlds, but without the resource extraction and slave-labour economy viewed in *Star Wars*. My students watched *Contact* and said it was 'spectacle trying to be festival'. One felt Jodie's character in the movie inspires people to have a greater vision, while Palmer stands as a reminder that one must not abandon one's faith in this technological world. Another saw the tribal face of the movie as clearly shown, when we see that the whole mission has international impact. As repeated many times in the movie 'If we are alone here, then it's an awful lot of waste of space.' I am made to understand that we as human beings should be involved in this 'festival' of finding the truth. The religious, moral issues raised by the so-called 'opinion leaders' of the public cast an opposition to this 'greater' issue of searching for the truth.

These four ideal type spectacles are not independent of one another. And indeed, they form hybrid types (see Table 7.2). Table 7.1 dimensions need some explanation.

Table 7.2 Nine types of movies reflecting global spectacles

	FRAGMENTATION			
	Biotech spectacle *Gattica* *Twilight of the Gods* *Twins* *Sleeper* *Boys from Brazil*	**Bio-eco inter-spectacle** *Medicine Man* *Silkwood* *China Syndrome* *Outbreak* *The Stand* *DNA* *Species* *Godzilla*	**Eco spectacle** *Armageddon* *Deep Impact*	
I N D I V I D U A L	**Bio-robo inter-spectacle** *Metropolis* *Modern Times* *Robocop* *Johnny Mnemonic* *The Stepford Wives* *Total Recall* *The Fly*	**Inter-spectacle** *Blade Runner* *Fifth Element* *Jurassic Park* *The Matrix*	**Eco-civics inter-spectacle** *Mad Max* *Rollerball* *Waterworld* *Postman* *Fire Below* *Towering Inferno* *Civil Action* *Soylent Green*	**C O M M U N I T Y**
	Consumption spectacle *The Game* *The 13th Floor* *eXistenZ*	**Cyber inter-spectacle** *Truman Show* *Pleasantville* *Enemy of the State* *Network*	**Tribal spectacle** *Star Wars* *Star Trek* *Contact*	
	STANDARDIZATION			

Fragmentation / standardization

Late global capitalism interlaces both fragmentation and standardization. Fragmentation according to Bauman (1997) and many others is the defining characteristic of postmodernity while for Kelly (1998) fragmentation is but one of the new economic rules of global capitalism. Best and Kellner's (1999a) critique of Kelly's book is that he does not look at the dark side of the spectacle of production and consumption. In movies such as *Armageddon* and *Deep Impact* the eco-system has its revenge on human systems of technology. Biotech, Eco, Consumption and Tribal ethics and catastrophes however are frequent themes in the science fiction movies of Table 7.1. Fragmentation/standardization is also closely associated with the diffuse spectacle, since the consumer experiences 'only a succession of fragments of this commodity happiness, fragments in which the quality attributed to the whole is obviously missing every time' (#65). In *The Game, The 13th Floor* and *eXistenZ*, the happiness of consumption turns nightmarish. Fragmentation is also a part of current organizational life, the counterpart to global capitalism's attempt to standardize production and consumption behaviour while retaining market share in firms like McDonalds and Disney. In spectacle theory, late capitalism is a move from flexible production to flexible consumption. Making the fragment appear to be the totality masks choice-making. The 'McMenu' is fragmenting regionally and internationally with more Cajun 'McRibs' choices in New Orleans and leaner 'McSalad' options for California. McDonalds is sold everywhere, but the burger itself is modified, even allowed in India to be vegetarian, in order to reach every fragmented life-space on the planet. The Disney theme park is a standard item, but varies significantly between the US, France and Japan. Part of the totality is convincing producers, consumers and investors that life circumstances are improving for the masses, and those not improving are victimizing their own progress. Products from standard science fiction movies such as *Star Wars* and *Star Trek* turn the characters into commodity symbols to adorn lunchboxes and T-shirts. The tribal characters also mark the popular culture's views on diversity and spirituality, 'may the force be with you'.

Individual / community

The second dimension recognizes that organizations, societies, families, networks, cultures are made up of individuals as well as communities. In *Star Wars*, various life-forms compete and co-operate in interplanetary and intertribal commerce. Individualism is focused on the me-generation of consumption-equals-happiness, where transformations of the body through the latest in surgical technology bring instant joy. Community here is defined as both human-tribal and more diverse biotic multi-species eco-system communities ('Eco' and 'Tribal'). Some movie spectacles celebrate individuals without communities, others absorb individual identities into a whole array of tribal identities. Both the diffuse and the concentrated spectacle forms sell us 'the image of the society happily unified by consumption' but the object made celebrity in the spectacle 'becomes vulgar as soon as it is taken home by its consumer' (##69, 70). The Biotech films raise serious issues about the ethics of genetic re-engineering. In particular, *Gattica* explores the ethics of using DNA profiling to determine patterns of employment and individual rights.

However, the typology of Table 7.1 quickly breaks down when we look at science fiction movies that fall between the proposed ideal types. Beyond diffuse and concentrated spectacle genres of the ideal types along two dimensions lies science fiction movies, the recent inter-spectacle movies, of which *The Matrix* is one we shall soon explore.

Inter-spectacle theory

Inter-spectacle is a nexus of multiple spectacle genres, as depicted in Table 7.2. What I see happening is the rhizomatic (Deleuze and Guattari, 1987) interaction of the four ideal type spectacles (Biotech, Eco, Consumption and Tribal) in the sci-fi movies envisioning the future of global capitalism. There are simple two-way interactions such as between Biotech and Eco, Biotech and Consumption, etc. And there are inter-spectacles of more than two dimensions. There are for example, science fiction movies at the centre of Table 7.2, such as *Blade Runner*, *The Fifth Element*, *Jurassic Park*, and *The Matrix* that for me are particularly inter-spectacle, capturing the interpenetration of each of the surrounding spectacles. *Blade Runner*, for example, is a Biotech spectacle, an Eco spectacle, a theatre of consumption and production, as well as a network of warring corporate tribes and shantytown communities. In *The Fifth Element* Bruce Willis drives his taxi in a *Blade Runner* that is a Biotech and Eco disaster world, but also one that is about to be annihilated in interstellar catastrophe. In *Jurassic Park*, Jeff Goldblum lectures about the chaos effects of attempts to plan and control DNA, as Biotech-engineered dinosaurs figure out ways to procreate and threaten the planet with Eco catastrophe. In *The Matrix*, there is the eco spectacle of biotechnology destroying the natural environment, imprisoning humans in virtual reality so that they can be used to power the computers, and tribes at war with agents of artificial intelligence. This is the movie I will now focus upon.

The Matrix *as inter-spectacle*

I will briefly review the storyline of *The Matrix* and then explore inter-spectacle implications for organization theory. *The Matrix* is the action-packed spectacle of cyber-tech, Biotech virtuality mixed with the parable of the Second Coming, Zen koan and an apocalypse yarn. This inter-spectacle was written and directed by Larry and Andy Wachowski and stars Keanu Reeves, Laurence Fishburne, Carrie-Anne Moss, Joe Pantoliano and Hugo Weaving. And there is gravity-free virtual-reality kung fu, choreographed by Hong Kong artist Woo-Ping Yuen.

The Matrix is inter-spectacle, crossing Virtual Reality and Cyberpunk Theatre with Eco apocalypse and Tribal warfare set in the year 2199. The film is a pastiche of many genres, including Hong Kong-style kung fu. Cast members reportedly trained for six months with a Hong Kong kung fu master. And *The Matrix* is an interpretation of our modern-day world of organizations 'in which ominous silhouettes and claustrophobic paranoia are around every corner' (Leong, 1999: 1). The labyrinthine plot parallels Burrell's (1998) book *Pandemonium*. Both invite us to descend into the dark side of postmodern organization life, to see beyond the glamorous promise of the control of chaos and the so-called 'empowered' choices among fragmented complexity. I will briefly touch upon the plot and characterizations of this sci-fi movie before moving to organizational implications.

The Matrix begins with Trinity, played by Carrie-Anne Moss, the first voice we hear in the movie; she is a leather and vinyl-clad woman doing super-human mid-air-suspension-kick-cop-in-jaw sequences. Keanu Reeves plays Thomas Anderson, a cubicle-office worker, software engineer for Metacortex, a distinguished software company by day and at night the hacker, Neo, who is desperately seeking the truth about something he's heard of in rumours: 'What is the Matrix?' Neo believes he is living a normal life in 1999, but begins to question what is real and what is not as he follows clues left for him:

Trinity: Wake up, Neo . . . The Matrix has you . . . Follow the white rabbit . . . Knock, knock, Neo.

Neo begins to follow the (Alice In Wonderland – little white rabbit) clues left by Trinity into an underworld where he uncovers the truth about the Matrix. Neo hacks his way through 'cyberspace for traces of a shadowy character called Morpheus, who in turn is somehow involved with a mysterious construct or theory or whangdoodle called the Matrix' (O'Hehir, 1999: 1). Morpheus, as played by Laurence Fishburne, turns out to be a cyber-guru and tribal leader who allows Neo to see another reality, a dark and eco-catastrophic postmodern reality where virtual and Biotech science have invented cyber-machines that have doomed both human and non-human ecology. A resistance group (led by the guru Morpheus) recruits Neo, believing him to be the 'chosen one' (a reference to the mythic Second Coming). The resistance group is trying to wreck the Matrix computer hardware in order to emancipate the deluded, dreaming human race. Neo is an unaware saviour.

The film is loaded with overt references to Carroll's *Through the Looking Glass*. Reality isn't what it's cut out to be. 'Neo is falling down the rabbit hole, and like Alice he has a choice, a blue pill to take him home, a red will take him to the truth' (Kayn, 1999: 1). *The Matrix* follows the theme of Lewis Carroll's Alice in Wonderland, through the looking glass, where Morpheus like the Caterpillar offers Neo two pills. 'One will return him to his drone existence, while the other will open his mind to the Matrix so he can learn what the hell is going on' (O'Hehir, 1999: 1). Neo pops the pill and discovers his own so-called life is a computer-generated and enhanced illusion; he and most everyone else has a (as in *Neuromancer* and *Johnny Mnemonic*) direct plug in his head, connecting him and most everyone else to the virtual reality of the Matrix (in *eXistenZ* the plug is at the base of the spinal cord). 'What is real and what is a dream?' As Morpheus explains: 'The Matrix is everything, it is all around us. It is the world that has been pulled over your eyes to shield you from the truth.' Parallels to Marx and Debord here are too obvious to state.

Computer artificial intelligence has taken over your human body, kept it in suspended animation, pumping in nutrients to keep you alive so you can generate electricity for the Matrix from your body chemistry, and keeping you happy and compliant by feeding you thoughts about actually living. Computer artificial intelligence has created an extensive earthly façade that dominates the 'real' world and makes humans the slave race, serving as living batteries to the machine. The hardware of the Matrix universe is powered by humans–batteries for its bioelectric energy.

The postmodern reality of the Eco disaster and the Cyber appropriate of reality is too intolerable for human consumption, so suspension in artificial virtual reality is a way to anaesthetize the human race. In order to keep people unaware of their slave-status, artificial intelligence constructed the Matrix, a virtual representation of late nineteenth-century Earth. Why all the *fin de siècle* deception? The virtual machines want to spare the humans the nightmare of a post-apocalyptic world in which much of the ecology has been destroyed by biowarfare.

The Sentient Agents also play out the Tribal war genre and seek Neo and the others who have escaped their virtual cages. The Sentient Agents are led by the Agent Smith (Hugo Weaving). Sentient Agents are intelligent programs within the Matrix that act to reinforce the artificial intelligence control of earth's populace. Neo joins with a few souls who have been awoken by an underground group seeking to liberate humanity from 'the Matrix', a vast virtual reality system which up until now, he had thought was 'the real world'. The Matrix is a reality ruled by virtual-intelligent computers where humans are bred to provide cheap and efficient power to its circuitry: 'It is the world that has been pulled over your eyes to hide the truth . . . a prison for your mind.'

The Matrix would remain mired in the dark side of the force, were it not for its mythical and religious subthemes. Andy and Larry Wachowski, who made this film, borrowed from two incompatible religious traditions: Buddhism, in particular Zen Buddhism, and Christianity (Rivera, 1999). Neo is the saviour. Morpheus speaks to Neo like the Zen master to his apprentice, answering with koans such as, 'I can only show you the door, you must walk through', and 'when the time comes, you won't need to dodge the bullet'. And they visit someone called the 'Oracle'. Buddhism, which teaches that 'salvation comes through the insight that human experience, including suffering, is illusory' (Rivera, 1999). There is also an Ahimsa reference, that suffering is the product of our attachments to these illusions, including the illusory idea of freedom (Rivera, 1999). These are the worldviews that make the movie fashionable and intelligible to its spectators.

The Buddhist theme does not provide sufficient appeal to the western audience who prefers heroes that take control of their realities. Enter Christianity, and the Oracle, foretelling a Second Coming, someone to lead the slaves out of their bondage. Neo may be the one, the messiah who will defeat the evil machines. Morpheus is convinced that Neo is 'the one'. The resistance movement hides in a place they call 'Zion'.

> For me, this theme is a derivative of several other movies. As one reviewer put it: *The Matrix* shamelessly plunders the sci-fi archives, filching plot elements from old *Twilight Zone* episodes, *The Terminator*, the books of William Gibson, among others. Furthermore, the Wachowski brothers have also thrown in

some overused Christian motifs, Lewis Carroll references, and bits of existentialist philosophy for good measure. Furthermore, they cast Keanu Reeves in the lead, not known for his great thespian skills and who hasn't been in a good movie in the past few years since *Speed*. All in all, it looked like *Johnny Mnemonic* all over again.

(Leong, 1999: 1)

The Matrix is also in the genre of several more films about virtual reality, namely David Cronenberg's *eXistenZ*, *Centropolis*, and *The 13th Floor*. There are also parallels to HAL, the computer in Stanley Kubrick's *2001: A Space Odyssey*, murdering the spaceship crew until astronaut Dave Bowman (Keir Dullea) disconnects it. In this genre of science fiction, artificial intelligence has evolved and become so powerful that shutting the machines down is no longer an option.

Rivera (1999) points out that

this plot detail comes straight from another Warner Bros. film: Alex Proyas' underrated masterpiece *Dark City*. The producers are Joel *Die Hard* Silver and co-producer: Andrew *Dark City* Mason. In *Dark City*, Andy and Larry Wachowski create a plausible and intelligent scenario where Neo's perception of his reality is challenged until he slowly realizes the truth. In these films, the stuff of which human consciousness is made, our perceptions and our memories, isn't to be trusted. They've been manipulated in order to control us.

(Rivera, 1999: 1)

But is it future or here and now?

Dialectics of myth and science

The Matrix also speaks to the *Dialectic of Enlightenment* (Horkheimer and Adorno, 1972). *The Matrix* storyline attempts to transcend the duality of thesis (mythic knowledge) and anti-thesis (enlightenment of science), and in the synthesis (Neo's Second Coming) science reverts to mythic. As Horkheimer and Adorno (1972: xvi) put it 'myth is already enlightenment and enlightenment reverts to mythology'. And 'Enlightenment intends to secure itself against the return of the mythic' through mathematics, abstract formal logic, systematics and demythologization (pp. 25–27). Ironically, it is a process that returns science to a mythic it never seems to transcend. And for Horkheimer and Adorno (1972: 87), the result is the extreme forms of terror-to-control the masses advocated by Hobbes and Machiavelli.

In the dialectic of myth and enlightenment, science seeks to master nature and to submit everything natural to the autocratic logic of science. 'Yet the fully enlightened earth', as in *The Matrix* movie, 'radiates disaster triumphant' (Horkheimer and Adorno, 1972: 3). In *The Matrix*, science in the form of AI-conspiracy has taken control of an earth parched by human technology and seeks if necessary the extermination of the pestilence, humans. Science as Matrix presents itself is both progress and salvation. But to do so it must disenchant the humans, ironically, by suspending them in a mythic world of (mythic) virtuality. But as Horkheimer and Adorno (1972: 4) foretold, 'the only kind of thinking that is sufficiently hard to shatter myths is ultimately self-destructive'. Science is fighting spiritual myth with virtual myth. Fear is everywhere (i.e. Matrix-agents fear the rebels will lift the yoke of carefully regulated virtual-illusion to expose totalitarian control by the battery-machine). Ironically, *The Matrix* believes human species are not prepared to live with chaotic existence, the apocalypse of post-nuclear disaster.

There is another interesting irony in *The Matrix*. The rebel tribe must disenchant both Artificial Intelligence agents and cyber-slaves of the virtual-real world of the Matrix and reveal it to be mythic-illusion. And to do so they must master both science and spiritual myth (discipline of kung fu, Rebirth and Second Coming as well as AI science and weapons of destruction). On his own mythic journey, Neo commits self-sacrifice in order to be born again as a saviour to the slaves and a destroyer of the Matrix. Neo will sacrifice his life to save Morpheus. And this sacrifice in Horkheimer and Adorno's (1972: 10) terms 'marks a step toward discursive logic'. That is, the duality of science and mythic (discourse narrative) is transcended in the moment of sacrifice, and science gets defeated by magic and rebel-science (e.g., Neo bends his body to the bullets as he controls time itself, slowing the bullets and even healing the virtual wounds to his body). In the concluding scene Neo (as mythic) embodies science (the AI-agent of the Matrix), literally diving headfirst into the agent's body. In this way, Neo transcends the duality (in theory) by not distancing himself from the scientific object (the Matrix). But there is more to it.

Neo and the rebels are bringing enlightenment to the slaves and AI-agents of the Matrix. Yet to do so, one could ask if the rebels don't become their very antithesis? As Horkheimer and Adorno (1972: 16) observe: 'Enlightenment is mythic fear turned radical.' The Matrix has attempted to move human civilization away from the chaos of its own barbarism (to self and planet) by cocooning all humans in the utopia of a virtuality machine (Horkheimer and Adorno, 1972: 17). The Matrix is 'an instrument of rational administration' by the enlightened AI, but ironically, 'they steer society toward barbarism' in the war of man to escape the imprisonment of the computing machine (Horkheimer and Adorno, 1972: 20). As the rebels free other cyber-slaves and take vengeance against the AI-agents, do they become the new sovereigns?

In sum, *The Matrix* can be read as the dialectic of thesis, anti-thesis and synthesis. In the end the rebels reassert spiritual domination over science. Will the rebels, turned sovereigns, use science to control humanity? As *The Matrix* demonstrates, most of humanity is content to live within the virtual walls of spectacle, preferring the illusion of steak to the 'real' taste of mush. The mix of Zen, kung fu, fundamentalism, and New Age spiritualism is not an integrated film-message. The movie does not reject science, it remasters it and sets it along a slightly different path. The final message is that it is by freeing our mind from spectacle that we attain freedom. Ironically, to free the mind, the rebels use virtual teaching machines and simulated combat arenas to learn to fight terror with terror. And they use New Age spiritualism, taking us along Neo's journey of self-discovery, revealing to us spectators that if we believe in ourselves, all is possible. We are left to sort out this ultimate irony: in the virtual machine we were interconnected to the one, and to resist that prison we are handed a new form of enlightenment, all are connected to one in the body of the spirit. Yet, do we not move from the prison of the utopia of the perfect virtual machine to another that seeks after our mind?

Organizational implications of *The Matrix* and inter-spectacle

If life imitates art, then it can be said that OT imitates the spectacle images of popular media culture. And popular culture, most notably science fiction movies, imitate the presumed future of organization turned spectacle. I think OT is already conversant with the spectacle futuristic science fiction images of basic spectacle genres Biotechnology (*Jurassic Park*), Cybernetics (*The 13th Floor*) and Ecological apocalypse/robotics (*Blade Runner*). While the apocalyptic plots have not happened in full regalia in our time, what has been implemented is the technology dreams that make them possible. Various science fiction films portray the theatrics of significant changes in technology (*Metropolis*), population (*Soylent Green*) and our (un) natural habitat (*Mad Max*) in tragic and satirical visions of late global capitalism and organizational life.

There is some speculative evidence that organizational life is rapidly imitating the artistry of science fiction. To the average spectator, this is just Hollywood science fiction, right?

> Wrong, says Kevin Warwick, a professor at the department of cybernetics at the University of Reading in England – the British equivalent of the M.I.T. Media Lab – who has spent his career working on robotics, creating machine intelligence and, most controversially, building human-computer implants for use in his own body.
>
> (Brown, 1999:1)

On April 20, 1998, Professor Warwick, inspired by Michael Crichton's book *The Terminal Man*' had a glass capsule about 23 millimeters long and 3 millimeters wide containing an electromagnetic coil and a silicon chip inserted in his arm (*Geek News*, 1999; Brown, 1999). The media calls him Professor Cyborg, since his chip is in contact with a computer making lights turn on and off when he enters and exits rooms and gives him a spoken, running tally of the mail in his e-mail box. As in the movie *Blade Runner*, Warwick keeps electronic pets, a 'seven dwarves' troupe of little wheeled robots with white faces and ultrasonic eyes who have been teaching themselves both individual and group behaviour. 'Our senses are restricted, they suit us as humans, but machines have the capabilities of sensing the world in ultrasonics, ultraviolet, infrared, X-ray, gamma ray,' Warwick explains (Brown, 1999: 3). And, as in the book *Neuromancer* by William Gibson,

Warwick foresees a day when computer users can jack in and visualize the computer reality in their head.

It would seem that computer and Biotech will alter the way organizations and our bodies exist in our lifetime. *Blade Runner, eXistenZ* and *The Matrix* are 'cyberpunk' visions of our organizational present (Newquist, 1999: 1). The Matrix creates a dark, depressing and apocalyptic universe.

Inter-spectacle science fiction movies also speak to an awakening of the consumer and spec-actor to the iron cage of spectacle existence. Tables 7.1 and 7.2 introduced some basic types of spectacles so that we might look more closely at inter-spectacle behaviour of organizations, doing global theatre on the global stage. Table 7.3 drops the movies to look at contemporary organizational life spectacles on our planet. My point is quite simple and quite radical. I think that organizations do not evolve and are quite artificial spectacles made to appear as natural and evolutionary. Corporations browse the centres of genetic diversity, helping themselves to a rich largess of genetic treasures, only to sell back the same in a slightly engineered and patented form, and at a hefty price – all for products that have been freely shared and traded among farmers and villagers for all of human history (Rifkin, 1998: 52).

Monsanto Corporation and other transnational corporations are rapidly patenting biotic materials to control seed production and to make agriculture dependent upon genetically engineered fertilizers and pesticides. Monsanto sells us a storyline, that world hunger will end, or that industrial pollution will end, so we do not examine too closely the downside of cybertech, biotech, and robotech production and consumption. In the near future, it will become extremely difficult to differentiate between virtual reality and reality, or between natural human and animal and genetically engineered species.

OT is what Best and Kellner (1999a: 8) call a 'quest to erase fundamental differences between humans, technology, and nature'. Our texts need to be rewritten and quickly. The use of organic metaphors like 'evolution', 'hive', 'swarm' and 'self-organizing' do not help to create a spectacle of spectacles, an inter-spectacle biotech, ecotech, bio-eco, bio-robo, and consumption spectacles in our books and teaching. In the new spectacles and inter-spectacles, we give MBAs a cosmology that scripts their role in biomimicry, while setting up cyber universities to make the transition seamless and non-self-reflexive.

Rifkin (1998) argues that each new era of technology development invents a cosmology that makes that reality into common sense. What I am calling for in OT is a questioning of the new cosmology from an inter-spectacle perspective.

There is some ground for this critique. Best and Kellner (1999a: 10), for example, point out that the fragmented, networked, soft-capitalism economy is the new metaphor 'appropriate for the present age, where all people, businesses, and nations are interlocked into a massive hive-like system of technology, economics, and communication.' Spectacle dramatizes the new metaphors of OT by making chaos, fragmentation and the postmodern a logic that does not have to be questioned. Putting these simple metaphors of OT into an inter-spectacle context allows for a critique of their political economy and ethical ambitions.

Table 7.3 Nine types of global spectacles

<table>
<tr><td colspan="5">FRAGMENTATION</td></tr>
<tr>
<td rowspan="10" align="center">I
N
D
I
V
I
D
U
A
L</td>
<td>Biotech spectacle
Genome Project
Genetic engineering
  industry
Gene patents by
  DuPont, Novartis,
  Upjohn, Monsanto,
  Eli Lilly, Rohm &
  Haas, and Dow
  Chemical
New firms like: Amgen,
  Organogenesis,
  Genzyme, Calgene,
  Mycogen, Myriad</td>
<td>Bio-eco
  inter-spectacle
Bio weapons industry
Monsanto terminator
  seeds
Chernobyl
Three Mile Island
Exxon Valdez
Aids, Malaria spreading</td>
<td>Eco spectacle
Ozone layer
Air and water quality
Deforestation
Desertification</td>
<td rowspan="10" align="center">C
O
M
M
U
N
I
T
Y</td>
</tr>
<tr>
<td>Bio-robo
  inter-spectacle
DNA computer chips
Robotic factories</td>
<td>Inter-spectacle
Rich versus poor
Science and mythic</td>
<td>Eco-civics
  inter-spectacle
McLibel
Green Peace
Save the Rainforest
World Vision
ISO 14000 standards</td>
</tr>
<tr>
<td>Consumption
  spectacle
Disneyland
Las Vegas (Mirage,
  Luxor, etc.)
Nike Town
Digital storytelling
  theatre
Shopping malls
Home shopping channel
Virtual corporations
Global division of labour
Knowledge workers
Word Wide Web
Telecommuting</td>
<td>Cyber
  inter-spectacle
Security guard industry
Surveillance industry
Prison industry
Clinton impeachment
Trial
OJ trial
Rodney King beating</td>
<td>Tribal spectacle
Shanty town slums
Peasantariat
Criminal families
Ethnic cleansing
Holocaust
Nomadic tribes</td>
</tr>
<tr><td colspan="3">STANDARDIZATION</td></tr>
</table>

To me *The Matrix* is a metaphor for our unquestioned assumptions about organizational and consumptive life modes. OT is a type of Pleasantville theory, an uncritical acceptance of metaphor as reality, as the story of reality. It is not making clear the differences between 'organizing' in the natural world and 'organizing' in the socio-economic and technical world (Best and Kellner, 1999a: 14). As OT adopts uncritically the language of socio-economic and technical, *The Matrix* points out the need to look at what happens when spirit (and ethics) is divorced from organization science. As Horkheimer and Adorno (1972: 92) point out, this does not mean that modern science is without ethics, only that when science as enlightenment shouts out mythic, to improve the validity of knowledge, it becomes the oppressive order it seeks to transcend. For example, the way in which organization science celebrates the ethics of the free competitive market without sufficient reflection on the social and ecological implications of biotechnology and virtuality machines.

Conclusions

The main point is that by equating organic-nature with organic-organization studies and technology as progress through industrial science, we do not see humans as agents of change in the ongoing inter-spectacle conditions of late capitalism.

To summarize, there is a rhizomatics of spectacle that is not being well addressed in organization theory. The spectacles are interpenetrating as we have explored in our survey of science fiction movies with blatant organization themes. What is at issue here is not the separate molar spectacles of Biotech, Eco, Consumption, of Net-Tribe in Table 7.1. Rather, what is curious is how these intersect to form bio-eco, cyber-eco, etc. It is inter-spectacle in Table 7.2 and translates into the context of new organization theories in contexts presented in Table 7.3.

There are intertextual links between the beleaguered office worker Neo, and Tony Perkins in Orson Welles' film of Kafka's *The Trial*. But, it also can be read as a statement about Marxist theory, people living the deluded dream-life produced by spectacle and inter-spectacle. The virtual illusion keeps people from rebelling against the machines that really run the show. The Matrix is an artificial intelligence with control over his life, making the population believe they are still in the year 1999, instead of 2199. Beyond spectacle and inter-spectacle, the Situationist International movement of the 1960s and 1970s called for a basic understanding of the individual in community and the fragmented life under mass production and consumption. Spectacle continues to haunt us in late capitalism and is reflected in the non-critical orientation to organization theory.

The challenge for OT is to peer beneath the inter-spectacle veil of promised utopia to fashion democratic and ecological ethics. The interface of critical theory (e.g. Horkheimer and Adorno) and postmodern theory (e.g. Debord) makes this veil more obvious. There are several reasons why OT does not peer beneath the veil, so obvious in *The Matrix* (Boje, 2000). First, much of what is taken as cases and examples in OT is lifted from the spectacle and public relations materials of corporate writers (consultants, CEOs, publicists and apologists). Second, universities in general, and business colleges, in particular, are entering into more financial relations with industry. Third, accreditation bodies of the Academy and the State are demanding that university knowledge be made more relevant to corporate careers and otherwise benefit industry. Fourth, there is a revival of naïve spirituality and even Social Darwinist epistemology in the business school that would make Nietzsche and Marx turn in their graves. Each of these developments makes it difficult to sustain a critical look beneath the veil of *The Matrix*.

Notes

I would like to thank Grace Ann Rosile and the editors of this book for their helpful comments on earlier chapter drafts.

References

Baudrillard, Jean (1992) *Hystericizing the Millennium*. Originally published in French as part of Jean Baudrillard, *L'Illusion de la fin: ou la grève des evenements*, Paris: Galilée. Translation by Charles Dudas, York University.

—— (1994) 'Plastic surgery for the other.' In Jean Baudrillard and Marc Guillaume, *Figures de l'alterité*, Paris: Descartes et Cie. Translated by Francois Debrix.

Bauman, Zygmunt (1997) *Postmodernity and its Discontents*, Washington Square, NY: New York University Press.

Best, Steven and Kellner, Douglas (1997) *The Postmodern Turn*, New York/London: Guilford Press.

—— (1999) 'Kevin Kelly's complexity theory: the politics and idealogy of self-organizing systems', OE, Volume 12, Number 2, pp. 141–62.

—— (1999b) 'Debord, cybersituations, and the interactive spectacle.' Accessed on the web, April 16, 2001, *http://www.uta.edu/huma/illuminations/best6.htm*

Boje, David M. (2000) *Spectacle and Festival of Organization: Managing Ahimsa Production and Consumption*. Book to be published by Hampton Press CA.

Brown, Janelle (1999) 'Professor Cyborg,' Salon. October 20, *http://www.salon.com/tech/feature/1999/10/20/cyborg/index.html?CP = POI&DN = 310*

Burrell, Gibson (1998) *Pandemonium: Towards a Retro-Organization Theory*, London: Sage.

Debord, Guy (1967) *La Société du Spectacle*, Paris, France: Editions Buchet-Chastel. Note it was reprinted in 1971 by Champ Libre (Paris). The first English translation was published by Black & Red in 1970. It was revised in 1977, incorporating numerous improvements suggested by friends and critics of the first translation. By convention, numbers refer to paragraphs in the 1967 version.

Deleuze, Gilles and Guattari, Felix (1987) *A Thousand Plateaus: Capitalism and Schizophrenia*, Minneapolis: University of Minnesota Press. Translated by Brian Massumi.

Firat, Fuat A. and Dholakia, Nikhilesh (1998) *Consuming People: From Political Economy to Theaters of Consumption*, London/New York: Routledge.

Geek News (1999) 'Question and answer with cybernetics professor Kevin Warwick.' September 22, *http://geeknews.net/interviews/kevinw.shtml*

Horkheimer, Max and Adorno, Theodor W. (1972) *Dialectic of Enlightenment*, New York: Herder and Herder. Translated by John Cumming from *Dialektick der Aufklarung* (1944).

Kayn, Ali (1999) Movie review of *The Matrix*, *http://www.festivale.webcentral.com.au/filmrvu/9904frvh.htm*

Kelly, Kevin (1998) *New Rules for the New Economy*, New York: Viking.

Kristeva, Julia (1986) 'Word, dialogue, and the novel.' In T. Moi (ed.), *The Kristeva Reader*, New York: Columbia University Press, pp. 35–61.

Leong, Anthony (1999) Movie review of *The Matrix*, *http://members.aol.com/aleong1631/matrix.html*

Marx, Karl (1867) *Das Kapital: kritik der politischen Oekonomie*, Hamburg: Verlag von Otto Meissner and New York: L.W. Schmidt. English version (1967) *Capital: A Critique of Political Economy*, Volume I: *The Process of Capitalist Production*, New York: International Publishers. Translated by Samuel Moore and Edward Aveling and edited by Frederick Engels.

Newquist, Kenneth (1999) 'Kicking cyberpunk into overdrive with The Matrix', *Nuke-Town Movie Reviews*, *http://www.nuketown.com/theatre/the_matrix/index.htm*

O'Hehir, Andrew (1999) 'The Matrix is a masterful sci-fi stew', Salon. April 2, *http://www.salon.com/ent/movies/reviews/1999/04/02reviewa.html*

Rifkin, Jeremy (1998) *The Biotech Century: Harnessing the Gene and Remaking the World*, New York: Tarcher/Putnam.

Rivera, Roberto (1999) 'Rethinking reality: review of Matrix', *http://www.boundless.org/departments/atplay/a0000115.html*

Part III

Is there in truth no beauty?

8 Reading *Star Trek*

Imagining, theorizing, and reflecting on organizational discourse and practice

Donncha Kavanagh, Kieran Keohane and Carmen Kuhling

Introduction

The argument we will develop here is that the popular culture phenomenon *Star Trek* (including the original television series, *The Next Generation, Deep Space Nine* and *Voyager*, and associated merchandise and paraphernalia) can be treated as a research resource; data, if you like, that if read and interpreted, can provide organizational scientists with important insights into contemporary problems and phenomena. We approach '*Star Trek*' (the inclusive term for the television series and its many spin-offs) as an 'expressive good', the product of a corporation in the entertainment industry, with a mass-market global consumer base. Conceived of in this way, it is as legitimate to take the scrutiny of *Star Trek* as seriously as any other management or marketing phenomenon. *Star Trek* is a particularly rich expressive good having held a central position in the popular culture market – a market notoriously prone to fads, fashions and short-term crazes – for the last three decades (a recent Harris Poll indicated that 53 per cent of the US public define themselves as *Star Trek* 'fans', while over 2 billion dollars has been spent on merchandise from the series).

When we say that products are 'expressive goods' we mean that in their production, in their circulation in the marketplace, and in the cycle of their consumption, they give expression to the prevailing social forces of the wider society of which that cycle is a part. That is, products are expressive of what consumers deem to be needful and desirable at that particular historical conjuncture, and of what governments and regulatory bodies establish as collective norms and principles. In sum, products, commodities, 'expressive goods' are *fetishes*. They are material objects that are much greater than their simple materiality. They are, in a sense, invested with, possessed of, and animated by the spirits that move society as a whole. They are expressive of the *Zeitgeist*, the spirit of the times. As points of condensation for wider historical and social forces, they are things into which and onto which we project our highest values, our deepest needs, our most passionate desires, our darkest fears and our most urgent anxieties. Indeed, the secret of the marketplace is that the product must be pitched, that the right spin must be put on the thing so that it catches the eye and stirs our desire to have it, to consume it, to be part of the world that it stands for. A BMW is more than a car. It is 'the ultimate driving machine', and it expresses prestige, power and a reality in which the owner of this product has already 'arrived' without ever driving at all.

In this chapter, we focus especially on the management and organizational issues of *Star Trek* in terms of how each of the four series represents an 'ideal type' of the dominant organizational ethos of its time.[1] For us, *Star Trek* provides a potent set of visual images, narratives and metaphors through which we can make sense of both theory and practice, and it also provides an ideal opportunity to work and play with the practices of theorizing and the fluid boundaries between organization theory, management studies and culture studies. As much as anything else, *Star Trek* is a story about a changing organization *at work*, dealing, albeit in caricature, with the types of issues that engage 'ordinary' people in their everyday lives. And like other popular cartoons – for example, *Dilbert* – its great attraction is its ability to represent, make visible and make available to a mass audience, for common conversation, organizational issues that are a prevalent, if not universal, part of viewers' experiences. Indeed, if we accept Hirschman and Sander's (1997) assertion that 'one potent approach for comprehending a society's values and beliefs is to examine the stories it tells' then it is surprising that *Star Trek* and similar stories haven't been studied to exhaustion by management and marketing scholars.[2]

A singular and valuable feature of *Star Trek* is that it has changed deliberately and radically over the last thirty years, reflecting broader changes in American (and wider) society over that time. As such, it provides a unique and rich longitudinal database of representations of (and inspirations for) management and organizational practices over an extended period. Thus, the paper is structured chronologically, as we examine the evolution of *Star Trek* and its various incarnations over time, from *The Original Series*, produced in the 1960s, to *Star Trek: The Next Generation*, to *Deep Space Nine*, to the latest series, *Voyager* (hereinafter we will refer to these as *TOS*, *TNG*, *DS9* and *Voyager*, respectively). We will discuss not only the changes between the series but also how these changes reflect and constitute changes in organizational theory and practice.

Our reading of *Star Trek* is obviously only one of many possible interpretations and we make no claim that it is the definitive or correct one. What is interesting for us, and hopefully for you, is that imaginative fictions like *Star Trek* can become resources that allow us to think ourselves away from the contexts of action and the mundane realities in which we are constrained to think and practice 'real' management. And this deliberate self-estrangement from the world (which, it must be stressed and made explicit to critics who, adopting the mantle of 'Science', would charge that science fiction is 'bad data' and 'soft science') is nothing but the original source of scientific objectivity specified by Bacon, and, as such, may provide us with the opportunity to creatively explore imaginative ways to deal with 'real' problems. In this way, science fictional utopias are a 'species of political epistemology' and a 'metaphor for potential histories' (Pfaelzer 1988: 289). In other words, such utopias can facilitate a critical imaginary and enable us to envision a variety of organizational alternatives with which we can assess our own management practices.

Star Trek – 1960s style

> A map of the world that does not include Utopia is not even worth glancing at, for it leaves out the one country at which Humanity is always landing. And when humanity lands there, it looks out, and, seeing a better country, sets sail.
>
> Oscar Wilde, *The Soul of Man Under Socialism* (1895)

The original series (*TOS*), produced in the 1960s, corresponds historically with the ideological climate surrounding the Cold War and the space race. At the time we were excited by space. We were on the threshold of what we thought was a new frontier – 'the final frontier' as Kirk narrates it, 'to boldly go where no man had gone before'. America would put a man on the Moon, and after that, the sky's the limit, literally. The onward march of human progress under American world leadership was assured, an assurance mirrored in Kirk's space-cowboy cockiness. In the Kennedy era American enterprise was at its zenith; this was the affluent society, and science, and specifically medicine, promised solutions to all problems. Mirroring this the authority of the Captain of the USS *Enterprise* was assured and underwritten by the clear, relentless logic of science officer Spock, the dedication of Dr 'Bones' McCoy, and the ingenuity of Scotty, chief engineer, who could always get more power from the thrusters. The command structure of the USS *Enterprise* was an idealized representation of American business in the post-war boom, from which the conflicts internal to American society had been eliminated.

In this utopian vision of an already present/future American society there is no class, or class ideological conflict, as in the affluent society which American post-war prosperity was delivering; everyone would (soon, any day now!) have more than plenty. Checkov, a Russian, sat at the helm with Sulu, an Oriental, and Uhuru, a Black woman, was communications officer. There is no racial, or gender conflict. In harmony with the Enlightenment, modern tradition in which *TOS* is rooted, rational thought and a progressive and developmental model of science and society are privileged. In Trek-Utopia, poverty, injustice, crime and alienation are eliminated through technology, progress and a secular, liberal, humanist mythology, while social harmony is achieved through celebrating and protecting individual identity and freedom. Thus, Trek-Utopia is comparable to earlier utopian visions like Fourier's writings from the 1820s and H.G. Wells' ([1905] 1967) *A Modern Utopia*, which were both antithetic to the more communistic utopias of the nineteenth century where collective solidarity was given precedence over individual freedom. Hence, Kirk is positively hostile to societies that efface human individuality and freethinking, and he is keen to restore individual freedom to any stellar 'utopian' societies that he considers 'dystopian'.

At the same time, there are strong similarities between *TOS*'s utopian vision and many of the communistic utopias in the literature, from Thomas More's original *Utopia* (1516), to Francis Bacon's *New Atlantis* (1622), to Cabet's *Voyage to Icaria* (1839). Most obviously, the whole sphere of the economic is absent in *TOS*, there being no money, property, production or commercial exchange, since replicator technology allows the instant 'production' of whatever you desire. Consequently, the Marxist critique of capitalism, and the ills of alienation, confrontation and class conflict, are waved away by technological progress, and, in the absence of money and property there's apparently neither crime nor greed.

Despite *TOS*'s emphasis on progress and change, there is no explanation of how the present reality was arrived at, besides some vague references to cataclysmic events in the past (reminiscent of the Hebrew prophets' utopian narratives which predicted that a small remnant of society would survive a catastrophic event and that these would live the perfect life). And for all its talk about progress, *TOS* is a strangely static place with each episode returning to a symbolic beginning where everything is much as it was before: a *perpetuum immobile*. A more fundamental anomaly is the contradiction between *TOS*'s belief in progress and change and its essentialist definitions of self and of human nature, which creates the continual tension between social order and individual freedom that runs through the series. It also means that *TOS* had a never-ending difficulty in dealing with issues of radical difference. Its message was always simple: women and ethnics have their places in society; as long as they are space secretaries, and say 'aye aye' to the captains of industry.

This brings us to the (ideal-typical) organization that is represented in *TOS*. In the Captain's chair sits the charismatic hero, a man who made his own way in the world, who took risks and interpreted the rules in his own way. An entrepreneur with flair and verve, for whom things always worked out right in the end, Kirk was the ideal type subject, the young white man, the cornerstone of the American ideology. This charismatic individual who headed up the organization relied on a hierarchical collective command structure, structured according to the principles of an ideal typical modern bureaucracy – highly qualified professional specialists, vocationally committed to their roles in the organization, engineering, medicine, navigation, science, communications, fields with clear and unambiguous jurisdictions, procedures, and protocols. Loyalty and solidarity were due not only to the Captain (the individual entrepreneur) but were now also, and more so, built into the structure of the firm, into the abstract rules of the organization, and into wider collective authorities: to one's office and rank, to one's duty to specific roles (i.e. to management); to the *Enterprise*, to Starfleet, to the Federation (i.e. to one's profession); and finally to the abstract and hypothetical values that the professional roles in the particular organization were institutional instances of: Spock's science committed to 'Reason', Bones' medicine to 'Life', Kirk's Captain to the abstraction of 'Progress' itself as an absolute value – 'to boldly go', the principle and the motive of Modernity.

In many ways, *TOS* reflects, describes, prescribes and inspires the 'classical' understanding of organizational life, which was articulated and invented between 1880 and 1960. The *Enterprise* – the name itself is significant – conforms to Fayol's ([1916] 1949) fourteen General Principles of Management more than any organization in the 'real' world: there is clearly a division of work; a belief in authority (including both the right to issue commands and responsibility for their execution); discipline (and, conversely, good leadership); unity of command (i.e. one boss); unity of direction (i.e. a single goal); the subordination of individual interest to general interest; a scalar chain (i.e. a hierarchical structure of authority); order (both material and social); equity; stability of tenure; a belief in initiative; an appropriate balance between centralization and decentralization; and *esprit de corps*. The one absent principle is 'remuneration'. Furthermore, by centring most episodes on a particular problem facing the triumvirate of Kirk, Spock and McCoy, *TOS* presents us with the classical understanding of organizations as being fundamentally about decision-making, in terms of the optimal reconciliation of the political, rational and emotional issues involved in strategic action (as depicted, for example, in Herbert Simon's ([1945] 1997) classic text, *Administrative Behaviour*). The *Enterprise* also reflected the classical and dominant view of organizations as essentially co-operative, task-focused, open systems that would only survive by staying in equilibrium with their environment, which, in turn, required strong management. For example, in his appropriately titled book of the period – *The Enterprise and its Environment* – Rice (1963) defines the primary task of the organization as 'the task that it must perform to survive' (p. 13) and the primary task of leadership as 'to manage the relations between an enterprise and its environment so as to permit optimal performance of the primary task of the enterprise' (p. 15).

The Next Generation (1987–94)

By the late 1980s space had become boring, and limited. Travel further than the Moon to planets in our solar system was prohibitive, not only for technological reasons, but because we knew enough about the barren emptiness of space to make such effort pointless. While millions world-wide watched Armstrong make 'a giant leap for mankind' nobody wanted to watch any longer when the giant leap turned out to be no more than the routine space trucking of the space shuttle, plonking satellites around the globe was no more exciting than a milkround, and along with the monotonous novelty of fifty-seven channels of SKY TV came the sinister threat of global surveillance and orbiting weapons systems targeting planet Earth.

   The Next Generation (*TNG*) expressed this new historical context. The remake expresses a nostalgia for an era when the future was larger and brighter. At a time when the American economy was in the throes of a transformation, when corporations were down-sizing, rationalizing, retooling, from the level of the firm right up to NAFTA and the IMF, *TNG* reinscribed the modernist ideal of a complex organization integrated by a perfectly functioning division of labour in a hierarchical collective command structure, wherein competent professionals filled the duties of their vocations. The self-assured manifest destiny of America leading a global programme of development, prosperity and democracy appeared irredeemably compromised by defeat in Vietnam, the failure of American-led modernization to bring prosperity to the Third World, and the tarnishing of democracy in American sponsorship of cruel and barbaric dictatorships in Latin America. America had to appear to disentangle itself from active interference in other cultures, thus the 'Prime Directive' of the new Starfleet, and the ideological pangloss, that God is in his Heaven and the Universe is unfolding as it should. In contrast to the original series, *TNG* settled into a period of consolidating explored space, where the Enterprise usually dealt with known enemies/allies and rarely left Federation territory. In this new setting, focus on the outer frontier shifted to inner frontiers, and *TNG* showed not battle with the Klingons or Romulans (who probably stood for the Russians in the original series) for control of the Quadrant, but negotiating treaties and respecting neutral zones, and more significantly, of negotiating social relations between different races (species). Klingons, Vulcans, Ferengi, Romulans, the Borg and so on who were characterized no longer by their absolute Otherness, their irreducible particularity as 'aliens', but as aspects of ourselves, members of a wider collective with whom we must negotiate and find common cause, rather than outsmart, defeat and demonstrate our superiority over, the characteristic stamp on the encounter with difference in the original series.

A good illustration of this new paradigm occurs in the fourth season of *TNG*, when a new species, the Cardassians, are introduced into the series. In the episode, 'The Wounded', a renegade Federation ship commanded by Captain Maxwell, a former war-hero, has gone into Cardassian space and is destroying Cardassian ships and stations, and the subsequent story revolves around Picard's ultimately successful attempt to talk him out of his violent actions. At the end of the episode a dejected Maxwell sings the Irish ballad 'The Minstrel Boy', the theme of which is the demise and usurpation of an old heroic code in a political world dominated by larger forces engaged in powerplays (Richards 1997: 26–7). The message is clear: in the world of the 1990s there is no place for the gung-ho approach of yesterday epitomized by the likes of Maxwell, Kirk and the Klingons, and, by extension, the US of the 1950s and 1960s which was all too ready to rush in with guns blazing after applying simplistic analyses to complex disputes in remote places like Vietnam and Korea. In this new era, American self-identity in international policy is refashioned from the cowboy to the policeman/diplomat whose primary responsibility is to ensure that the balance of power remains intact in the new global order.

From an organizational perspective, we may interpret the different species in the series as instances of Weber's three types of authority systems – the rational, traditional and charismatic – while recognizing that the empirical world never maps neatly onto any taxonomy of ideal types. For us, the Federation represents *rational-legal bureaucracy*, which 'is capable of attaining the highest degree of efficiency, and is in this sense formally the most rational known means of exercising authority over human beings' (Weber [1921] 1968: 223). In contrast, the Klingon Empire, with its emphasis on custom and honour, typifies Weber's *traditional* authority structure, wherein age-old rules and powers are primary. And we interpret the Ferengi, who always threaten to destabilize the status quo, as representative of Weber's *charismatic* authority structure – remembering that, for Weber, a charismatic leader may not necessarily have outstanding traits. In particular, the Ferengi exemplify how difficult it is to perpetuate charismatic authority without transforming it into either traditional or rational-legal authority. Another recurring theme in *Star Trek*, following Weber, is that both charismatic and traditional authority are much inferior to rational authority – the future, according to Weber, 'belongs to bureaucratization' ([1921] 1968: 1401). At the same time, Picard, as charismatic leader, also serves to counterbalance the dehumanizing and petrifying tendencies of legal-rational authority that Weber saw as the fatal flaw in modern civilization; that through rationalization we might become 'specialists without spirit, hedonists without heart' trapped in an iron cage of rationalized acquisitiveness of our own devising. In the ideology of *TNG*, modernity is saved from this fate by the agency of the charismatic hero (Picard) who, when the circumstances demand, is prepared to defy Starfleet Command, and reassert the principles of liberal humanism against the overbearing forces of rationalization. This recurring theme of *TNG* is best exemplified by the episode in which Starfleet want to disassemble Data, to study him, and Picard refuses to allow the procedure, defying the prevailing technocratic rationality in the name of the individual's right to integrity and self-determination.

It is also important to note that the Ferengi, Klingons and Federation co-exist and define one other through their mutual relationships. Thus, since *TNG* – more so that *TOS* – is about the totality of relations between different species, it also reflects a more sophisticated understanding of social and national (US) identity in the 1990s: society is now characterized by complex antagonisms; other cultures are no longer represented simply as less developed, or as more technologically advanced than our own, but rather as being 'different', requiring a hermeneutic and reflexive orientation rather than competitive confrontation: we can learn more about ourselves and one another from our encounters with one another. This 'reflexivity' is the self-correcting principle at the heart of modern society, and 'reflexive modernization' lauded by Beck, Giddens and Lash (1994) will allow us to continually improve, and to keep on boldly going where no one has gone before, ultimately to a new point of harmonic convergence, where all difference disappears in a unified and unifying cosmic consciousness, a globalist sensibility in a globalized New World Order.

The nostalgic redemptive fantasy represented in *TNG* was that the postmodern American social organization was self-correcting, and a society that had momentarily lost its bearings and directions could re-collect for itself its first principles, and get back on an even keel. This was the gauntlet thrown down by Q, the postmodern Man become God, omnipotent, omniscient, but not all good, to whom Picard replied that with resolve, determination and self-confidence in the principles of Enlightenment reason that had brought us this far, we would weather the storm and go on striving to become the best that we can be. The world had changed, but perhaps not fundamentally.

This robust and reassuring assertion of 'plus ça change, plus c'est la même chose' was expressed in *TNG* in the portrayal of women. The prominence of women in *TNG* reflected on the one hand their new position in public life in American society, and on the other, *TNG* reinscribed the persistence of gender hierarchy and confinement to traditional roles in the sexual division of labour in modern society in general, and in the modern complex organizations in particular. Women (and other minorities) were in the workplace, but the old order was intact. Dr Beverley Crusher, the professional working mother in the caring profession; Guinan, the archetype of the Black Earth momma, ageless and wise; Geordi, the young Black man, seeing the world through the colour-blind visor, the 'neutral' discourse of engineering. Deanna Troy represented emotion, communicativeness, sympathy, empathy, appetite, luxurious eroticism, sexuality and allure. These qualities had their place in the contemporary organization, but confined to the expanded professional role of personnel and human resource management. This paralleled the Bush rhetoric of a kinder gentler America, and the institutionalization in the American workplace of not just employee welfare, but of counselling, addiction treatment and so on, in a curious amalgam of reform and elaboration of power and subjectifying self-regulation. *TNG* flirted briefly with a female mould-breaker, Tasha Yar, survivor of sexual abuse, security officer and deflowerer of Data, but she became a lesbian pop icon before lesbian chic came in, and had to be iced, underlining the conservative moment in postmodernism in the wider culture.

Organization and management studies exhibited similar shifts in the form and content of their discourses between the 1960s and the 1990s. With hindsight, we can identify the late 1970s, when Burrell and Morgan (1979) published *Sociological Paradigms and Organisational Analysis*, as the point in time when organization studies discovered warp drive, as it were, powering the discipline into strange new worlds. From then on there was less certainty about the discipline, as the flaws in the macho-mechanical, functionalist paradigm became more obvious, and as the complexity of organizational life demanded a more sophisticated, more subtle form of theorizing through which different stories could be told and different perspectives acknowledged (Morgan 1986). Increasingly, organizational theorists began to focus on the cultural and symbolic sides of organizing (Pettigrew 1979, Smircich 1983, Hofstede 1980, Pondy 1983), and even in the discipline's intellectual core – in sub-fields like decision-theory and strategic management – instrumentalism and teleological thinking were coming under attack by writers such as March and Olsen ([1976] 1979), who drew attention to the irrationality and ambiguity that is intrinsic to decision-making, and Quinn (1980) and Mintzberg and Waters (1985) who saw decision-making as a process of 'logical incrementalism' where strategic actions 'emerge' without deliberate design. For Quinn, Mintzberg and others, goals, plans and missions were instances of a teleological understanding of decision-making, which was inherently inadequate in a reality where ends were either adjusted to suit means or emerged through opportunistic or non-rational processes. Allied to this critique was a deeper, critical reflection about the discipline itself, its relationship to management practices, and the deleterious effects of the management paradigm on minorities, women, the environment, the family and foreign communities (Alvesson and Willmott 1992). And once organization studies joined the postmodern carnival (Cooper and Burrell 1988), the centripetal forces of the pomo-Ferris wheel threatened to tear the discipline asunder (Cannella and Paetzold 1994, Pfeffer 1993). This is not to say that the classical, rational-instrumental understanding of management was ditched. Far from it. There was, and still is, a focus on the organization in its environment and – *vide* the 1980s interest in Quality – an enthusiastic repackaging and updating of old ideas from classical management thought. Yet, in much the same way that the Ferengi and Klingons joined the *Enterprise* in *TNG*, ideas that were previously alien to management studies came to be an accepted part of its now-fragmented identity (Whitley 1984). Not surprisingly, the pressing need to think in relational terms meant that the *network* came to be the dominant metaphor and motif in not only organizational theory and practice (Powell 1990, Nohria and Eccles 1993), but also across the social sciences in the 1990s (Araujo and Easton 1996). This interest in networks was reflected in *TNG*, where a new species, the Borg, took the relational and network ideas, currently in vogue in the literature, to their diabolical and fantastic conclusions. Since the Borg represent one of the most enduring and critical mirrors that *TNG* held up to contemporary society and organization studies, we will now discuss their significance in more depth.

The Borg were introduced in a 1989 episode in which Q – an omnipotent deity/trickster who continually chides Picard about humanity's arrogance – sends the *Enterprise* seven thousand light years away, 'to give you a taste of your future', after Picard refuses to allow him to join the crew. They immediately encounter a cube-shaped ship, from which two Borgs – hybrid organic and artificial life forms – appear on the *Enterprise* and begin draining information from the ship's computers. Once their data survey is complete, the Borg vessel demands the surrender of the *Enterprise*. The Borg state that they are intent on perfecting the standard of life of every species they encounter through assimilating each one into the 'Borg Collective', a giant, hive-like, cybernetic network of technologically-linked cyborgs in which each being shares the thoughts and feelings of each and every other member. The Borg is so integrated and collective that individual cyborg/ humanoids do not register as individuals: through assimilation, individuality, the Self, is necessarily sacrificed.

The Borg Collective may be variously interpreted, but, as organic/mechanical hybrids – they are 'cyborgs' (or cy/borg) – they certainly reflect Haraway's (1985) questioning of the essentialist boundaries of the modern project. For example, when an Away Team from the Enterprise beams aboard the Borg ship, they find that infants are cybernetically fused with machines soon after birth, and, tellingly, there are no females. Thus, the potency of the Borg threat to the Enterprise is a metaphor for the cyborg's threat to the modern, humanist paradigm where essentialist models of the self, and apparently inviolable boundaries – such as between the human and the non-human, leader and follower, individual and society, whole and part, mind and body, culture and nature, male and female – are subverted. In Haraway's (1985: 178) words, cyborgs 'make very problematic the statuses of man or woman, human, artefact, member of a race, individual entity, or body', and, while this may contain a radical promise of emancipation, this development is profoundly ambiguous, as, like the Borg, cyborgs represent the 'final imposition of a grid of control on the planet' (1985: 154).[3]

Another interpretation is to see the Borg as the Federation, or, more precisely, to see it as what the Federation will become in the future if it continues along its present path of development. The Borg's motivation is identical to the Federation's – 'we mean you no harm', 'we only wish to improve quality of life' – and the *Enterprise*, like the Borg ship, is an organic-mechanical-cybernetic entity, as indeed are some of the crew (Geordi La Forge has a prosthetic visor, Picard has an artificial heart). The clear message is that the Borg ship *is* the *Enterprise*, and they only meet because Q sends the ship forward in *time* as well as in space. Thus, understood as an ideal type of the worst elements of science, the Borg represent the ascendance of one side of the Dialectic of the Enlightenment (Horkheimer and Adorno 1973): the victory of Instrumental Rationality and the concomitant oppression of the the political and ethical dimensions of the Enlightenment project. In other words, the *Enterprise*'s encounter with the Borg can be interpreted as a vivid illustration of the twentieth-century critique of Enlightenment thought. If the Federation portrays a utopian, modern future, then the Borg depicts a dystopian world that has lost its humanity to technological consciousness, driven only by the imperative of rationalized acquisition; we could become, as Goethe and Weber predicted, 'specialists without spirit, hedonists without heart, a nullity that imagines it has attained a level of civilisation never before achieved' (Weber [1930] 1958: 182). Thus, the Borg are an almost perfect pop culture representation of Weber's central critical image of modern existence, the infamous 'iron cage', wherein all natural and social relations are dominated by the principle of rational instrumentalism. Developing Weber's stark prognosis of the fate of modernity, the Borg are the *différance*, the unsaid but ever-present dystopia, that inheres within all utopian visions. George Kateb (1963: 231), in his critique of utopian texts, might well have been speaking about the Borg when he observed that

> [t]here is one text or another on hand to demonstrate the logical conclusion of each part of the utopian program. Virtue can become automatism, painlessness can become animality, equality can become uniformity or truncation, stability can become stagnation, efficiency can become compulsive routine, social rationality can become social textureless, harmony can become lifelessness.

Similarly, the Away Team's discovery of the Borg nursery is a reference to Habermas' critique of the colonization of the primary, language-based institutions of the life-world, such as family and community (Deetz 1992). Habermas' argument is that the corporation's narrow set of human needs – money and power – is normally counterbalanced by the more meaningful life-world, but that as bureaucratic institutions grow, the life-world becomes 'overloaded' – so, for example, we go to professional counsellors rather than family or friends for help during trying times. At the extreme we end up destroying the natural environment and narrowing the human character, creating a dismal 'carceral' society (Foucault 1977). We become Borg. Interestingly, Habermas' solution to this problem – communicative action – is played out in *TNG* when Picard goes to Guinan, whose race was previously attacked by the Borg, for help. Picard, the latter-day Renaissance Man, asks, 'how can we reason with the Borg?' to which Guinan answers simply: 'you can't.' The clear message is that in the extreme, the product of reason – the Borg – becomes unreasonable, or alternatively that Enlightenment reason itself contains the possibilities for multiple – utopian or dystopian – rationalities.

Deep Space Nine (1993–9)

When the third *Star Trek* series, *Deep Space Nine* (*DS9*) began broadcasting in 1993, the world had changed, fundamentally, and nostalgic reverie for a golden age of *Star Trek* cannot mask that. *Deep Space Nine* stands as a 'reality check' against the dream of a harmonious New World order brought about by reflexive modernization. Deep Space Nine is an immobile space station in deep space, signifying that *DS9* is about stasis: instead of boldly going forward, *DS9* is bogged down, stuck at the cross-roads of time and space. As such, it represents the aspects of contemporary history that are locked in antagonisms for which there is no resolution – former colonial overlords, Cardassians, are held in hostile contempt by their former subjects, the Bajorans; opposites that stand variously, depending on the contextualization, for Blacks and Whites, West Bank Arabs and Israeli Zionists, Jews and anti-Semites, the New Independent States and Russians. And *DS9* is Beirut, Sarajevo, an NYPD precinct station, or a shopping mall in the bad-lands of LA, or any of the infinite number of theatres of conflict in contemporary society, where the ideal of a future society is lost to the day-to-day practicality of muddling through. *DS9* is a post-colonial wasteland, akin to multi-ethnic post-colonial London where the 'frontier' talks back and the 'native' is ready to resist anything resembling a colonial presence. The hapless, motley assortment of races and species that comprise contemporary cities are preyed upon by unscrupulous wheelers and dealers, and wandering warmongers of varying hues of barbarity. The frame that holds both the show and these theatres of conflict together is security and crisis management by a team restructured by affirmative action and political correctness: the stoic Black chief, the angry young woman, the donkey-working Irish engineer, the naive, trimmed-down-to-size British doctor, and the stern, unwavering hand of the Constable, as impotent and directionless in determining the shape of a grander scheme of things as the UN Security Council in the Balkans. The central feature is no longer the bridge – symbolizing command and control – but a 'promenade' and bar where different races mingle. Unlike Kirk and Picard, Commander Sisko is only nominally in control, and relies on a large network of informers. The station, originally built by the Cardassians, has an alien quality to it: and is always on the brink of war and conflict as revivals of religious nationalisms sweep the Klingon and Bajoran home worlds. In this context, the Prime Directive is rarely mentioned.

An interesting aspect of *DS9* is that while there was no commerce in *TOS* or in the earlier series of *TNG* – the 'replicator' having made production and exchange redundant – the old logic of commerce reappears with a vengeance in *DS9*. Life in the station is centred on the 'promenade', full of shops, gambling houses and business establishments, while, early on, Jean-Luc Picard predicted that Deep Space Nine would become a 'a centre for commerce'. Money, issues of 'free trade' and the exchange of commodities, often weapons, and especially the precious metal 'latinum', play a central role in the relations between the Ferengi, the Federation, the Cardassians, and other trading species. (The availability of replicator technology exemplifies the type of amnesia and paralogy that is tolerated within the world of *Star Trek*.)

Within organization studies, we can understand *DS9* as representing the small but growing number of post-colonial texts that first began to appear in the late 1980s (Anzaldúa 1987, Said 1989, Spivak 1988, García-Canclini 1995) and which now constitutes a definite stream in contemporary discourse as evidenced by some recent publications (Calás and Smircich 1999, Calás 1994, Reed 1996). It also reflects the long-standing critique that anthropology – and *Star Trek* is founded on the concept of anthropological exploration – has a colonizing and domineering dimension leading it to inexorably consume alien cultures. Moreover, the anthropologist – like the Federation/Borg – is no benign culture-junkie; rather s/he is voyeuristic, selfish, arrogant and an insidious instrument through which one group or society dominates another, and, in particular, is one element underpinning the ascendancy of the Occident (Clifford and Marcus 1986, Fox 1991, Grimshaw and Hart 1994, Tyler 1987: 92).

An important aspect of the post-colonial literature is that it allows, demands even, that the native speaks back, a theme that also runs through *DS9*. For example, the pilot episode includes a scene where Major Kira, a female Bajoran officer on the space station meets Dr Bashir, a young English doctor from the Federation. Kira is a veteran of the Bajoran war against the Cardassians, and she also distrusts the Federation, believing that they too may be colonizers. Their exchange goes as follows:

Doctor Bashir: I didn't want some cushy job or research grant. I wanted *this*: the farthest reaches of the galaxy; one of the remotest outposts available. This is where the adventure is; this is where the heroes are made. Right here. In the wilderness.
Major Kira: *This wilderness is my home!*
Doctor Bashir: (stutters)
Major Kira: The Cardassians left behind a lot of injured people. *You* can make yourself useful by bringing your Federation medicine to the natives. You'll find them a friendly, simple folk.

This exchange is reworked in a manner of sorts by writers like Anzaldúa (1987), who produced a multi-lingual, hybrid text that seeks not only to give the native a voice but also provides a different story about the genealogy and rationale behind the existence of a particular setting. Thus, the space station in *DS9* might very well still be the *Enterprise*, except this time interpreted by a (post-colonial) Other.

The implications of post-colonial theory for organization studies are only beginning to be worked through, but it seems clear that since hybridity is a root metaphor of the literature – the post-colonial is a hybrid place – then hybrid notions and hybrid forms of theorizing will be required. Thus, we can anticipate that new contact zones between disciplines will be explored, that new modes of re-presentation will be utilized (Krug 1998), and that previously opposing categories will be commingled as theorists rake through the ashes of those 'bonfires of the certainties' that have engulfed the social sciences (Law 1994: 248).

Voyager (1995–present)

Voyager, the fourth incarnation of *Star Trek*, is the present phase of the product. The product has been significantly reworked, and now expresses the new shape of American society generally speaking, and the problems and dilemmas of contemporary organizations more particularly. *Voyager* is trying to return home, no longer boldly going, we are now trying to find our way back, to reunite, to reconcile, to settle down and to live happily ever after. The command structure of *Voyager* is in place, but like the contemporary organization and the wider society, it is a house divided. It is a Starfleet ship, but half the crew are Maquis, a renegade outlaw band who will not do things 'by the book', but have their own rules and codes of practice. On *Voyager*, the Federation's bureaucracy, alliances, treaties, diplomacy, family ties and the other institutional configurations of a complex interplanetary society are gone. Similarly, contemporary organizations are far from smoothly functioning bureaucracies, but are marked by competing internal narratives; and the rules of the organization are contested on the basis of solidarities – such as gender, race and ethnicity – that fall outside of the formal parameters of the organization. In the classical model, represented by *TOS* and nostalgically reinscribed by *TNG*, such alternate bases from which power could be based and exercised were irrelevant, but the contemporary organization that doesn't reckon with the new culture wars, and actively take them into account and negotiate them, will find itself in motivational crisis, and indeed in serious legal trouble faster than you can say 'glass ceiling'. Similarly, what characterizes life on *Voyager*, as it does in the contemporary workplace, from the sweatshop to the Oval Office, is the fluidity of barriers between public and private roles, and the way in which, contrary to the classic modern model, issues that may have been previously held to be matters of private life, intrude into the workplace. Thus it is not only a question of women being on the bridge in command positions – so long as they acted like men! – but rather, sexuality in its widest senses must be accommodated in the new organization. Maternity leave, child care provision, protocol for relations amongst staff members, these are the issues at the heart of the internal politics of the world's banks and businesses, and governing the transgressions of roles is what is really at stake in the Clinton/Lewinsky affair. Moreover, in a postmodern world, appeals to an Archimedian point are meaningless, just as for those on the *Voyager*, appeals to the Federation's ideas of right and wrong are redundant: the only fixed point in this decentred universe – for those in the *Voyager* – is the *Voyager*. Hence, the moral of this story is that we must muddle through, creating a local programme of action that, while we know it can always be deconstructed, still provides meaning and sustenance amidst the mundane chaos of existence.

Captain Catherine Janeway, committed to running a Starfleet ship, no longer only consults and then makes executive decisions (the classic modern model of managerial power, and the model represented by Kirk and Picard) she must also foster collective agreement with her crew. Thus, power is a matter of persuasion, agreement and hegemony, rather than executive decision, calculated judgement based on the best available information. On Janeway's *Enterprise*, the internal problems of the organization are just as formidable as the external ones. Families are divided, with little hope of reconciliation, where previously family life was irrelevant to the concern of the organization. In *TOS* and *TNG* the crew were single, or as professionals their vocation to their work took priority over all else. On *Voyager*, heroic Medicine is a chimera. The 'human(e)' doctor is dead, and the Emergency Medical Hologram, working in narrower confines must work up from being a holo sham to more humane standards, as technical competence is not enough to meet the health needs of contemporary American society. In both these respects the problems of *Voyager* express the concerns of social welfare and public health care provision that were at the heart of the Clinton presidency.

Voyager also represents the most explicit attempt to confront the intrusion of sexuality and gender issues into the workplace. As such, it continues and develops the theme that emerged in *TOS* of women/the sexual/the unconscious as both an ominous *and* delightful Other: a primal and chaotic force liable to disrupt the social order and undermine the judgement of captain and crew, *and* a necessary element making adventures in space and organizational life much more fun. Although forward-thinking for its time, *TOS* reflected conventional gender ideology wherein the crew was predominantly male, and where fears/desires for the alien/Other frequently posed as female reflected the segregated spheres of masculine and feminine life-world apparent at that time. Although Roddenberry himself initially cast the First Officer as female, he ultimately capitulated to the predominant gender thinking of the time wherein women exhibited power only through their sexuality. Leaders and decision-makers were predominantly men, and women in the workplace were but an extension of the care-giving role in the home.

In contrast to this association between masculinity and power, *Voyager* experiments with various ways of conceiving of powerful women. Whereas Kirk's authority was based predominantly on individual loyalty to a flawed but archetypal masculine leader, and Picard's authority rested upon a masculinity based predominantly on faith in his measured reason and reflection, Captain Janeway is a complex yet convincing woman in authority and represents a new departure where the radical distinction between personal and professional life has become more fluid and malleable. As well, *Voyager* presents versions of female leadership that are more convincing: unlike in previous series wherein characters such as Troi (*TNG*) and Uhuru (*TOS*) dress in revealing clothes and frequently defer to male authority, the female characters Janeway, Torres, Kess – and Seven – are both more central to the storylines, and more complex and compelling, enabling us to imagine a contemporary version of powerful femininity that neither emulates male authority nor reverts to archaic feminine stereotypes. Rather, traits culturally perceived as feminine are portrayed as strengths: Janeway's sensitivity to the personal dilemmas of her crew heightens her effectiveness as Captain; Torres' vulnerability does not interfere with her performance as a good chief engineer; and Kess' intuitive and empathic abilities enable her to outwit powerful enemies. Perhaps the most recent and most interesting character, Seven of Nine, has the most ambiguous status as simultaneously Borg/human/female, and is perhaps a clear example of the variety of sometimes clashing identities and ethnicities represented by the new-found hybrid identities discussed earlier, as well as a recognition of the various contradictory and complex positions women occupy with regards to their relationship to core/periphery: Seven is both colonized and colonizer, abused and abuser, human and Borg. As a female archetype, she is both masculine and feminine: physically strong yet lonely and isolated because of psychological abuse suffered during her time as Borg.

The centrality of sexual issues in this series – such as Kess' pregnancy, Torres' negotiation of advances from her Vulcan co-worker, Janeway's treatment of Chakotay's affection for her when they are stranded alone, and Kim's attraction to Seven – all illustrate the 'return of the repressed', the personal, sexual and emotional life of the crew. This emphasis mirrors the emerging understanding in organizational life of the significance of these issues within presumably rational structures. And rather than portraying these issues as problematic, as something peripheral to work life, or simplistically as harassment, *Voyager* illustrates how the personal constantly intrudes in and redefines the professional, and cannot be compartmentalized away or legally prohibited, again reflecting current themes in the organizational literature on sexuality (Hearn *et al.*. 1989, Witz and Savage 1992).

Reflections

The fact that the four shows (*Star Trek – The Original Series*, *The Next Generation*, *Deep Space Nine* and *Voyager*) co-exist in the same time/space continuum (re-runs of *TOS* and *TNG*, and back-to-back scheduling of *DS9* and *Voyager* on Sky and the national and global networks) is also interesting. It expresses the extent to which the past protrudes into the present, and illustrates an aspect of the postmodern condition, which is that (at least) four distinctive, divergent ideological moods can be operative at the same time. Nevertheless, this diversity does not mask the common themes that run through *Star Trek*'s various incarnations, and, as we have attempted to demonstrate, which also run through the evolution of management and organization discourse.

Of course, Star *Trek* is a fantasy rather than a manifesto for social change, and one must not forget that. But the gap between science fiction and science fact should not be overstated either. Fiction (from 'ficto') means 'to make', 'to create', and the same impulse to creatively and imaginatively reinvent our environment(s) and ourselves underpins both professional 'real-world' management practice, and imaginary, fantasy-world management scenarios. Rather than thinking of a hard distinction between management science in practice and management science fiction, we suggest that these realities from 'other dimensions' are not entirely alien to one another. Rather, we suggest that these are not alternate but *intersecting* universes, realms of fact and fiction that interpenetrate one another: our 'fictional' management scenarios mirror 'real' management problems, and vice versa.

Again, we find cognate themes in the parallel universe that is organization and management studies. Like *Star Trek*, organization and management studies is now a menagerie of different, but vaguely similar, research paradigms, illustrated by the co-existence of 'management' texts that interpret the significance of ANOVAs and Cronbach-alpha coefficients, and others that interpret the significance of Supernovas and Klingons in the Alpha Quadrant. This is to be welcomed and indeed the increasing complexity, uncertainty and diversity of Star Trek over the last thirty years is a good metaphor for the evolution of organization theory over the same period. Finally, it is our hope that *Star Trek* and other 'expressive goods' will continue to be used as a rich resource for knowing about management and for exploring contact zones between different disciplines and communities of practice.

Notes

1 For a selected bibliography of sociological interpretations of *Star Trek*, see Harrison *et al.*. (1996, Appendix B).
2 See Hassard and Holliday (1998) for a recent and rare study of representations of work and organizations in popular culture. The special issue of *Organization* (1999, 6, 4) on Science Fiction and Organizations also marks an interesting new trend in theorizing about organizations.
3 For further discussion on cyborgs, science fiction and organization, see Parker (1999).

References

Alvesson, M. and Willmott, H. (eds) (1992) *Critical Management Studies*, London: Sage.
Anzaldúa, G. (1987) *The Homeland, Aztlan, El Otro Mexico*, San Francisco: Spinsters/Aunt Lute Books.
Araujo, L. and Easton, G. (1996) 'Networks in Socioeconomic Systems', in D. Iacobucci (ed.) *Networks in Marketing*, London: Sage.
Beck, U., Giddens, A. and Lash, S. (1994) *Reflexive Modernization: Politics, Tradition and Aesthetics in the Modern Social Order*, Oxford: Polity Press.
Burrell, G. and Morgan, G. (1979) *Sociological Paradigms and Organisational Analysis*, London: Heinemann.
Calás, M. (1994) 'Minerva's Owl? Introduction to a Thematic Section on Globalization', *Organization*, 1, 2: 243–8.

Calás, M. and Smircich, L. (1999) 'Past Postmodernism?: Reflections and Tentative Directions', *Academy of Management Review: Special Issue on Theory Development*, 24, 4: 649–71.

Cannella, A.A. and Paetzold, R.L. (1994) 'Pfeffer's Barriers to the Advance of Organizational Science: A Rejoinder', *Academy of Management Review*, 19, 2: 331–41.

Clifford, J. and Marcus, G.E. (eds) (1986) *Writing Culture: The Poetics and Politics of Ethnography*, Berkeley, Calif.: University of California Press.

Cooper, R. and Burrell, G. (1988) 'Modernism, Postmodernism and Organisational Analysis: An Introduction', *Organisation Studies*, 9, 1: 91–112.

Deetz, S. (1992) *Democracy in an Age of Corporate Colonization*, Ithaca, New York: State University of New York Press.

Fayol, H. ([1916] 1949) *General and Industrial Management*, London: Pitman.

Foucault, M. (1977) *Discipline and Punish: The Birth of the Prison*, Harmondsworth: Penguin.

Fox, R.G. (ed.) (1991) *Recapturing Anthropology: Working in the Present*, Santa Fe, NM: School of American Research Press.

García-Canclini, N. (1995) *Hybrid Cultures*, Minneapolis: University of Minnesota Press.

Grimshaw, A. and Hart, K. (1994) 'Anthropology and the Crisis of the Intellectuals', *Critique of Anthropology*, 14, 3: 227–62.

Haraway, D. (1985) 'A Manifesto for Cyborgs: Science, Technology and Socialist Feminism in the 1980's', *Socialist Review*, 15, 80: 65–107.

Harrison, T., Projansky, S., Ono, K.A. and Helford, E.R. (1996) *Enterprise Zones: Critical Positions on Star Trek*, Boulder, Colo.: Westview Press.

Hassard, J. and Holliday, R. (eds) (1998) *Organization-Representation*, London: Sage.

Hearn, J., Sheppard, D., Tancred-Sherriff, P. and Burrell, G. (eds) (1989) *The Sexuality of Organization*, London: Sage.

Hirschman, E.C. and Sanders, C.R. (1997) 'Motion Pictures as Metaphoric Consumption: How Animal Narratives Teach us to be Human', *Semiotica*, 115, 1/2: 53–79.

Hofstede, G. (1980) *Culture's Consequences: International Differences in Work-Related Values*, London: Sage.

Horkheimer, M. and Adorno, T.W. (1973) *Dialectic of Enlightenment*, London: Allen Lane.

Kateb, G. (1963) *Utopia and its Enemies*, New York: Free Press of Glencoe.

Krug, K. (1998) 'A Hypermediated Ethnography of Organizational Change: Conversations in the Museum of Anthropology', unpublished Ph.D. thesis, University of British Columbia.

Law, J. (1994) *Organising Modernity*, Oxford: Blackwell.

March, J.G. and Olsen, J.P. (eds) ([1976] 1979) *Ambiguity and Choice in Organizations*, Bergen: Universitetsforlaget.

Mintzberg, H. and Waters, J. (1985) 'Of Strategies, Deliberate and Emergent', *Strategic Management Journal*, 6, July/September: 257–72.

Morgan, G. (1986) *Images of Organization*, Beverly Hills: Sage.

Nohria, N. and Eccles, R.G. (eds) (1993) *Networks and Organizations*, Boston: Harvard Business School Press.

Parker, M. (1999) 'Manufacturing Bodies: Flesh, Organization, Cyborgs', in J. Hassard, R. Holliday and H. Willmott (eds) *Organising the Body*, London: Sage.

Pettigrew, A. (1979) 'On Studying Organizational Cultures', *Administrative Science Quarterly*, 24, December: 570–81.

Pfaelzer, J. (1988) 'The Changing of the Avant-Garde: The Feminist Utopia', *Science Fiction Studies*, 15, 3: 282–94.

Pfeffer, J. (1993) 'Barriers to the Advance of Organizational Science: Paradigm Development as a Dependent Variable', *Academy of Management Review*, 18, 4: 599–620.

Pondy, L.R. *et al.*. (ed.) (1983) *Organizational Symbolism*, Greenwich: JAI Press.

Powell, W.W. (1990) 'Neither Market nor Hierarchy: Network Forms of Organization', in B.M. Staw and L.L. Cummings (eds) *Research in Organisational Behaviour*, Volume 12, Greenwich, CT: JAI Press.

Quinn, J.B. (1980) *Strategies for Change: Logical Incrementalism*, New York: Irwin.

Reed, M. (1996) 'Organizational Theorizing: A Historically Contested Terrain', in S. Clegg, C. Hardy and W. R. Nord (eds) *Handbook of Organization Studies*, London: Sage.

Rice, A.K. (1963) *The Enterprise and its Environment*, London: Tavistock Publications.

Richards, T. (1997) *The Meaning of Star Trek*, New York: Doubleday.

Said, E.W. (1989) 'Representing the Colonized: Anthropology's Interlocutors', *Critical Inquiry*, 15: 205–25.

Simon, H. A. ([1945] 1997) *Administrative Behavior*, New York: The Free Press.

Smircich, L. (1983) 'Concepts of Culture and Organizational Analysis', *Administrative Science Quarterly*, 28, 3: 339–58.

Spivak, G.C. (1988) 'Can the Subaltern Speak?', in C. Nelson and L. Grossberg (eds) *Marxism and the Interpretation of Culture*, Urbana: University of Illinois Press.

Tyler, S. (1987) *The Unspeakable: Discourse, Dialogue and Rhetoric in the Postmodern World*, Madison: University of Wisconsin Press.

Weber, M. ([1921] 1968) *Economy and Society*, Totowa, NJ: Bedminister Press.

Weber, M. ([1930] 1958) *The Protestant Ethic and the Spirit of Capitalism*, New York: Macmillan.

Wells, H. G. ([1905] 1967) *A Modern Utopia*, Lincoln: University of Nebraska Press.

Whitley, R. (1984) 'The Fragmented State of Management Studies', *Journal of Management Studies*, 21, 3: 331–48.

Wilde, O. ([1895] 1914) *The Soul of Man Under Socialism*, London: Arthur L. Humphrey.

Witz, A. and Savage, M. (1992) *Gender and Bureaucracy*, Oxford: Blackwell.

9 From the Borgias to the Borg (and back again)

Rethinking organizational futures

Chris Land and Martin Corbett

Introduction

Representations of organizational futures tend to emphasize post-industrial conceptualizations such as the informated organization (Zuboff, 1988), the knowledge-creating company (Nonaka and Takeuchi, 1995), the virtual organization (Davidow and Malone, 1992) or the networked organization (Dutton, 1999). In these accounts the role of technology is often central and yet the relationship between the social and technological elements of the organization is poorly understood. In organization studies, technology has tended to be marginalized, allowing the discipline to maintain its implicitly human-centred perspective. In short, textbook organization theory has failed to rise to the challenge presented by technology to organizations and to theories of organization. Instead, the discipline has retreated to a comfortable position of liberal humanism where the sovereign, individual subject is retained as the object of study.

This paper traces the humanist trajectory of organization theory back and forth through time from the fifteenth-century Italy of the Borgias to Starfleet's encounters with the Borg between Stardates 42761.3 and 50984.3. Whilst both the Borgias and the Borg are generally presented as enemies of humanism, the Borgias have provided a template for effective leadership and management in humanist organization theory. The Borg, on the other hand, present a real threat to this humanist agenda. The paper develops this theme by drawing comparisons between the ways that Starfleet and the writers of *Star Trek: The Next Generation* (*ST:TNG*) and *Star Trek: Voyager* have dealt with the threat of the Borg and the ways in which contemporary organization theory is dealing with technologically fetishistic, and equally threatening, trends such as knowledge management.[1]

Although there are clear similarities between the reactionary strategies of Starfleet and organization theory, we have not yet given up hope that there might be an alternative. Rather than coming down on the side of either technology or humanism we conclude the paper by bringing the whole non-human/human dualism into question and propose the cyborg as an alternative to both the Borg and the Borgias. In this sense, the paper lays the groundwork for an anti-humanist theory of organization and technology.

A search for origins: the renascent human

The key ideological revolution of the European Renaissance in the mid-fifteenth to mid-sixteenth century was the construction of a worldview in which the human took centre stage. Machiavelli placed the human at the centre of politics; science developed into the construction of truth according to humans' observation rather than according to God's creation; legal rules rather than God's will became the fundamental concern of the judiciary; and artists produced paintings to be seen from the perspective of the human observer rather than God.

This humanist philosophy displaced God at the centre of all things in favour of the human. Not just any human mind you, but the individual who was 'self-made' and 'made their mark' on the world. More significantly perhaps, the humans at the centre of Renaissance humanism were those who self-consciously created, through the application of tools and knowledge of natural laws, a 'second' nature for themselves. This 'second' nature, as Kaufman (1993) notes, is based on human mastery and control of nature. Furthermore, Heller (1978) argues that this idea of mastery paralleled the discovery of the concept of humanity and the idea of the progression and development of humanity. Although mathematics and technologies were fundamental to this development, the important role of certain remarkable individuals in creating human history was also emphasized (as evidenced in the popularity of the printed autobiography, the civic honours bestowed on Great Artists and Architects, and in the works of Shakespeare at this time).

The Borgias, most notoriously Rodrigo (Pope Alexander VI), and two of his children Cesare and Lucrezia, were supreme examples of Renaissance humanism. In under a century the Borgias grew from an obscure fief in Spain to a position of supreme power in Europe, and this was due in no small measure to the charismatic personalities of the leading figures in the family. Rodrigo, Cesare and Lucrezia were all highly emotional, almost 'driven' people. They were of striking appearance, possessed by voracious sexual appetites, killed their enemies with cruel disdain, and possessed finely honed political skills of manipulation and deceit. These flamboyant people were perhaps the founder members of the Renaissance 'cult of the personality', whilst their achievements in establishing a powerful Papal State are recognized to this day.

The success of the Borgia's organization was based on strong charismatic leadership buttressed by an inner circle of trusted family members, and a ruthless determination to expand and colonize. Civilian employees of 'BorgiaCo' were kept in place through terror and desire; whilst military employees were kept in place by firm discipline and monetary reward. The Borgias led by example and commanded great loyalty. Machiavelli was so impressed by the Borgia organization that he wrote one of the first management texts – *The Prince* – praising the managerial skills of Cesare Borgia. The book is still in print today (Machiavelli, 1998).

The Borgias fascinated not only Machiavelli but most of the Italian court in the fifteenth century, and all of the characteristics which enthralled 500 years ago still captivate organization theorists today. The Borgias' use and abuse of power, their charismatic leadership and expansionist strategic management, their use of technologies as prosthetic extensions of human agency and mastery, and above all, their remarkable organizational and human resource management skills have been divorced from their violent abuse by the family and, suitably reterritorialized and repackaged in business and organization theory texts, are now sold as desirable, reproducible management qualities (e.g. Jay, 1987).

Indeed, the humanism born in the Renaissance, exemplified by the Borgias, still finds resonance 1,000 years into the future – in the world of *ST:TNG*. Here the humanism has a distinctly ninteenth-century (and noticeably more benign) flavour. For example, in the *ST:TNG* episode 'Descent: Part One' (in which the Borg feature prominently), Commander Data (an android) plays cards with holograms of Isaac Newton, Albert Einstein and Stephen Hawking. As Boyd (1996) argues, this scene is very much in keeping with the nineteenth-century humanist view that a series of Great Minds create continual progress in science and technology and that Great Men create history. The homage to nineteenth-century humanism is more overt in the two-part episode 'Time's arrow' in which Mark Twain ends up on board the Starship *Enterprise*. Within hours of his arrival, all of his concerns and fears about the dark Borgia-like aspects of liberal humanism (domination, exploitation, inequality) are banished and he embraces a utopian future in which all differences and inequalities (not just between humans but between all major known life-forms) appear to have been abolished through the application of benign leadership and legal-rational authority.

Ameliorating the threat of radical otherness 1: *ST:TNG*'s response to Borganization from 'Q, who?' to 'First Contact'

So far we have looked at ideas of the universal 'human' that began to coalesce in the Renaissance and, almost paradoxically, are exemplified by the Borgias. It is the very universality of this humanism that made possible the emancipatory projects of the Enlightenment. If all humans are equal because under the skin they are essentially the same, then it is possible to see systematic social inequalities and seek to liberate those who are not treated equally. The effect of this equalizing however is to homogenize humanity and preclude the possibility of radical or essential difference. Within the category 'human' there can be no essential differences, only accidental ones, which are really no difference at all. A similar liberal humanist ideology underwrites *ST:TNG* and the Borg present a serious threat to this ideal. When the Borg are first introduced to *ST:TNG* viewers, they have the appearance of a radical Other. The Borg have no gender, no leader, no individual identity. They are the antithesis of humanity with their fetishistically technologized bodies and hive mentality. This difference not only threatens the crew of the *Enterprise* with an enemy they cannot reason with but presents a very real difficulty for the script writers of *ST:TNG*: 'the transformations that the Borg undergo during their six appearances on the show reveal the difficulty of representing radical difference in a humanist utopia dependent on . . . essentialist notions of the 'self' and human nature' (Boyd, 1996: 96).

These transformations move the Borg from the position of difference found in 'Q, who?' and 'The best of both worlds: Parts one and two', through the development of individual identity in 'I, Borg' and the consequences of this individualization in 'Descent: Parts one and two'. The early, radical Borg are irreconcilable with *ST:TNG*'s whole ideological message and Starfleet's strategies for countering threat. The Borg simply cannot be reasoned with. The only way that this threat can be managed is to humanize the collective and endow it with (at least the potential for) individual identity and agency.[2]

In 'Q, who?', Starfleet encounter the Borg for the first time. In this episode, an 'Away Team' headed up by Rijker are beamed aboard the Borg cube[3] and discover the Borg nursery where individual baby Borg are being grown and fitted with implants. It would seem the Borg collective has no need for humans at all. It scavenges the universe for technologies and raw materials to steal. As we move through 'The best of both worlds: Parts one and two', Picard is kidnapped by, and assimilated into, the collective so that he can act as the Borg's ambassador to the human race, which it now wants to assimilate. The Borg are no longer just interested in technology but seek to incorporate others' technological *and biological* 'distinctiveness' into their own. With this move we are encouraged to forget the Borg nursery and view Borganic reproduction as entirely parasitic on other species. The 'Borganization' expands and evolves by assimilating the identities and collective knowledge of other species. By the end of 'The best of both worlds: Part two', we know that even when Picard has been fully assimilated, the old Picard is still there beneath all the implants and prostheses. This opens the possibility that individual members of the Borg could be persuaded to remember who they 'really are'.

Indeed, this is precisely what happens in 'I, Borg' when the crew of the *Enterprise* respond to a distress call and encounter a Borg crash site with an 'adolescent male' Borg still alive.[4] After bringing this Borg back on board, the *Enterprise* is faced with a dilemma. If the Borg – named Third of Five – remains on board then the rest of the collective will soon come looking for him. Despite their previous encounter, the *Enterprise* is still unprepared to fight such a powerful enemy. On the other hand, the captive Borg presents unparalleled possibilities for studying the Borg and finding a weak spot. Commander LeForge is given this task and eventually finds a bug in their 3D processing of abstract, geometrical models. Third of Five will now be exposed to a complex optical illusion and returned to the collective, effectively introducing a disabling virus into the collective mind. This has the potential to annihilate the Borg entirely. Although some of the crew have a few qualms about such a blatant act of genocide (particularly Commander LeForge who has befriended Third of Five and renamed 'him' Hugh), Picard is insistent upon the Borg's destruction. Picard only changes his mind at the very last minute when Hugh recognizes him as 'Locutious of Borg' (the name Picard was given while assimilated). In order to test Hugh, Picard orders the Borg to assist him in taking over the *Enterprise*. Hugh refuses and in doing so uses the word 'I', as opposed to the collective 'we' for the first time. Picard takes this as a sign that Hugh has developed a genuine sense of self-identity and so has a claim to human rights. At the end of this episode, Hugh decides to return to the collective rather than risk the lives of his new friends and Picard concludes by wondering whether:

> perhaps, in that short time before they purge his memory, the sense of individuality which he has gained with us might be transmitted through the entire Borg collective, every one of the Borg being given the opportunity to experience the feeling of . . . of . . . singularity. Perhaps that's the most pernicious programme of all; the knowledge of self being spread throughout the collective in that brief moment might alter them forever.

In 'Descent: Parts one and two', we meet Hugh again. It seems that individuality did spread when he returned to the Borg and his group were severed from the larger collective like a gangrenous limb. Newly individualized, these Borg were lost, alone and confused. Without the benevolent authority of Starfleet to guide them, they fell under the influence of Commander Data's evil android 'brother', Lore. In the conclusion to this two-part episode, Lore is overcome and killed with the help of Hugh and his group. With their evil leader dead and their resentment at what Starfleet did to them finally overcome, it seems likely that the Borg will continue to function as a group of individuals, possibly with Hugh as their leader.

The humanization of the Borg is continued in the film *First Contact* where we discover that the collective had a leader all along: the sinisterly sexualized Borg queen. Interestingly, for the purposes of the film the scriptwriters decide not to continue with Hugh as leader, but to posit an evil, female leader who was there all the time suppressing the natural individuality of those she assimilated.[5] This stands in striking contrast to the positive spin given to Hugh's (male) leadership potential.

Of course, the naturalization of gendered authority is nothing new to *Star Trek*. In *Star Trek II: The Wrath of Khan* the naturalized, patriarchal authority of Kirk was juxtaposed with the slovenly, bad leadership of Khan (Corbett, 1998a). Indeed, Khan was another unnatural 'child of technology' much like the Borg only with genetic engineering instead of nano-tech implants. But, if Khan was a bad father, he has nothing on the Borg Queen as bad mother. For she has never let her children off the apron strings and allowed them to develop an adult sense of self. Throughout *First Contact*, the Borg Queen's otherness and bad leadership are emphasized. She sacrifices many of the collective in a subterfuge to divert Starfleet from her real mission – actions more becoming of a Lucrezia Borgia than a loving mother. Most importantly she disturbs the 'natural order', not only by her 'unnatural' female leadership and techno-fetishistic sexuality, but through her attempts to seduce Data and give him 'real' human flesh and sensations. Fortunately, at the end of the film, Data sacrifices his new-found organic flesh to release a necrotic liquid, catching the queen unawares and dissolving her organic components. The 'natural order' of human and machine is restored as Picard climbs above the danger, Data is returned to his 'pure' artificial form, and the unnatural Borganization is destroyed. All that is left of the Borg Queen at the end of this final conflict is a shining, chrome skull reminiscent of *The Terminator* when the eponymous cyborg emerges from the fire purified of his all-too-human flesh. Still connected to this skull are a few twitching, metallic vertebrae. Humanely, Picard picks up what is left of the queen and breaks her neck.

With the end of *First Contact* the threat of the Borg has been thoroughly neutralized. They are now just like any other species that the *Enterprise* might encounter. They have agency, individuality and a leader who can be either reasoned with or executed. By literally decapitating the Borg's leader and breaking her neck, Picard has decapitated the entire Borg collective. Without a leader the Borg are no longer a real danger.

Assimilating the 'Other': Seven of Nine and renaissance humanism as patriarchal authority

A more recent figuration of the Borg can be found in *Star Trek Voyager* (*Voyager* hereafter). In a series of episodes, including 'Scorpion: Parts one and two', and 'The Raven', the character Seven of Nine is introduced. At first, Seven of Nine appears as a threat to the crew of *Voyager*, who have to fight off a Borg attack to avoid being assimilated into the collective. As the episodes unfold, however, she[6] is steadily humanized and eventually becomes a regular member of the crew. Even the apparently radical difference of the Borg can now be assimilated into the Starfleet collective and once again the individual human subject can take centre stage.

Where *ST:TNG* and *Voyager* differ is in the humanism that they represent and oppose to the Borg. Whereas *ST:TNG* holds nineteenth-century America as its touchstone (Boyd, 1996), *Voyager* explicitly harks back to the Renaissance as the origin of humanity. The links between the Borgias and the Borg are played out on screen as Captain Janeway humanizes Seven of Nine by taking her to the holodeck where she runs a simulation of Leonardo da Vinci's workshop. By keeping in touch with the origins of humanism in this way, Janeway has been able to find an authentically human space within an otherwise technologically threatening world.[7] When Seven of Nine is introduced to this space, she finds it hard to understand. With time however she is able to make contact with her human side, bring her nano-technological implants under control, and reject the collective.

This transformation does not happen all at once. By connecting to Leonardo ('the Master'), and through him to a humanist tradition running some 800 years back in time and space, Seven of Nine is reconnected to the human race and thereby Starfleet.[8] Even so, this founding father is not enough to fully reinstate her humanity. For this she must also be reconciled with her biological father and the nuclear family. This happens in 'The Raven' when the nanocites still inside her respond to the call of a Borg ship in the vicinity. It transpires that the signal came from a shipwreck – the *Raven* – on a nearby planet. Once Seven is on the ship memories from her childhood start to return and she realizes this was the place where she grew up and, whilst still a little girl, was captured by the Borg.[9] Once these memories have returned Seven is finally free of her Borg programming and can return to Voyager with the knowledge of her real origins. Reterritorialized by the Oedipal nuclear family she is at last a human and can take her place as part of Starfleet.

What both stories emphasize is the need for Seven's human identity to be validated by a patriarchal male, whether the lost father on the Raven or a founding father of humanism, like Leonardo. In both cases the validity of her human identity is dependent upon authorization by a phallic authority to which she will always be Other. Her difference as Borg has been replaced by gender difference, which liberal humanism has long since learned to assimilate.

Ameliorating the threat of radical otherness 2: technology and organization theory

Let us move away from futuristic sci-fi towards present-day organization theory. What should be clear from the discussion so far is that the Borg represent a clear threat to *Star Trek*'s humanism. The key to this threat is the Borg's technological hybridity. Their collective, hive-like, mind is perhaps what makes them especially alien, but even this is a product of information and communication technologies (ICT). This section of the paper argues that in both *ST:TNG* and organization theory, technology is treated as extensive (i.e. as a tool that simply extends human capabilities). This is a move which denies the intensive aspects of technology and the ways in which prostheses reconfigure their 'users' to such an extent that this distinction becomes meaningless.

In its most simple guise, organization theory takes one of two main approaches to technology: 'technological determinism' and 'organizational choice' (Scarbrough and Corbett, 1992). Technological determinism has a long pedigree in the social sciences, stretching from Marx's historical materialism (Carling, 1993), through to Lynn White's reduction of Feudalism to the development of the stirrup (White, 1962). Most often cited as representing this tradition in organization theory is Joan Woodward's (1965) study of the impact of different types of production technology on the social organization of production. Whereas technological determinism sees social organization as being determined (albeit 'in the last instance') by technology, the organizational choice perspective, epitomized by Buchanan and Boddy (1983), suggests that technology is the result of managerial choice. Both perspectives see technology as entirely distinct from the organization.

These two camps are somewhat out of vogue at present, with organizational researchers increasingly professing some form of social constructivism or social shaping of technology (Dutton, 1999; MacKenzie and Wajcman, 1999; Webster, 1996). What the social constructivist perspective has in common with technological determinism and organizational choice is a distinction between the social and the technical. Even where the discourse refers to 'blurred boundaries', the analysis tends towards social determinism. Where social shaping theorists move from analysis to prescription, they tend to talk of achieving 'fit' (Williams, 1999) in a similar way to the socio-technical systems approach pioneered by the Tavistock Institute (Cherns, 1976).[10]

The underlying theme in all of these approaches is that technology, including

ICT, is treated simply as a tool or extension of essentially human capacities. Human-centred design assumes a stable, coherent unitary and centred human subject, despite the fact that technology reconfigures the human as much as the other way round (Corbett, 1998b). This was a point noted as early as the 1930s, but largely ignored by contemporary organization theory:

> Civilisation itself has become a machine that does, or tries to do, everything in a mechanical fashion. We think only in horse-power now; we cannot look at a waterfall without mentally turning it into electric power; we cannot survey a countryside full of pasturing cattle without thinking of its exploitation as a source of meat-supply.
>
> (Spengler, 1932: 94)

A more recent example, connected to the etymological origins of the term organization as 'to endow with organs' (McLean and Hoskin, 1998), is the human heart. Once we know that the heart functions as a pump for circulating blood, we can create an artificial heart to do this job. Once it can be replaced, the heart itself becomes a pump and nothing more.[11] It is in precisely these terms that we now think of hearts. The naturalness of this functionalist thinking is even carried over into *ST:TNG*. In the episode 'Tapestry', we discover that Captain Picard has an artificial heart: the result of losing his head, thinking with his 'heart' and getting into a fight in his youth.

The retreat from 'becoming' technology (in a Deleuzian sense) to a safe distinction between the human (or social) and the technical means that we never effectively theorize this complexity. To bring this discussion back to the Borg, the next section examines the recent popularity of knowledge management in organization theory and finds the spectre of the Borg lurking behind its utopian and technocentric rhetoric. Following from this comparison of knowledge management and the Borg, we compare attempts to redress this technocentrism and recentre 'the human' in the knowledge management literature with the transformation of the Borg in *ST:TNG*.

The Borg and knowledge management

> Try to imagine an organization whose members are in constant telepathic contact with one another. New ideas created by an individual are broadcast simultaneously to every part of the enterprise. No learning is ever lost – the workforce becomes a huge memory bank, recording and relaying data. Communication barriers simply disappear. Knowledge – and the ability to retain, share and apply it – becomes the most important asset of the business.
>
> (Scarbrough, 1999: 68)

In the above we are invited to imagine the future organization represented in the knowledge management literature. It takes no great leap of imagination to see similarities with the Borg: 'This may seem like science fiction but this kind of imagery is driving much of the growing interest in knowledge management' (Scarbrough, ibid.: 68).

Definitions of knowledge management are varied. Some focus on facilitating innovation in high-tech industries (Leonard and Sensiper, 1998), whilst others highlight the importance of customer information to marketing and competitive advantage (Finerty, 1997). Still others are concerned with the management of expertise in project-based work where there is a risk of 'reinventing the wheel' every time a group encounters a novel problem. This approach emphasizes the importance of utilizing individuals' or groups' learning and experience and making that knowledge available to others in the organization. It is a formalized vicarious learning process reminiscent of the Borg's instantaneous adaptation of shield defences to new weapons. What all of these approaches to knowledge management have in common is a heavily technological bent. As Hugh Willmott puts it: 'ICT + new work organization = knowledge management' (1998: 25).

In a recent review of the knowledge management literature, Scarbrough, Swan and Preston (1999) found that the majority of articles have appeared in the IS/IT literatures with nearly 70 per cent of articles in 1998 appearing in such literatures. This is quite understandable when one considers the widespread belief that the advent of ICT has heralded the dawning of a 'knowledge society' (Drucker, 1988), 'information society' (Webster, 1995) or 'post-industrial society' (Bell, 1974). What these conceptions share is an emphasis on the changing nature of society and economic relations due to the development of ICT. Central to these changes are the increasing importance of information and knowledge.[12] The association of information, knowledge and ICT has, in turn, influenced where knowledge management has found its most receptive audience: amongst IT professionals and management consultants.

One effect of this technocentricism in knowledge management has been the privileging of codifiable, or 'explicit' knowledge that can be stored on computerized databases and intranets to be retrieved by others as and when it is needed.[13] Even the most stalwart critics of rationalist approaches to knowledge management privilege explicit, governable knowledge over more personal, tacit or embodied forms. In their highly influential book *The Knowledge-Creating Company*, Ikujiro Nonaka and Hirotaka Takeuchi spend a considerable amount of time insisting upon the importance of 'tacit knowledge' to the knowledge creation process. Even they, however, finish up emphasizing the ultimate centrality of abstracted, codified, 'explicit knowledge':

> The quintessential knowledge-creation process takes place when tacit knowledge is converted into explicit knowledge. In other words, our hunches, perceptions, mental models, beliefs, and experiences are converted into something that can be communicated and transmitted in formal and systematic language.
>
> (Nonaka and Takeuchi, 1995: 230–1)

In other words, it is not really knowledge if it remains tacit. Only explicit knowledge has any real importance. They are, of course, right to note that too much emphasis has been placed on the transfer and storage of explicit knowledge without having sufficiently addressed the problem of extracting that knowledge from the actual, embodied activities of workers. However, their concept of the 'high-density field' where this knowledge extraction/conversion occurs, once again draws us inexorably closer to the Borg: 'A high-density field is the place where the conversion is triggered through some sort of dialogue. It is here that crew members begin constructing a common language and synchronizing their mental and physical rhythms' (Nonaka and Takeuchi, 1995: 231).

The synchronization of 'mental and physical rhythms' is what the Borg are all about. Indeed, it is almost universally the case that if one extrapolates from the knowledge management literature in order to envisage the future organization, one is left with the image of the Borg. However, as we have seen, their image does not sit well with humanist utopias such as the knowledge-creating organization with its empowered, fulfilled workers and knowledge-sharing, democratic participation. Indeed, the technocentrism of much of the knowledge management literature can be quite explicitly dehumanizing with its predominant metaphors of knowledge 'mining' and 'extraction' (Finerty, 1997; Scarbrough *et al.*, 1999). With this kind of discourse running riot, there is a very real risk that mainstream organization theory will find its own, supposedly liberal, agenda brought into question.

The limits of Starfleet's humanist utopia were exposed by its inability to represent the Borg without first humanizing them. Organization theory's inability to theorize technology, and technocentric innovations like knowledge management, similarly expose the discipline's own limits (for an overview see McLoughlin, 1999). This can be illuminated by drawing comparisons between recent strategies in organization theory to rehumanize knowledge management, and the strategies employed by the script-writers of *ST:TNG* to contain the Borg and assimilate them into the humanist world of Starfleet.

Ameliorating the threat of radical otherness 3: knowledge management' s retreat to liberal humanism

In their review of knowledge management, Scarbrough *et al.*. (1999) argue that the

> philosophy of knowledge management has the potential to exploit, control, automate and devalue the employee and sits uncomfortably with the dominant values and goals of [People Management] which include fairness in the employee relationship and an emphasis on the human quality of work.
>
> (Scarbrough *et al.*., 1999: 27)

Their main point is that knowledge management needs to pay more attention to people management issues.[14] By ignoring the human factors involved in organizing, and seeking simplistic, technocratic, best practice solutions to the perceived problem, knowledge management is turning its back on the whole of the human-centred tradition of social science, sociology and psychology that gave birth to modern organization studies. Rather than taking issue with such a critique, we want to consider the value of such a reactionary retreat to a position of liberal humanism.

Scarbrough *et al.*. (ibid.) conclude that successful knowledge management initiatives must pay keen attention to employee commitment, the maintenance of a supportive culture and strong leadership. We are back to the Borgias again! The parallel, reactionary movements of *Star Trek* and organization theory are represented in Figure 9.1.

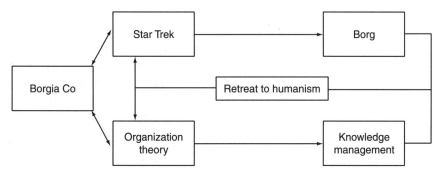

Figure 9.1 From the Borgia to the Borg and back again

None of this is to deny that the court of the Borgias were highly successful on many counts. One need only think of the creativity of Leonardo da Vinci whilst in the service of Cesare Borgia, or Machiavelli's attempts to codify best practice for a prince and so share his knowledge with future generations of rulers and diplomats, to realize that theirs was a highly successful organization both in terms of knowledge creation and retention. However, this vision of leadership is somewhat at odds with the technologically mediated, rational organization of today's knowledge management literature. Is it really possible to simply turn our back on technology and insist that the human at the centre of organization studies is some kind of universal constant? By connecting to a tradition of liberal humanism that harks back to the Renaissance, these reactionary moves in knowledge management essentialize both human and technology thereby blinding us to the codetermination of these categories. Paradoxically, if an insistence on an essential human identity prevents us from effectively theorizing technology and difference, humanism can have quite inhumane consequences. In *ST:TNG* the dehumanizing impact of new technology was limited and defused by the scriptwriters' recentring of the human. But can we be sure that the same strategy will work in organization studies?

From Borgia to Borg to cyborg: toward an anti-humanist organization theory

This paper has presented a series of dualisms clustered around the distinction between the human and technology. In doing so we have suggested that both organization theory and *Star Trek* have tended to privilege the human over the technological. In critiquing this move our intention has not been to suggest that we should embrace the Borg, or knowledge management, in their more techno-centric manifestations, but to question the *a priori* division of the field into two seemingly exclusive positions. The real problem then, is not the solution to the question of the human-technology relationship, but the question itself.

Retreating to a humanist position based upon a dualism of human or non-human is problematic on two counts. First, as we have noted with regard to the Renaissance and the Borgias, the human is not a universal but a historically specific construction (see also Porter, 1997). Second, the non/human dualism is a 'badly analysed composite' (Deleuze, 1991). The non-human pole of the dualism already contains the idea of the human as it is defined as that which is not human. In this sense there is no real (qualitative) difference between the human and the non-human. At best there is only a difference of degree: more or less human. Either way, the question of the human remains. In this sense the determinism/choice, technology/human, knowledge management/organization theory, Borg/Starfleet, Borg/Borgia oppositions are all manifestations of a badly analysed composite – non/human. Choice is limited to a simple for or against. Rather than resisting Borganization, humanism is the principle that makes it possible.

There are two main issues at stake here. One is the refusal to engage with difference – with the Other. The second is the impossibility of thinking otherwise: of moving beyond simplistic ontological dualisms. In respect of the first, engaging with the Other, it is clear that both Starfleet and organization theory have failed. When faced with a difference that threatens their most basic assumptions they can only see a problem to be overcome. Starfleet never attempts to understand or engage with the Borg, only to render them manageable according to their stand-ard operating procedures. Similarly, organization theory has not attempted to understand technology on its own terms. Instead it has either projected humanist fears onto it or dismissed it as irrelevant.[15] *ST:TNG* exemplifies this projection.

In their initial configuration the Borg appear as frighteningly Other. They are obsessed with technology and have no human concerns. This creates problems both for the crew of the *Enterprise* and the script-writers. Because of this the Borg are slowly but surely humanized until they have been defeated ('First contact') or fully assimilated into Starfleet as crew members (*Voyager*). Either way the Borg can now be re-presented within a humanist framework.

But what of their original form? At first the Borg's difference, their Otherness, was exemplified by their lack of gender, leadership or individual identity. In a sense this is not Other at all, but the ideal of the politically correct subject of contemporary liberal humanism. It is the ideal embodied in the Universal Dec-laration of Human Rights.[16] With no identity or gender there can be no dis-crimination. Without leaders, the ideal of democracy has been realized and there can be no oppression. From this perspective the Borg simply represent the 'dark shadow' of humanism. There is no real dualism, just a badly analysed composite that never moves outside of a framework constituted by humanism itself. There is no engagement with the Other.

This leads us to the second problem with the non/human dualism: the impossibility of thinking otherwise. As soon as one accepts this dualism, the only choice left is which pole to inhabit, which side to support: human or anti-human. By problematizing the non/human dualism we have attempted to show that neither side is desirable. What is needed is an alternative that lies beyond dualisms. Rather than antihuman-ism, we are proposing an anti-humanism that refuses to subscribe to the lines of engagement set out by humanism. Anti-humanism does not attempt a third way that includes, or assimilates, both sides of the dualism (from 'either–or' to 'both–and'). Rather, it problematizes the very act of division. Along with Bourdieu (1989) we see ontological dualisms as colluding adversaries which serve to limit the range of the thinkable. We need to uncover what lies ' "between" the between' (Deleuze and Parnet, 1987: xii). It is in this borderland that we find the dangerous figure of the cyborg.

The cyborg offers us an alternative to the Borg versus human battle lines drawn up by *Star Trek* and the knowledge management debate. It is a figure radically different from either Starfleet commanders or the Borg. It is a heterogeneous, hybrid figure that holds no truck with BorgiaCo and Oedipal patriarchy, and so rejects its military origins (Haraway, 1991). Most importantly, the cyborg is neither human, machine, nor human-and-machine combined. It is a multiplicity that rejects the individualization imposed by both mechanism and humanism. It is the assemblage that produces both 'human' and 'technology'. Both are effects produced by cyborganization. The cyborg cuts across the non/human dualism and rejects the essentialist purity of *being* human in favour of *becoming* cyborg, an assemblage comprising (amongst other things) human bodies without fixed identity or sole claim to the site of agency.

Although it began life within feminist science studies (Kirkup *et al..*, 2000), the cyborg showed due disrespect for boundaries, and travelled swiftly through much of social theory, philosophy and psychology (see Gray, 1995). It has now made tentative moves into organization studies within the folds of 'cyborganization theory' (e.g. Cooper and Law, 1995; Parker and Cooper, 1998; Wood, 1998). From this theoretical perspective, the cyborg offers a radically different way of theorizing organization as arenas where agency is distributed among people and things, and bounded order is always temporary.

Whilst the ethical and moral implications of an anti-humanist organization theory deserve careful consideration (see Parker, 1998), we hope that this paper has at least demonstrated the need for such a theoretical turn if we are to escape the binary bind of humanism versus mechanism and think difference on its own terms. The Borg (as represented in 'Q, who?') may well turn out to be the organizational form of the future. Who knows? Certainly not the humanist organization theorists (and their *ST:TNG* script-writing allies) who have rendered themselves incapable of analysing such a form. It is hoped that cyborganization theory will be able to offer some insight into the future of organizational theory and practice before it is assimilated.

Notes

1 Thanks to Rebecca Dale for first drawing our attention to the connections between the Borg and knowledge management discourse.

2 The following discussion owes much to Katrina Boyd's (1996) reading of the Borg and *ST:TNG*.

3 The Borg space-craft is a perfect cube, not so subtlety emphasizing their alien Otherness and unnaturalness.

4 No longer are the Borg genderless, as they were proclaimed in 'Q, who?' (although see note 6). Once Picard had been assimilated no such ambiguity could be tolerated. The idea of a neutered Captain would upset the patriarchally validated authority structure of Starfleet far too much.

5 In this sense the Borg Queen plays upon the archetype of the archaic mother discussed by Barbara Creed (1989). As represented in horror and sci-fi, this figure becomes distorted from the mother/goddess as source of all life, to a 'monstrous feminine' smothering those in her care. Rather than giving birth to distinctive entities (individualization), the mother expands to absorb her offspring back into herself (assimilation).

6 By this point the Borg are clearly gendered, a trend that began with Hugh in 'I, Borg' who is introduced as 'a male adolescent'. It is worth noting, however, that even in 'Q, Who?', the first episode to feature the Borg, Q introduces the Borg as genderless but subsequently refers to a particular Borg as 'he'.

7 Of course, 'The Master's Workshop' is nothing but a highly advanced technological simulacra so there is nothing authentic about this setting at all. Leonardo himself is now just a hologram operated by an artificial intelligence. As is so often found in *Star Trek*, the show's technologically advanced settings continually serve to problematize and displace the human subject that the liberal, humanist narrative attempts to recentre. These discrepancies are perhaps one of the greatest values of SF for an organization theory trying to understand technological advance, as they serve to illuminate both the problems that a modern, humanist, academic discipline can have theorizing technology and also point towards some of the strategies that organizations develop to cope with these discrepancies. Scott Bukatman (1993), in particular, discusses the ways in which the technologically advanced settings and language of sci-fi writings serve to continually unsettle the reader's taken-for-granted assumptions about referentiality, and the relationship of signs to any stable signified. This epistemological relativization is also played out on the ontological level by the holographic simulations of virtual reality (VR) on *Voyager*'s holodecks.

8 As Amelie Hastie (1996) notes, 'Starfleet' is often equated with 'human', for example in an episode of *ST:TNG* when Deana Troi reveals that she is half Betazoid, half human by noting that her father was a Starfleet officer, i.e. a human. These sort of slips reveal the homogeneity that belies Starfleet's apparent heterogeneity and species (i.e. racial) diversity.

9 The links between these scenes and recovered memory syndrome may also prove an interesting site for investigation. Certainly there are links between sexual abuse and the terrorization of a small child by the Borg who penetrate her with nano-technological implants. *Raven* emphasizes the naturalness of the traditional nuclear family from which Seven of Nine was torn, and the unnaturalness of the Borg who have destroyed this natural unit and replaced it with a horrific, unnatural, forced unity. The Borg, it seems, do not make good parents.

10 A particular problem with these approaches is that, by separating the social from the technical, they tend to have a very limited account of technology. The very theories and methodologies developed to ensure socio-technical 'fit' are both technical and social, a reflexivity that is rarely acknowledged by those making these suggestions. This is a problem that is found throughout organization studies: what is the status of theory? If we look to the recommendations of early organizational theorists like F.W. Taylor (or

more recent innovations like just-in-time, lean production or total quality management), theory itself is clearly a form of technology.

11 Thanks for Gibson Burrell for providing this example.

12 Although it is a hotly debated topic in the knowledge management field, we will not consider the relationship between data, information and knowledge in this paper except to note that they are often treated interchangeably or placed in a simple hierarchy with more information leading to more knowledge, so long as it is effectively utilized.

13 Clearly, the predominance of technocentric knowledge management owes much to the traditionally technocratic nature of management. Although there have been moves away from extreme forms of bureaucratic organization and scientific management, much of the same technical rationality can be seen in more contemporary approaches to organizational management, for example business process re-engineering (Hammer and Champy, 1995) which has been a very influential precursor to knowledge management.

14 These conclusions are doubtless influenced by the fact that their report was commissioned by the Institute of Personnel and Development, but the conclusions seem worthy of attention regardless of their intended audience.

15 A similar point is made in Stanislav Lem's novel *Solaris*. The entire novel is set on board a station hovering above a planet: Solaris. The crew of the station, only three, are all scientists attempting to understand the apparent intelligence of the planet's living ocean. Rather than engage with this difference, however, the scientists only succeed in projecting their own, all too human concerns onto the planet. This is reinforced and reflected by the main character (Kris) and his relationship with his now deceased wife, brought back from his unconscious by Solaris' ocean.

16 Thanks to Iain Munro for this point.

References

Bell, D. (1974) *The Coming of Post-Industrial Society*, London: Heinemann.

Bourdieu, P. (1989) 'Scientific field and scientific thought', in S. Ortner (ed.) *Author Meets Critics: Reactions to Theory in Anthropology Since the Sixties*, Ann Arbor, Michigan: University of Michigan Press.

Boyd, K.G. (1996) 'Cyborgs in utopia: the problem of radical difference in *Star Trek: The Next Generation*', in T. Harrison, S. Projansky, K.A. Ono and E.R. Helford (eds) *Enterprise Zones: Critical Positions on Star Trek*, Boulder, Colorado: Westview Press.

Buchanan, D.A. and Boddy, D. (1983) *Organisations in the Computer Age*, Aldershot: Gower.

Bukatman, S. (1993) *Terminal Identity: The Virtual Subject in Post-Modern Science Fiction*, Durham, North Carolina: Duke University Press.

Carling, A. (1993) 'Analytical Marxism and historical materialism: the debate on social evolution', *Science and Society*, 57, 31–65.

Cherns, A.B. (1976) 'Principles of sociotechnical design', *Human Relations*, 29, 783–92.

Cooper, R. and Law, J. (1995) 'Organisation: distal and proximal views', *Research in the Sociology of Organisations*, 13, 237–74.

Corbett, J.M. (1998a) 'Sublime technologies and future organisation in science fiction film, 1970–95', in J. Hassard and R. Holliday (eds) *Organisation / Representation: Work and Organisations in Popular Culture*, London: Sage.

Corbett, J.M. (1998b) 'Reconstructing human-centred technology: lessons from the Hollywood dream factory', *AI and Society*, 12, 214–30.

Creed, B. (1989) 'Alien and the monstrous feminine', in A. Kuhn (ed.) *Alien Zone: Cultural Theory and Contemporary Science Fiction Cinema*, London: Verso.

Davidow, W. and Malone, M. (1992) *The Virtual Corporation: Structuring and Revitalizing the Corporation for the 21st Century*, London: Harper Business.

Deleuze, G. (1991) *Bergsonism*, London: Zone.

Deleuze, G. and Parnet, C. (1987) *Dialogues*, London: The Athlone Press.

Drucker, P. (1988) 'The coming of the new organization', Harvard Business Review, January–February, pp. 45–53.

Dutton, W.H. (ed.) (1999) *Society on the Line: Information Politics in the Digital Age*, Oxford: Oxford University Press.

Finerty, L. (1997) 'Information retrieval for intranets: the case for knowledge management', *Document World*, 2, 2–34.

Gray, C.H. (ed.) (1995) *The Cyborg Handbook*, London: Routledge.

Hammer, M. and Champy, J. (1995) *Reengineering the Corporation: A Manifesto for Business Revolution*, London: Brealey.

Haraway, D. (1991) *Simians, Cyborgs, and Women: The Reinvention of Nature*, London: Free Association Books.

Hastie, A. (1996) 'A fabricated space: assimilating the individual on *Star Trek: The Next Generation*', in T. Harrison, S. Projansky, K.A. Ono and E.R. Helford (eds) *Enterprise Zones: Critical Positions on Star Trek*, Boulder, Colorado: Westview Press.

Heller, A. (1978) *Renaissance Man*, London: Routledge.

Jay, A. (1987) *Management and Machiavelli: Power and Authority in Business Life*, London: Hutchinson Business Press.

Kaufman, T.D. (1993) *The Mastery of Nature: Aspects of Art, Science and Humanism in the Renaissance*, Princeton, NJ: Princeton University Press.

Kirkup, G., Janes, L., Woodward, K. and Hovenden, F. (eds) (2000) *The Gendered Cyborg: A Reader*, London: Routledge (in association with the Open University).

Leonard, D. and Sensiper, S. (1998) 'The role of tacit knowledge in group innovation', *California Management Review*, 40, 112–32.

Machiavelli, N. (1998) *The Prince*, Oxford: Oxford Paperbacks.

MacKenzie, D. and Wajcman, J. (eds) (1999) *The Social Shaping of Technology* second edition, Buckingham: Open University Press.

McLean, C. and Hoskin, K. (1998) 'Organizing madness: reflections on the forms of the form', *Organisation*, 5, 519–41.

McLoughlin, I. (1999) *Creative Technological Change: The Shaping of Technology and Organisation*, London: Routledge.

Nonaka, I. and Takeuchi, H. (1995) *The Knowledge-Creating Company: How Japanese Companies Create the Dynamics of Innovation*, Oxford: Oxford University Press.

Parker, M. (1998) 'Judgement Day: cyborganisation, humanism and postmodern ethics', *Organisation*, 5, 4, 503–18.

Parker, M. and Cooper, R. (1998) 'Cyborganisation: cinema as nervous system', in J. Hassard and R. Holliday (eds) *Organisation/Representation: Work and Organisations in Popular Culture*, London: Sage.

Porter, R. (ed.) (1997) *Rewriting the Self: Histories from the Renaissance to the Present*, London: Routledge.

Scarbrough, H. (1999) 'System error', *People Management*, 8 April 1999, 68–74.

Scarbrough, H. and Corbett, J.M. (1992) *Technology and Organisation: Power, Meaning and Design*, London: Routledge.

Scarbrough, H., Swan, J. and Preston, J. (1999) *Knowledge Management: A Literature Review*, London: The Institute of Personnel and Development.

Spengler, O. (1932) *Man and Technics*, New York: Alfred A. Knopf.

Star, S.L. (1991) 'Power, technology and the phenomenology of conventions: on being allergic to onions', in J. Law (ed.) *A Sociology of Monsters: Essays on Power, Technology and Domination*, London: Routledge.

Webster, F. (1995) *Theories of the Information Society*, London: Routledge.

Webster, J. (1996) *Shaping Women's Work: Gender, Employment and Information Technology*, Harlow: Addison Wesley Longman.

White, L. (1962) *Medieval Technology and Social Change*, London: Open University Press.

Williams, R. (1999) 'The social shaping of technology', in W.H. Dutton (ed.) *Society on the Line: Information Politics in the Digital Age*, Oxford: Oxford University Press.

Willmott, H. (1998) 'Here today, gone tomorrow?', *Knowledge Management: A Real Business Guide*, London: Caspian Publishing.

Wood, M. (1998) 'Agency and organisation: toward a cyborg-consciousness', *Human Relations*, 51, 1209–26.

Woodward, J. (1965) *Industrial Organisation: Theory and Practice*, Oxford: Oxford University Press.

Zuboff, S. (1988) *In the Age of the Smart Machine: The Future of Work and Power*, New York: Basic Books.

10 Of Philip K. Dick, reflexivity and shifting realities

Organizing (writing) in our post-industrial society

Christian De Cock

Imaginations of the future, like imaginations of the past, are devices for living in the present.

(March, 1995, p. 427)

I don't accept the judgement that in using images and metaphors of other worlds, space travel, the future, imagined technologies, societies, or beings, science fiction escapes from having human relevance to our lives. Those images and metaphors used by a serious writer are images and metaphors of our lives, legitimately novelistic, symbolic ways of saying what cannot otherwise be said about us, our being and our choices, here and now. What science fiction does is enlarge the here and now.

(Le Guin, 1994, p. 5)

'But are you writing something *serious?*' Note the word. Fuck. If they couldn't get us to write serious things, they solved the problem by decreeing that what we were writing *was* serious.

(Dick, 1991, p. 152 note from 1978[1])

Philip K. Dick, organization studies and me

I have to admit I have some slight misgivings about writing an 'academic' chapter on Philip K. Dick. Not that I am the first to do so. In the twenty years or so since his death, Philip K. Dick has attracted a small army of interpreters. He has been seen as a prophet of hyperreality and as a gnostic visionary of the suburbs (Starr, 1993). In discussions on the internet he is often referred to as the 'Godfather of Cyberpunk'. Certainly, Dick created a body of fiction that brings to life the indeterminacy between originals and simulacra that is the hallmark of virtual reality – both as metaphor and as technology – of post-industrial society (Sutin, 1995). Dick's landscapes tend to be highly commercialized spaces in which the boundaries between autonomous individual and technological artefact have become increasingly permeable (Hayles, 1999). But more of this later. My misgivings have to do with the fact that Dick, a writer who spent most of his life working within the tight confines of the pulp markets, felt animosity toward 'mainstream' academicians who sought to adopt SF, as it were, and make it respectable or important (notwithstanding the fact that, at the same time, the lack of mainstream attention for his work was a source of pain for him). The following extract of an unpublished book review captures this animosity:

> If SF becomes annexed to the academic world it will buy into its own death . . . Professor Warrick's pound-and-a-half book with its expensive binding, paper, and dust jacket staggers you with its physical impression, but it has no soul and it will take our soul in what really seems to me to be brutal greed. Let us alone, Dr. Warrick; let us read our paperback novels with their peeled eyeball covers. Don't dignify us. Our power to stimulate human imagination and to delight is intrinsic to us already. Quite frankly, we were doing fine before you came along.
>
> (Dick, 1980/1995, pp. 97–8)

So why write this article? A healthy (?) obsession with Dick's œuvre I suppose, coupled with the comforting realization that Dick contradicted himself so many times in his lifetime. But to truly answer this question I have to tell the brief story of Philip K. Dick, organization studies and me.

My introduction to the world of Philip K. Dick began in 1985 when I was given two Dick books – *Ubik* and *Flow My Tears, the Policeman Said* – as a birthday present. The girl in question was from Metz, a very Dickean connection as I found out later,[2] the books were written in French and published in flashy golden covers (as far as you can get from the peeled eyeball covers as possible). I remember reading them (my French was a lot better then than it is now), being pretty impressed with *Ubik* especially, and then filing the books away in my SF collection. Fast forward to 1992. This is the year I started my Ph.D. studies. I came across the *Rethinking Organization* book by Reed and Hughes, and to my surprise two of my favourite chapters briefly referenced this SF author I vaguely remembered reading a few years earlier (Burrell, 1992, p. 177; Turner, 1992, p. 56). I then bought one of Dick's short story collections (perhaps in the hope of using it for my Ph.D. studies – I wisely didn't). And suddenly I was addicted. The next couple of years I tried to collect as many Dick books as possible, including the English editions of my birthday books. A moment I recall with particular fondness is finding a perfect copy of *Now Wait for Last Year* in a car boot sale for 10p. This sudden obsession was not uncommon as I discovered later:

> In my role as editor of the Philip K. Dick Society Newsletter, I frequently get letters from people who just a few months ago discovered Dick's work and have now read fifteen books and must obtain all the others. He tends to be read as he wrote: in large doses.
>
> (Williams, 1986, p. 142)

Then came the call for papers, first for the special SF issue of *Organization* in 1997, later for this book. This got me reading Dick's collected philosophical writings and his *Exegesis*, as well as some literary criticism of Dick's work. So, you see, the link between organization studies and Philip K. Dick is self-evident to me. Of course, this still does not provide an answer to the question: 'How to write something meaningful?'

An academic book presupposes a particular style that does not necessarily do justice to the work of Dick (although Dick himself has written some pretty high-brow stuff). After some pondering I decided upon the following strategy. After introducing the problematic from the perspective of organization studies – the growing awareness of the tenuous nature of organizational reality and the difficulty we have in constructing texts that deal with this tenuous reality in a reflexive way – I explore the key characteristics of Dick's novels and the essence of his writing techniques. This is followed by a discussion of *Ubik* to give the reader a flavour of a typical Dickean novel. I conclude with the logical, but rather too predictable, discussion of the importance of Dick for the field of organization studies. Of course, it would be nonsensical to suggest that we can 'apply' Dick in the way it has happened with Foucault, Derrida or Elias, but to name a few. Yet there is something curiously attractive about an author who used the most trashy tropes of a genre (SF) to create a body of work that both transcends and invigorates that genre. Could this point to an analogue in organization theory that might enable us to frame new possibilities of writing or reading organizational narratives? Perhaps.

Modes of organizing, modes of theorizing and this thing called reality

'As Marx might have said more generally, 'all that is built or all that is "natural" melts into image' in the contemporary global economies of signs and space' (Lash and Urry, 1994, p. 326).

The opinion seems to be broadly shared among both academics and practitioners that traditional conceptions of effective organizing and decision-making are no longer viable because we live in a time of irredeemable turbulence and ambiguity (Gergen, 1995). The emerging digital or 'new' economy seems to be a technologically driven vision of new forms of organizing, relying heavily on notions of flexibility as a response this turbulence. Corporate dinosaurs must be replaced with smart networks that add value. Words such as 'cyberspace'[3] and 'cyborganization' drip easily from tongues (e.g. Parker and Cooper, 1998) and 'the organization' becomes more difficult to conceptualize as it 'dissipates into cyberspace' and 'permeates its own boundaries' (Hardy and Clegg 1997: S6). Organizations are losing important elements of permanence as two central features of the modern organization, namely the assumption of self-contained units and its structural solidity, are undermined (March, 1995). Even the concept of place becomes increasingly phantasmagoric as locales get thoroughly penetrated by social influences quite distant from them (Giddens, 1990).

In this new organizational world 'reality' seems to have become only a contract, the fabrication of a consensus that can be modified or can break down at any time

(Kallinikos, 1997) and the witnessing point – the natural datum or physical reference point – seems to be in danger of being scrapped (Brown, 1997). This notion that reality is dissolving from the inside cannot but be related with feelings of disorientation and anxiety. Casey (1995, pp. 70–1), for example, provides a vivid description of the position of 'the self' within these new organizational realities. This is a world where everyone has lost a sense of everyday competence and is dependent upon experts, where people become dependent on corporate bureaucracy and mass culture to know what to do. The solidity (or absence of it) of reality has of course been debated at great length in the fields of philosophy and social theory, but it remains an interesting fact that organizational scholars have become preoccupied with this issue in recent years. Hassard and Holliday (1998), for example, talk about the theoretical imperative to explore the linkages between fact/fiction and illusion/reality. It is as if some fundamental metaphysical questions have finally descended into the metaphorical organizational street.

Over the past decade or so, many academics who label themselves critical management theorists and/or postmodernists (for once, let's not name any names) have taken issue with traditional modes of organizing (and ways of theorizing about this organizing) by highlighting many irrationalities and hidden power issues. These academics have taken on board the idea that language has a role in the constitution of reality and their work is marked by a questioning of the nature of reality, of our conception of knowledge, cognition, perception and observation (e.g. Chia, 1996a; Cooper and Law, 1995; Czarniawska, 1997). Notwithstanding the importance of their contributions, these authors face the problem that in order to condemn a mode of organizing or theorizing they need to occupy an elevated position, a sort of God's eye view of the world; a position which they persuasively challenge when they deconstruct the claims of orthodox/modern organizational analyses (Parker, 2000; Weiskopf and Willmott, 1997). Chia, for example, writes about the radically untidy, ill-adjusted character of the fields of actual experience – 'It is only by . . . giving ourselves over to the powers of "chaos", ambiguity, and confusion that new and deeper insights and understanding can be attained' (Chia, 1996b, p. 423) – using arguments which could not be more tidy, analytical and precise. This of course raises the issue of reflexivity: if reality can never be stabilized and the research/theorizing process 'is always necessarily precarious, incomplete and fragmented' (Chia, 1996a, p. 54), then Chia's writing clearly sits rather uncomfortably with his ontological and epistemological beliefs. In this he is, of course, not alone (see, e.g., Gephart *et al..*, 1996; Cooper and Law, 1995).

This schizophrenia is evidence of rather peculiar discursive rules where certain ontological and epistemological statements are allowed and even encouraged, but the reciprocate communicational practices are disallowed. Even the people who are most adventurous in their ideas or statements (such as Chia) are still caught within rather confined communicational practices. To use Vickers' (1995) terminology: there is a disjunction between the ways in which organization theorists are ready to see and value the organizational world (their appreciative setting) and the ways in which they are ready to respond to it (their instrumental system). When we write about reflexivity, paradox and postmodernism in organizational analysis, it is expected that we do this unambiguously.[4] And yet, the notion that 'if not consistency, then chaos' is not admitted even by all logicians, and is rejected by many at the frontiers of natural science research – 'a contradiction causes only some hell to break loose' (McCloskey, 1994, p. 166).

Coming to grips with Philip K. Dick's shifting realities

> I am a fictionalizing philosopher, not a novelist; my novel & story-writing ability is employed as a means to formulate my perception. . . . I think I understand the common ingredient in those whom my writing helps: they cannot or will not blunt their own intimations about the irrational, mysterious nature of reality, &, for them, my corpus of writing is one long ratiocination regarding this inexplicable reality, an investigation & presentation, analysis & response and personal history.
>
> (Dick 1991, p. 161, note from 1978)

> There is no worse mistake than taking the real for the real . . .
>
> (Baudrillard, 1994, p. 61)

The increasing awareness of the tenuous nature of (organizational) reality and the difficulty organizational scholars experience in constructing texts that deal with this tenuous reality in a reflexive way creates a space to reflect on the work of Philip K. Dick. Dick fully accepts that the late modern condition attendant on the ever-expanding proliferation of realities cannot be undone or overcome (i.e. going back to one reality which replaces values with facts) but has to be faced, tolerated and worked through. In book after book, Dick portrays an elemental estrangement of reality. Dickian characters find themselves trapped in hallucinations or fake worlds of various kinds, often without knowing it or, if knowing it, without being able to do anything about it. And it is not only worlds that are fake. Objects, animals, people may also be unreal in various ways (Aldiss, 1979). There can be no longer any talk of returning to nature or of turning away from the 'artificial', since the fusion of the natural with the artificial has long since become an accomplished fact (Lem, 1984). As Dick himself suggested in a reflective essay:

> What we are seeing is a gradual merging of the general nature of human activity and function into the activity and function of what we humans have built and surrounded ourselves with. . . . As the external world becomes more animate, we may find that we – the so-called humans – are becoming, and may to a great extent always have been, inanimate in the sense that *we* are led, directed by built-in tropisms, rather than leading.
>
> (Dick, 1972/1995, pp. 183–7)

Up to the late 1950s Dick could be characterized as a writer of mainly antiutopian SF. From then onwards he developed a penchant for plots that emphasized metaphysical speculations without providing any moral or onto-logical solutions (Sutin, 1995). Not surprisingly, he was initially considered some-thing of an odd figure by the SF community (Sutin, 1991). The convention of SF in the 1950s and 1960s required rational accounting for events that were quite improbable and even seemingly at odds with logic and experience. Thus, although SF stories depicted an imaginary reality, their authors were often at pains to create characters who embodied familiar values, outlooks and manner-isms. For example, John W. Campbell's magazine *Astounding Stories* insisted that writers postulate one outlandish circumstance – the 'what if?' clause – and rigor-ously follow the laws of science from there (Starr, 1993). Authors such as Asimov, Heinlein and Bradbury, remained faithful to these requirements of scientific accuracy and plausible prophecy. Not so Dick.

What Dick offers is not so much the future foreseen, as future shock, a projec-tion of the fears and fascinations proper to the human individual in our times. The plots of most of his SF novels are moved from page to page by doubt and by the collapse of the characters' and author's assumptions as to what is going on, forcing new hypotheses and new plot developments. Dick's characters generally begin as naive realists, firmly convinced that their perceptions provide them with knowledge about what is actually present in the world around them. But then they are usually thrown into an encounter where both external reality and their own identities are drastically questioned. As Dick forces his characters to confront these questions, he portrays the basic dilemma of our post-industrial society: we can no longer tell the illusory from the substantial; we no longer have an absolute basis for knowing what is real or what is human. For Dick, 'the clear line between hallucination and reality has itself become a kind of hallucination' (Warrick, 1983, p. 205). Dick's inability to experience the solidity of any one reality becomes fertile soil for the creation of endless alternate realities, each at last as convincing as the one that went before and each containing some primal error, something 'out of joint', and the location of that error can never be decided upon. Everything may be dissolved, invaded and subtly infiltrated or discovered to be a fabrication. In stories like 'Breakfast at Twilight' and 'The Hanging Stranger', what is truly chilling is not that the ordinary human person and environment can be manipulated into inhumanity or into naturalizing evil conditions as normal, but that the ordinary human person and environment is not substantially 'there' to be manipulated (Palmer, 1995).

Any analytic discussion of Dick's work makes it sound to be grim and unappealing. On the surface, it may be; yet it must also be said that Dick is often amazingly funny. As his characters confront exasperating hallucinations and inter-secting time-sequences, they respond with a typical blend of desperate specula-tion, cautious empathy and brittle humour (Starr, 1993). The terror and the humour are fused. It is in this rare quality that Dick's work resembles Kafka's, producing a 'Ghastly Comedy of bafflement' (Aldiss, 1979, p. 58).

On Dick's writing techniques: the writing that cannot be written

> And this is how it is: if only you do not try to utter what is unutterable then *nothing* gets lost. But the unutterable will be – unutterably – *contained* in what has been uttered!
>
> (Wittgenstein[5])

> All languages of heteroglossia, whatever the principle underlying them and making each unique, are specific points of view on the world, forms for conceptualising the world in words, specific world views, each characterised by its own objects, meanings and values. As such they all may be juxtaposed to one another, mutually supplement one another, contradict one another and co-exist in the consciousness of real people. . . . They may all be drawn in by the novelist for the orchestration of his themes and for the refracted (indirect) expression of his intentions and values.
>
> (Bakhtin, 1981, p. 292)

> I certainly see the randomness in my work, & I also see how this fast shuffle of possibility after possibility might eventually, given enough time, juxtapose & disclose something important, automatically overlooked in more orderly thinking . . . . Since nothing, absolutely nothing, is excluded (as not worth being included) I proffer a vast mixed bag – out of it I shake coin operated doors & God. It's a fucking circus. I'm like a sharp eyed crow, spying anything that twinkles & grabbing it up to add to my heap.
>
> (Dick, 1991, p. 147, note from 1978)

The way Dick expresses his philosophical ideas is unusual, to say the least. His maddeningly profuse plots make a mockery of traditional criteria of 'good' writing. The plots may limp or soar, but they seldom hang together. To keep all the loose ends tied up would violate verisimilitude in the service of consistency, for the Dickian universe has ambiguity and indeterminacy at its core. Put simply, Dick writes about an untidy world in an untidy way, thus sacrificing consistency at the immediate level of plot developments or even a single novel, for meta-consistency when we come to consider his œuvre in its totality. This provides an interesting way of 'working through' the reflexivity struggle in organizational analysis, without necessarily pointing to any clear solutions. Dick effortlessly incorporates in his stories the values of pluralism and fragmentation and an ironic admission of the ephemerality of things, values which attracted many organizational scholars to postmodernism (Kilduff and Mehra, 1997).

Dick's narrative polyphony approximates the heteroglossia Bakhtin (1981) had in mind. Dick's novels are not exclusively human centred. They include other beings, other aspects of being. They may deal with relationships between people but may also explore the relationship between a person and something else: an android, a machine, a society. In Dick's fictions a creature that resembles a pudding or an insect may qualify as human even when something that looks, walks and talks like a man does not. But the acknowledgement of 'The Other' goes even further than that. A novel by Dick is not bound – and often is not – to be understood, because of its peculiar maximum span of meanings and because Dick never ridicules trash. In a Dickian universe, there are many realities, most of them equally valid, but none of them an overview of the whole. At any given moment, a character may gather the focus of attention around her; but the immediate reality is apt to dissolve into an equally valid alternate reality in which she/he/it has no significance whatsoever. A pluralous sense of meaning emerges as characters exchange views and interactively direct the storyline. This allows the reader to empathize with all the focal characters, be they villains or heroes, for Dick has no black and white villains and heroes. In Dick's collective, non-individualist world everybody, high and low, destroyer and sufferer, is in an existential situation which largely determines his/her actions; even the arch-destroyer Palmer Eldritch is a sufferer (Suvin, 1983).

Perhaps no better visual images catch the essence of a Dickian narrative structure than Chinese calligraphy, where a configuration of curved and straight lines forms a network. All parts are connected to all other parts, but not directly. By linear threads or veins, one can zigzag a way through the plot, but one is not given the hub of a central narrative view (Warrick, 1983). This is not to say that Dick's writing is 'clever' in the traditional technical sense. His novels are easy to read and sometimes verge on the clumsy. As Disch (1983, p. 14) sympathetically commented: '[Dick is] capable of whole chapters of turgid prose and of bloopers so grandiose you may wonder, momentarily, whether they're not just his little way of winking at his fellow laborers in the pulps.'

Dick employs glaring clichés of trash (e.g. the usual SF props of precognition, time travel, androids . . .) to tackle exceedingly complex philosophical problems. This trashy surface allows his novels to survive in different ways in the reader's environment, either semiotically (awareness of the resurrection of metaphysical values) or semantically (very entertaining, if a bit disjointed) understood. Thus the novels contain some sort of double encoding which Lem (1984, pp. 85–6) explained as follows:

> If many coloured flags are put upon the masts of a ship in the harbour, a child on the shore will think that this is a merry game and perhaps will have a lot of fun watching, although at the same time an adult will recognize the flags as a language of signals, and know that it stands for a report on a plague that has broken out on board the ship.

Of course this makes judgement work very difficult. What constitutes a good Dickean story? Dick, even by his own admission,[6] certainly produced a lot of very mediocre stories and novels, but in his best novels (e.g. *Ubik, Martian Time Slip, The Three Stigmata of Palmer Eldritch*) he creates something very special indeed. To quote Lem (1984, p. 74) again:

> Dick has invented an extremely refined tactic: he uses elements of trash . . . so

that he leads to a gradual resurrection of the long-extinct, metaphysical-exotic values. In a way he makes trash battle against trash . . . Dick succeeds in changing a circus tent into a temple, and during this process the reader may experience catharsis. It is extremely difficult to grasp analytically the means that make it possible for him to do so.

What is inconsistency in literature after all? It is a symptom either of incompetence or else of repudiation of some values (such as credibility of incidents or their logical coherence) for the sake of other values. There is no universally valid answer to the question whether it is permissible to sacrifice order for the sake of vision in a creative work, everything depends on what kind of order and what kind of vision are involved. Disorienting as Dick's narrative technique may be, it is essential if his project of imperfection is to be credible. His images are opposed to all that is finished and polished and are ultimately expendable in his impossible quest for 'the writing that cannot be written':

> The greatest incentive to write is that you can't figure out the universe. And you keep trying to do it by writing about it. You can coerce it into making sense by writing a book that makes sense, but what happens is, your books don't make any sense either.
>
> (Interview with Dick, in Williams, 1986, p. 98)

This impossible contradiction of 'the writing that cannot be written' forces a recognition of challenge, subversion because standard language or interpretative tools or intellectual categories are being jammed by the dissonance – the subaltern voice – in the work itself (cf. Bernard-Donals, 1998, on Bakhtin's work). The impossibility of imposing consistency on the text compels us to seek its global meanings not in the realm of events themselves, but in that of their constructive principle, the very thing that is responsible for lack of focus. For Dick there is a mysterious chaotic quality in the universe which is not to be feared. His best novels embody this inexplicable quality and thus defy analysis (Bishop, 1983).

> Ultimately, one intuits rather than analyzes Dick's meaning. The totality of his complex fictional gestalt cannot be grasped by a mere part-by-part discussion. We must temper our analysis with a more or less intuitive groping if we are to find our way to the power and insight of the fiction.
>
> (Warrick, 1983, p. 196)

One of the attractions of Dick's novels – and the most probable reason for my collection fever – is that they all have points at which they interrelate. The consensus among critics (Aldiss, 1979; Bishop, 1983; Warrick, 1983; Lem, 1984) seems to be that his books overlap and have a cumulative impact that is very different from what can be found and pointed to in any individual Dick novel. But that is quite enough analysis; time for the promised introduction to *Ubik*.

Ubik

Since *Ubik* was the first of Dick's books I ever read, it is only appropriate that I use this novel to give the reader a flavour of Dick's shifting realities. Dick offers us here some kind of a Pirandelloesque ontology, where characters search not only for their author but also for their world. Like so many of Dick's novels, *Ubik* centres on the 'reality problem'. Information spontaneously intrudes into the world of the characters, indicating that their world is not what they think it is; in fact, it indicates that their world is not even there at all – some kind of world is there, but not the one they are experiencing. The characters never stop trying to make sense of a reality that grows progressively harder to grasp, but their efforts are always doomed to failure. Hollis lures Runciter, Joe Chip and a staff of inertials (gifted psychics who can neutralize the psychic talents of others) to a death trap on Luna, and the resultant explosion casts them into a radically trans-formed reality that may or may not be controlled by Pat Conley or Runciter or Hollis or someone or something else. It's never quite clear who survived (if any-one) and who lies hallucinating in cold pac. The characters engage in a battle not only for their lives, but also to save the basic categories of existence as they are trying to make headway through a world that is becoming ever more primitive.[7] Every time they/we think they/we can make some sense of the situation, the plot takes a turn that leaves them/us utterly bewildered. Needless to say that neither the characters nor the readers are able to discover any final, comprehensive meaning.

The world of *Ubik* is thoroughly saturated by commodities that foreground their status as quasi-living signifiers. Not only do doors threaten to sue and coffee pots demand money for services rendered; telephone and TV sets occasionally adopt a will of their own and, much to human characters' confusion, transmit their messages in a way only very dubiously related to any human agency. A crass materialism has supplanted spiritual resilience as our chief 'reality support' and Ubik seems to signify all manner of capitalist predation. An epigraph in the form of an advertising jingle opens each chapter. These commercials which have noth-ing to do with the narrative sell Ubik as the best beer, the best instant coffee, etc. Ubik first appears in the narrative when Joe Chip finds himself watching a televi-sion commercial and listening to a 'hard eyed housewife' extolling its virtues: 'I came over to Ubik after trying weak, out of date reality supports.' The meaning of Ubik is mysteriously changed when in the final epigraph we find the following proclamation, creating a strange juxtaposition of religion with capitalist con-sumerism, 'I am the word and my name is never spoken, the name which no one knows. I am called Ubik, but that is not my name. I am. I shall always be.'

The novel provides no clues as to why Ubik changes from signifying the worst excesses of capitalism to standing for a ubiquitous God. The final reference to Ubik in the narrative is an ironic comment on divine intervention: after the attractive young woman, who has materialized from the future to bring Joe Chip a spray can of Ubik, disappears, leaving him in the middle of trying to invite her to dinner, he discovers a message on the can: 'I THINK HER NAME IS MYRA

LANGLEY. LOOK ON REVERSE OF SIDE OF CONTAINER FOR ADDRESS AND PHONE NUMBER.'

Dick and the discursive universe of organization studies

> It is precisely the fleeting, relationally responsive events that our current referential-representational forms of rationality render invisible to us, and exclude from both rational discussion and attention. It is the urge towards both mastery and control implicit in all our current methodologies that leads us to banish particularised perceptions by ordering them into comprehensible and meaningful regularities.
>
> (Shotter and Billig, 1998, p. 27)

> I felt that the universe was so constructed that I could never really naturally follow the directions on anything and arrive easily and without effort at the right end. I think this is a learning thing, that the instructions that are easy for normal children are difficult for some children; they perceive a little differently, so that the ordinary instructions like 'color all the ducks yellow' somehow confuses some children for some perceptual reason.
>
> (Interview with Dick, in Williams, 1986, p. 156)

Up until a few years ago it would have been hard to imagine what role Dick's work could have played in the area of organization studies. However, recent developments, such as the turn towards the humanities (Zald, 1996), the popularization of postmodern discourse (Boje *et al..*, 1996; Kilduff and Mehra, 1997) and the interest in narrative fiction (Easton and Araujo, 1997; Phillips, 1995), make Dick's work meaningful or at least plausible within an organizational context, although it certainly maintains a defamiliarization value. Now that we are encouraged to view organizing as an 'active and dynamic process of identity-construction and reality-configuration and, therefore, an ontological activity' (Chia, 1997, p. 699), Dick's preoccupations with the 'reality problem' have acquired a new relevance and urgency and may help us come to terms with the chimerical components of our existence. At the very least, an appreciation of Dick's work may open up new arenas of intertextuality, pointing to new ways of seeing organizational processes and talking/writing about them.

Of course we will never be able to simply 'apply' Dick. His approach is the pure antithesis of the analytical framework. Do not turn to him for coherence or certainty. Dick sees any theoretical formulation that attempts to act as an all-encompassing, all-explaining hypothesis as a manifestation of paranoia (Easterbrook, 1995). We should be content with the mysterious, the meaningless, the contradictory. Emphasis in his stories is often on the gesture, the single action which may possibly be clever and moral enough for its insertion into the whole situation to, as it were, catch the whole situation off guard and make a difference (Dick, 1972/1995). But if this is a weakness, it is also a source of strength.

Notwithstanding the increasing ontological and epistemological sophistication in organization studies, the field still values simplification and systematization which translates in the demand for structured and precise explanations. Although it has become more accepted to perceive social reality 'not as natural, rational, and self-evident but as arbitrary, and exotic' (Alvesson, 1996, p. 111), acting upon that perception has remained as hard as ever. The field of organization studies is still haunted by formulae (see, e.g., Locke and Golden-Biddle, 1997; Golden-Biddle and Locke, 1993). There is much to be said for formulae. They fulfil expectations and make the whole academic performance easier for writer, reviewer, editor and reader (cf. Aldiss, 1979), but they also bring self-imposed limits to our areas of inquiry and perhaps, more importantly, in their emphasis on analytical clarity they function more as obscuring than revealing devices (Bourdieu, 1992; Burrell, 1996). As Clegg and Hardy (1996, p. 694) suggested, 'Analysis requires the death or at least the mutilation of that which is analysed. As researchers develop their understanding, they seem to become further removed from the subjects, less able to engage in conversation with them.'

Dick's writing may provide an antidote for the self-imposed and pre-established limits organizational scholars still suffer from. I indicated throughout this chapter that it is very difficult to grasp analytically what makes Dick's stories so compulsive to read or why he is considered to be 'one of the greatest experimental writers of our time' (Baudrillard, 1991, p. 312). Perhaps we should not even try. Only when texts are infinitely equivocal, forever supplementing their original message with noise supplied by the reader, do they remain saved from being consigned to obsolescence. I therefore very much like the description of the 'destructive drug-fuelled lunatic and 5-cents-a-word hack'[8] one of the editors suggested. It is this aspect of Dick that is in danger of getting lost in any 'academic' analysis of his work. Dick never set out to rewrite the rules of the SF genre – he remained faithful to its most trashy tropes – and yet he managed to create a body of work that scarcely fits within the genre. I am not sure what form an analogue in organization studies might take, but it would surely not be subject to the charge of 'self-referential intellectualism' critical management studies have suffered from (Fournier and Grey, 2000). Rather than taking the 'high road' of reifying managers as some kind of 'barbarian elite' (cf. Anthony, 1998), and denouncing modernist epistemologies while still applying (and demanding) rational and sequential argument, we might want to take the 'low road' of full engagement with the trashier tropes of our particular genre (as found, for example, in newspaper and magazine articles, and television programmes exploring/exploiting happenings in the organizational sphere). Could we use some of the glaring clichés typifying the discourses of 'e-business' and 'virtual organizations' to tackle fundamental organizational issues, turning the circus into a temple as it were? This might require a mix of 'investigation & presentation, analysis & response & personal history' (Dick 1991, p. 161, note from 1978). Perhaps we should break with the implicit rule of our field, the analogue of Campbell's 'what if?' clause, that we have to explain organizational phenomena all the time,[9] and foster instead the evocative ability which made Dick's utopias so startling and terrifying.[10] Thus, rather than try and *persuade* readers, we would try to *move* and *thrill* them. The difficulty in developing such approaches is illustrated by the fact that this chapter sticks pretty much to the tried-and-trusted academic formulae, although it does contain a small personal history. Ultimately, it is only fitting – dare I suggest Dickean – to provide no real conclusion and let Philip K. Dick provide the last reflection on Philip K. Dick.

> This little section appears ahead of the text of the novel [*The Three Stigmata of Palmer Eldritch*]. It *is* the novel actually. . . . Seventy-five thousand words, which I labored over many months . . . is merely there to provide background to the one small statement in the book that matters. . . . It goes as follows, and this is all I actually have to say or want ever to say:
>
> I mean, after all; you have to consider, we're only made of dust. That's admittedly not much to go on and we shouldn't forget that. But even considering, I mean it's a sort of bad beginning, we're not doing too bad. So I personally have faith that even in this lousy situation we're faced with we can make it. You get me?
>
> (Dick, 1972/1995, p. 206)

Notes

1 Throughout the text I will refer to the date of the original writing and then that of my particular edition.

2 Dick was a guest of honour at the September 1977 SF festival at Metz – probably one of the first times he received such massive recognition – and would have returned there in 1982 (Dick, unfortunately, died on 2 March, 1982).

3 'Cyberspace' was, of course, a concept first coined in a SF novel. In *Neuromancer* (1984), William Gibson produced a concept that was at once recognizable, and made possible the cognition of a whole new arena of the life world that had already been constructed unconsciously by an array of convergent information-processing technologies (Welchman, 1997).

4 Not that this is explicitly stated. Sometimes adventurous communicational practices are encouraged in editorial guidelines but then reviewers' comments come back: 'what are the key points you want to get across, present a clear argument, I like your idea but . . .' which forces us to repudiate certain values such as paradox, ambiguity, inconsistency. Thinking of our careers of course we comply. And yet, it has been suggested (in a very unambiguous way of course) that if language attempts to be too precise, then meaningful statements about organizational functioning appear unlikely; insightful models will tend to be somewhat ambiguous, vague and imprecise (Astley and Zammuto, 1992; Davis, 1986).

5 From a letter to Engelmann written in 1917 and reproduced in Monk's (1990, p. 151) biography.

6 'In 1953 I started writing the worst trashy stuff you ever read, and none of that stuff is in print. In 1953 I sold twenty-seven stories, and twenty-six of the twenty-seven were rotten, worthless pieces of fiction' (an interview quote from 'The Mainstream that Through the Ghetto Flows: An Interview with Philip K. Dick', http://www.missouri.edu/~moreview/interviews/dick.htm).

7 For example, Joe Chip's multiplex FM tuner regresses into a cylinder phonograph

playing a shouted recitation of the Lord's prayer. The regression of forms is a theme used by Dick to great effect in several other novels (e.g., in *Counter-Clock World*).

8 In the early 1960s Dick popped amphetamines like crazy and channelled the released energy into an astonishingly large creative output (during 1963–4 he wrote ten novels in just under two years, many of which are now acknowledged classics).

9 This suggestion is far from revolutionary. Hunter (1985: viii) describes in some detail how Wittgenstein seemed to make some point of avoiding explaining what he wished to say:

> He prescribed work programmes, but did not explain how to carry them out, or in what way he thought their results would be relevant; he asked questions but did not answer them; posed questions he thought ought not be asked, without saying so until much later, and then only indirectly; asked apparently rhetorical questions when it turned out he thought they called for careful answering.

Latour (1988) suggests that 'The ideal of an explanation is not to be reached, not only because it is unreachable, but because it is not a desirable goal anyway' (p. 164). Providing an explanation is working at empire-building.

10 Srinivas (1999) reminds us of one of Dick's characters in *The Man in the High Castle* who notes 'the power of fiction, even cheap popular fiction to evoke' (p. 125). Reflecting on that novel, Dick (1977/1995) later expressed his disinterest in explanation: 'When he [Mr. Tagomi] looked up, he was in another universe. I didn't explain how or why this happened because I don't know, and I would defy anyone, writer, reader, or critic, to give a so-called "explanation"' (Dick, 1977/1995, p. 237).

References

Aldiss, B. W. (1979). *This World and Nearer Ones: Essays Exploring the Familiar*. London: Weidenfeld & Nicolson.

Alvesson, M. (1996). 'Developing Programmatic Research'. In P. J. Frost and M. S. Taylor (eds), *Rhythms of Academic Life: Personal Accounts of Careers in Academia* (pp. 107–17). Thousand Oaks: Sage.

Anthony, P. (1998). 'Management Education: Ethics versus Morality'. In M. Parker (ed.), *Ethics & Organizations* (pp. 269–81). London: Sage.

Astley, W. G. and Zammuto, R. F. (1992). 'Organization Science, Managers, and Language Games'. *Organization Science*, 3(4), 443–60.

Bakhtin, M. (1981). *The Dialogic Imagination: Four Essays by M. M. Bakhtin*. Austin: University of Texas Press.

Baudrillard, J. (1991). 'Simulacra and Science Fiction'. *Science-Fiction Studies*, 18, 309–13.

Baudrillard, J. (1994). *The Illusion of the End*. Cambridge: Polity.

Bernard-Donals, M. (1998). 'Knowing the Subaltern: Bahktin, Carnival, and the Other Voice of the Human Sciences' (pp. 112–27). London: Sage.

Bishop, M. (1983). 'In Pursuit of "Ubik"'. In M. H. Greenberg and J. D. Olander (eds), *Philip K. Dick: Criticism and Interpretation* (pp. 137–47). New York: Taplinger.

Boje, D. M., Fitzgibbons, D. E. and Steingard, D. S. (1996). 'Storytelling at Administrative Science Quarterly: Warding off the Postmodern Barbarians'. In D. M. Boje, R. P. Gephart Jr and T. J. Thatchenkery (eds), *Postmodern Management and Organization Theory* (pp. 60–92). Thousand Oaks: Sage.

Bourdieu, P. (1992). 'Thinking About Limits'. *Theory, Culture & Society*, 9, 37–49.

Brown, D. (1997). *Cybertrends: Chaos, Power and Accountability in the Information Age*. London: Viking.

Burrell, G. (1992). 'Back to the Future: Time and Organization'. In M. Reed and M. Hughes (eds), *Rethinking Organization: New Directions in Organization Theory and Analysis* (pp. 165–83). Newbury Park/London: Sage.

Burrell, G. (1996). 'Normal Science, Paradigms, Metaphors, Discourses and Genealogies of Analysis'. In S. R. Clegg, C. Hardy and W. R. Nord (eds), *Handbook of Organization Studies* (pp. 642–58). London: Sage.

Casey, C. (1995). *Work, Self and Society After Industrialism*. London: Routledge.

Chia, R. (1996a). 'The Problem of Reflexivity in Organizational Research: Towards a Postmodern Science of Organization'. *Organization*, 3, 31–58.

Chia, R. (1996b). 'Teaching Paradigm Shifting in Management Education: University Business Schools and the Entrepreneurial Imagination'. *Journal of Management Studies*, 33, 409–28.

Chia, R. (1997). 'Thirty Years On: From Organizational Structures to the Organization of Thought'. *Organization Studies*, 18(4), 685–707.

Clegg, S.R. and Hardy, C. (1996). 'Conclusion: Representation'. In S.R. Clegg, C. Hardy and W.R. Nord (eds), *Handbook of Organization Studies*) pp. 676–708). London: Sage.

Cooper, R. and Law, J. (1995). 'Organization: Distal and Proximal Views'. *Research in the Sociology of Organizations*, 13, 237–74.

Czarniawska, Barbara (1997). *Narrating the Organization: Dramas of Institutional Identity*. Chicago: University of Chicago Press.

Davis, M. S. (1986). 'That's Classic! The Phenomenology and Rhetoric of Successful Social Theories'. *Philosophy of Social Science*, *16*, 309–44.

Dick, P. K. (1953/1990a). 'Breakfast at Twilight'. In *Second Variety*, Volume 2, *The Collected Stories of Philip K. Dick* (pp. 267–84). London: HarperCollins.

Dick, P. K. (1953/1990b). 'The Hanging Stranger'. In *The Father Thing*, Volume 3 *The Collected Stories of Philip K. Dick* (pp. 28–43). London: HarperCollins.

Dick, P. K. (1962/1992). *The Man in the High Castle*. New York: Vintage.

Dick, P. K. (1964/1990). *Martian Time Slip*. London: VGSF.

Dick, P. K. (1964/1991). *The Three Stigmata of Palmer Eldritch*. New York: Vintage.

Dick, P. K. (1966/1975). *Now Wait for Last Year*. St. Albans: Granada.

Dick, P. K. (1967/1990). *Counter-Clock World*. London: Grafton.

Dick, P. K. (1969/1991). *Ubik*. New York: Vintage.

Dick, P. K. (1972/1995). 'The Android and the Human'. In L. Sutin (ed.), *The Shifting Realities of Philip K. Dick: Selected Literary and Philosophical Writings* (pp. 183–210). New York: Vintage.

Dick, P. K. (1974/1996). *Flow my Tears, the Policeman Said*. London: Voyager.

Dick, P. K. (1976/1995). 'Man, Android, and Machine'. In L. Sutin (ed.), *The Shifting Realities of Philip K. Dick: Selected Literary and Philosophical Writings* (pp. 211–32). New York: Vintage.

Dick, P. K. (1977/1995). 'If You Find This World Bad, You Should See Some of the Others'. In L. Sutin (ed.), *The Shifting Realities of Philip K. Dick: Selected Literary and Philo-sophical Writings* (pp. 233–58). New York: Vintage.

Dick, P. K. (1980/1995). Book Review of *The Cybernetic Imagination in Science Fiction*. In L. Sutin (ed.), *The Shifting Realities of Philip K. Dick: Selected Literary and Philosophical Writings* (pp. 96–8). New York: Vintage.

Dick, P. K. (1981/1992). *Valis*. London: Grafton.

Dick, P. K. (1991). *In Pursuit of Valis: Selections From the Exegesis*. Novato, CA: Underwood-Miller.

Disch, T. M. (1983). 'Toward the Transcendent: An Introduction to "Solar Lottery" and

Other Works'. In M. H. Greenberg and J. D. Olander (eds), *Philip K. Dick: Criticism and Interpretation* (pp. 13–25). New York: Taplinger.

Easterbrook, N. (1995). 'Dianoia/Paranoia: Dick's Double "Impostor"'. In S. J. Umland (ed.), *Philip K. Dick: Contemporary Critical Interpretations* (pp. 19–41). Westport: Greenwood Press.

Easton, G. and Araujo, L. (1997). 'Management Research and Literary Criticism'. *British Journal of Management*, 8, 99–106.

Fournier, V. and Grey, C. (2000). 'At the Critical Moment: Conditions and Prospects for Critical Management Studies'. *Human Relations*, 53(1), 7–32.

Gephart Jr, R. P., Thatchenkery, T. J. and Boje, D. M. (1996). 'Conclusion: Restructuring Organizations for Future Survival'. In D. M. Boje, R. P. Gephart Jr and T. J. Thatchenkery (eds), *Postmodern Management and Organization Theory* (pp. 358–64). Thousand Oaks: Sage.

Gergen, K. J. (1995). 'Global Organization: From Imperialism to Ethical Vision'. *Organization*, 2, 519–32.

Gibson, W. (1984). *Neuromancer*. London: Victor Gollancz.

Giddens, A. (1990). *The Consequences of Modernity*. Cambridge: Polity.

Golden-Biddle, K. and Locke, K. (1993). 'Appealing Work: An Investigation of How Ethnographic Texts Convince'. *Organization Science*, 4(4), 595–616.

Hardy, C. and Clegg, S. (1997). 'Relativity Without Relativism: Reflexivity in Post-Paradigm Organization Studies'. *British Journal of Management*, 8, S5–S17.

Hassard, J. and Holliday, R. (1998). 'Introduction'. In J. Hassard and R. Holliday (eds), *Organization-Representation* (pp. 1–15). London: Sage.

Hayles, N. K. (1999). *How We Became Posthuman: Virtual Bodies in Cybernetics, Literature, and Informatics*. Chicago: University of Chicago Press.

Hunter, J. M. F. (1985). *Understanding Wittgenstein*. Edinburgh: Edinburgh University Press.

Kallinikos, J. (1997). 'Classic Review: Science, Knowledge and Society: The Postmodern Condition Revisted'. *Organization*, 4, 114–29.

Kilduff, M. and Mehra, A. (1997). 'Postmodernism and Organizational Research'. *Academy of Management Review*, 22, 453–81.

Lash, S. and Urry, J. (1994). *Economies of Signs and Space*. London: Sage.

Latour, B. (1988). 'The Politics of Explanation: An Alternative'. In S. Woolgar (ed.), *Knowledge and Reflexivity: New Frontiers in the Sociology of Knowledge* (pp. 155–76). London: Sage.

Le Guin, U. K. (1994). *A Fisherman of the Inland Sea*. New York: HarperCollins.

Lem, S. (1984). *Microworlds: Writings on Science Fiction and Fantasy*. London: Harcourt Brace Jovanovich.

Locke, K. and Golden-Biddle, K. (1997). 'Constructing Opportunities for Contribution: Structuring Intertextual Coherence and "Problematizing" in Organizational Studies'. *Academy of Management Journal*, 40, 1023–62.

McCloskey, D. N. (1994). *Knowledge and Persuasion in Economics*. Cambridge: Cambridge University Press.

March, J. G. (1995). 'The Future, Disposable Organizations and the Rigidities of Imagination'. *Organization*, 2, 427–40.

Monk, R. (1990). *Ludwig Wittgenstein: The Duty of Genius*. London: Vintage.

Palmer, C. (1995). 'Philip K. Dick and the Nuclear Family'. In S. J. Umland (ed.), *Philip K. Dick: Contemporary Critical Interpretations* (pp. 61–79). Westport: Greenwood Press.

Parker, M. (2000). *Organizational Culture and Identity*. London: Sage.

Parker, M. and Cooper, R. (1998). 'Cyborganization: Cinema as Nervous System'. In J. Hassard and R. Holliday (eds), *Organization-Representation* (pp. 201–28). London: Sage.

Phillips, N. (1995). 'Telling Organizational Tales: On the Role of Narrative Fiction in the Study of Organizations'. *Organization Studies*, 16(4), 625–49.

Shotter, S. and Billig, M. (1998). 'A Bakhtinian Psychology: From Out of the Heads of Individuals and into the Dialogues Between them'. In M. M. Bell and M. Gardiner (eds), *Bahktin and the Human Sciences* (pp. 13–29). London: Sage.

Srinivas, N. (1999). 'Managers as Androids: Reading Moral Agency in Philip Dick'. *Organization*, 6(4), 609–24.

Starr, A. (1993). 'The God in the Trash'. *The New Republic*, June (http://blake.oit.unc.edu/nr/articles/pkdick.htm).

Sutin, L. (1991). *Divine Invasions: A Life of Philip K. Dick*. New York: Carol Publishing.

Sutin, L. (1995). 'Introduction'. In L. Sutin (ed.), *The Shifting Realities of Philip K. Dick: Selected Literary and Philosophical Writings* (pp. ix–xxix). New York: Pantheon.

Suvin, D. (1983). 'Artifice as Refuge and World View: Philip K. Dick's Foci'. In M. H. Greenberg and J. D. Olander (eds), *Philip K. Dick: Criticism and Interpretation* (pp. 73–95). New York: Taplinger.

Turner, B. A. (1992). 'The Symbolic Understanding of Organizations'. In M. Reed and M. Hughes (eds), *Rethinking Organization: New Directions in Organization Theory and Analysis* (pp. 46–66). Newbury Park/London: Sage.

Vickers, G. (1995). *The Art of Judgment: A Study of Policy Making*, London: Sage.

Warrick, P. S. (1983). 'The Labyrinthian Process of the Artificial: Philip K. Dick's Androids and Mechanical Constructs'. In M. H. Greenberg and J. D. Olander (eds), *Philip K. Dick: Criticism and Interpretation* (pp. 189–214). New York: Taplinger.

Weiskopf, R. and Willmott, H. (1997). 'Turning the Given into a Question: A Critical Discussion of Chia's Organizational Analysis as Deconstructive Practice'. *Electronic Journal of Radical Organization Theory*, 3(2), (http://www.mngt.waikato.ac.nz/ejrot).

Welchman, A. (1997). 'Funking up the Cyborgs'. *Theory, Culture & Society*, 14, 155–62.

Williams, P. (1986). *Only Apparently Real: The World of Philip K Dick*. New York: Arbor House.

Zald, M. N. (1996). 'More Fragmentation? Unfinished Business in Linking the Social Sciences and the Humanities'. *Administrative Science Quarterly*, 41, 251–61.

11 'I am a man, and nothing human is alien to me'

Alienation and freakishness

Warren Smith

Aliens and alienation

Alienation is perhaps the emblematic condition of the organized society. Industrialization forced physical, mental and spiritual dislocation; a process whereby identities, communities and work practices were relentlessly detached from the natural and metaphysical essentials that had long provided stability. This was man's (and of course it was male) work. The growing efficacy of his rational techniques gave him confidence in his capacity to impose his will upon those forces that were once seen as unchallengeable. Modernity was about making them yield.

The concerns of science fiction are frequently those of modernity. Much science fiction explores, and often critiques, the consequences of our techno-rational methods. In classics like *The Shape of Things to Come*, *Brave New World* and *Metropolis*, it has portrayed the dystopian consequences of our ambitions. Sometimes an alien figure acts as an embodiment of these conditions. Its appearance usually serves to symbolize humanity's problematic relationships with its various Others. It is a force, perhaps created by man, but which quickly runs out of control. Something once of man but which both rejects and is rejected by him.

Of course Mary Shelley's *Frankenstein*, one of a number of texts identified as the source of the science fiction genre, is an obvious example. Both Levine (1979) and Baldrick (1990) argue that *Frankenstein* provides a metaphor for industrial production. It suggests the production of something that moves out of control. Victor Frankenstein struggles not only in the act of creation, unable to contain the forces he tries to harness, but with the monster that he creates. He creates something alien, but is quickly alienated by it. This experience is as Marx warned, 'By acting on the external world and changing it, he at the same time changes his own nature' (1975: 173). Our labour becomes, 'an object, an external existence, but that it exists outside him, independently of him and alien, and begins to confront him as an autonomous power, that the life which has bestowed on the object confronts him as hostile and alien' (Marx, 1975: 132).

Karel Capek's creation of the *Robot* in his play *R.U.R.* serves to make this point explicitly. From '*robota*' meaning compulsory labour, and '*robotnik*' meaning workman, Capek's *robots* are chemically produced synthetic beings whose emotions are seen to inhibit their role as tools of production. In a satire of scientific manage-ment, the robots rebel and destroy their human managers, sparing only the con-struction manager who works with his hands. Capek seeks to highlight what he sees as under threat in industrialized society, 'at the moment the robots launch their attack, that something immeasurably great and priceless is at stake: that is, humanity-man-we-ourselves' (Capek quoted in Hawkins-Dady, 1992: 696).

But alienation is not simply a condition of industrialized production. So much of humanity's development is tied up with the process of alienation. The essence of alienation, as Schacht (1970) points out, is the signification of distance or separation, between two or more objects. This began with the fall from paradise. Our separation from God compelled us to the existential anxieties of a mortal existence. In this sense alienation is man's chronic mortal state, his eternal condi-tion. Once man was split from the divine, alienation spread; we were separated from God, separated from our traditions, divided, accounted for and controlled. This process became central to modernity as it steadily demarcated new frontiers (Bauman, 1987, 1991).

Demarcation inevitably involved exclusion. But for the enlightened few, who could still sense, or perhaps construct, a golden past, this was something to be transcended. These were, to use Johnson's (1973) phrase, 'mediating elites'. For them, alienation implied awareness of various ontological questions, most fun-damentally the 'nature of man'. This is the sense of what it is that we are alien-ated from. This provided a sense to alien experiences that were otherwise sense-less, to reacquaint the struggling, alienated mass with a distant past (and future) where forgotten meanings might be reclaimed. These mediating elites have taken many different forms. But over time as they have multiplied, it has become harder, even for them, to remember what it was that had been lost. The dissolution of the boundaries of identity is emblematic of postmodernity. This sees the loss of the ontological essentials that made alienation meaningful. For example, one prime alienating force, technology, is no longer as it was under industrial production. Rather than act on the body, it infuses and absorbs it. For Baudrillard (1988: 14) this means that it lacks the constitutive conditions of alienation. In the relation-ship between workers and traditional machines, there is no ambiguity whatsoever. He notes that

> The worker is always estranged from the machine, and is therefore alienated by it. He keeps the precious quality of alienated man to himself whilst new technology, new machines, new images, interactive screens, do not alienate me at all. With me they form an integrated circuit.

Hence, 'the secret of the interface is that the Other is within it virtually the Same – otherness being surreptitiously confiscated by the machine' (pp. 5–6).

In science fiction, the technologized confusion of identities has been frequently associated with the cyborg (see for instance Land and Corbett, this volume). Assisted by Donna Haraway's (1991) social scientific version, the fluidity of the cyborg body denies the possibility of a ready differentiation between self and

other. Instead the cyborg recognizes the complicated process of identity formation, thereby deconstructing traditional entities, 'The constant exchange of
organic and synthetic body parts can produce rewritings of the body's social and
cultural form that are directly related to the reconstitution of social identities'
(Tomas, 1995: 114–15). Rather multiple formations are possible; a return to some
'original' state is no longer possible, nor desired. In allowing a disembodied future,
cyborgs resist a utopian, unifying, 'original' figure (Squires, 1996: 207). For Haraway (1991) it is a creature of a postgender world, unable to be seduced into
believing that difference can be appropriated to fulfil a higher unity. Instead it
embraces only the idea of partial identities, encouraging the construction of
partial connections with others.

And yet in much science fiction the cyborg remains defined by its boundaries.
Whilst the cyborg superficially captures the Baudrillardean technological death of
human subjectivity, in practice it usually provides a figure searching for its half-
remembered humanity. As both Telotte (1995: 22) and Land and Corbett (this
volume) point out the trend in cyborg cinema is toward rendering the artificial as
ever more human. Though the boundary between humans and machine is initially weakened, it is often reasserted. Cyborgs are seen to dwell on what it means
to be human; eventually it is human consciousness that is redemptive. The human
will remains present in the cyborg, and is instrumental in prompting it to break
free from its programming (Holland, 1995: 160). Hence Robocop breaks free
from OCP to reclaim his identity as Murphy. Sometimes the simple vulnerability
of flesh leads to salvation. Roy Batty, the leader of the renegade replicants in *Blade
Runner* (1982), finally concedes the value of human life at the point of his own
death. Again in the *Robocop* series, the cyborg is considered truly 'human', and
therefore accorded appropriate respect by his fellow officers, only after he is
dismembered in the second film. Similarly in *Aliens* (1986), the android Bishop
receives Ripley's gratitude only after being decapitated.

When Halberstam and Livingston (1991: 13) ask, 'Does posthumanity prop
itself up against a human body or does it cannibalise the human?' they produce a
dichotomy that, like the cyborg, fails to capture what we experience as alienation.
Alienation is not a state of being, but a process. We know enough to feel separation, even perhaps to desire its difference, but not enough to control its effects. In
this respect, alienation is not therefore about separation, but the tensions involved
in making sense. Neither the cyborg, nor conventional alien invasion narratives
where the 'unknown' invades the 'known' are therefore persuasive symbols. Dery
(1999: 50–1) nicely employs the example of Munch's *Scream* to typify the 'intro-
verted, alienated psychology of modernism'. This is literalized in Munch's paint-
ing by the circular movement of the viewer's eye. This device makes the world
revolve around the screamer. His/her emotions affect everything we see, the hills,
the sky, the screamer's body. Dery (1999) compares this presentation with the
postmodern self. Now we are turned inside out. The self is thoroughly colonized
by the media reality spectacle emanating from what was once 'outside'. Instead of
the subjective experience colouring perception, the outside floods in 'drowning
out' our mental voices.

Whilst Dery's (1999) example is well drawn, it underplays the process of alienation and the sensations that come with it. It suggests that the alien overcomes us;
that we are colonized. Instead alienation is a process that moves through us whilst
we dimly trace its movement. Nevertheless there are alien bodies that produce
these tensions; aliens that unsettle and discomfort rather than invade. This is the
alien as influenced, or perhaps rather read-through, by a more traditional, even
pre-modern, concept, the freak.

The alien as freak

The exceptional body has a well-established place within society. However its
function has changed over time. Early civilizations saw the monstrous as an
expression of divine will which could be interpreted in one of three ways; as a sign
of God's wrath, as a reminder that each birth is as miraculous as the original
creation, or as an omen intended for good (Fiedler, 1978). Indeed the word *monster*
derives from the Latin *monstra* meaning to warn/show/sign, a root of the modern
verb *to demonstrate*. But as the power of the divine became less forceful and pervasive, the freak became indicative of nature's somewhat whimsical fecundity. In
both of these cases, the freakish body as divine will or nature's fancy, man's role
was simply to accept; to marvel, perhaps fearful, but the condition was as it was
meant to be. Regarding it as a somehow unintended departure from what should
be was clearly inappropriate. The attribution of intent, either divine or natural,
meant that these extraordinary outcomes could not be seen as abnormal. This
worked against a notion of normality from which we might feel alienated.

But the impulse of modernity is not acceptance. Whilst early science was some
way away from discovering the causes of the freakish body, let al.one proposing
intervention, it could at least begin to record and classify. This was *teratology*, the
science of classifying the monstrous form (see Bloomfield and Vurdubakis, 1999).
First formulated by the French zoologist Isidore Geoffroy Saint-Hilaire in 1832,
teratology demythologized the freak by recasting it as pathological. Teratology dis-
engaged the freak from divine intent or natural wonder. However the inability of
science to provide explanation, at least until the advent of genetics, meant that the
freak remained detached from any organized response. Science had started to
suggest that exceptional bodies were departures from normality. But it could not
say why. We could continue to stare but through different eyes; still fascinated, but
now convinced that these were pitiful mistakes. As Thomson (1996: 3) writes,

> the prodigious monster transforms into the pathological terata; what was
> once sought after as revelation becomes pursued as entertainment, what
> aroused awe now inspires horror; what was taken as a portent shifts to a site
> of progress. In brief, wonder becomes error.

The ongoing but uncompleted modernist project of the body created a space
between two traditions, the past narrative of respectful wonder and the developing narrative of scientific error. The lack of a coherent institutional treatment of

the exceptional body meant that cues for reaction and response were inevitably confused. Modernization was a disorientating experience. Mass production and scientific management prized sameness, whilst social dislocation separated families from traditional affiliations. The need to 'fit in' was increasingly predicated on physical appearance. This created both the conditions of alienation and heightened the sense of normality on which difference depended. This uncertainty meant that many reactions were both viable and permissible, pity, fear, wonder, disgust, even lust. This was the foundation of the freak show, 'redolent with the older authority of the prodigious, infused with the fitfulness of the fanciful, and susceptible to the certainties of scientific positivism, the singular body on exhibit was ripe for reading' (Thomson, 1996: 4). Yet the freak show could only exist in this transitional space. Gradually science assumed a more secure grip as the laws of genetics were applied to human traits and the discovery of the endocrine system was linked to growth and sex characteristics. The exceptional body became 'deviant' or 'sick', claimed by the medical profession and displayed by appointment only (Bogdan, 1988: 64). Outsiders were to give science their support, and its subjects their pity. The famous example of John Merrick, the Elephant Man, is a good example. 'Saved' from the exploitation of the increasingly disreputable freak show, he was claimed by the medical profession and given shelter, his gentle nature and good manners allowing him compassion. Simple gawping was not allowed. Access to Merrick was granted via the presentation of 'appropriate' motives.

When the social contexts supporting the freak show changed, the desire for such wonders explored other outlets. Science fiction was one such arena. Many of the characters in science fiction are, in essence, freaks. A good example is the super-hero. The super-hero is usually a troubled, marginal figure that battles with the exceptional qualities of their alien, naturally or artificially mutated bodies. As Bukatman (1994: 94) explains, the body of the super-hero,

> is enlarged and diminished, turned invisible or made of stone, blown to atoms or reshaped at will. The body defies gravity, space and time; it divides and conquers; it turns to fire, lives in water, and is lighter than air. The body takes on animal attributes; it merges with plant life and melds with metal. The body is asexual and homosexual, heterosexual and hermaphrodite. Even the mind becomes a body, telepathic, telekinetic, transplantable, and controllable.

This difference creates problems for both the super-hero's place in society and 'normal' society's treatment of him/her. Even heroic figures are perennial outsiders forced to protect or conceal their identity. Whilst serving for humanity's benefit they often suffer misrepresentation, misunderstanding and resentment. In the comic book and recent feature film, the *X-Men* constitute a new minority group. Created by a rogue chromosome, they are mutant humans with special powers. Faced with increasing bigotry and hostility from the 'normal' populace, the *X-Men* are recruited and trained by Professor Charles Xavier to fight bigotry and promote tolerance. In their efforts they are frustrated not only by a hostile government but a group of mutant supremacists, led by Magneto, who strive to subjugate the human race.

In fact, there has always been something science fictional about the freak. The exhibited spectacular body was often framed by hypothetical explanations of cause and effect. One of the ways in which the freak show extended its life as moral sensitivities changed was by couching its language, its style of presentation, in the language of science. The task of the showman was to intertwine unbeliev-able wonders with scientific accounts of veracity. Freak shows were therefore museums and the showman was a 'lecturer' often titled 'Professor' or 'Doctor'. But this methodology was not purely passive, a means of deflecting moral criti-cism. This mode of presentation heightened sensation. The skill was to accentu-ate the unresolved space in which the show thrived. In this respect, the freak show did not depend on authenticity, but the debate that surrounded authenticity. It is revealing that one of the most famous characters was called simply 'What is it?' This succinct 'come on' crystallizes perfectly our problematic engagement with these alienating figures. We have to work hard at assessing and managing our reactions.

In her essay 'The Imagination of Disaster', Susan Sontag (1971) discussed the nature of our engagement with the alien inhabitants of science fiction. This is, she argues, the,

> undeniable pleasure we derive from looking at freaks, beings excluded from the category of the human. The sense of superiority over the freak conjoined in varying proportions with the titillation of fear and aversion makes it pos-sible for moral scruples to be lifted for cruelty to be enjoyed. The same thing happens in science fiction films. In the figure of the monster from outer space, the freakish, the ugly, the predatory, all converge – and provide a fantasy target or righteous bellicosity to discharge itself, and for the aesthetic enjoyment of suffering and disaster.
>
> (Sontag, 1971: 316)

But this is both an undifferentiated and remarkably detached view of the alien as freak. Sontag speaks only of the monstrous 'Other', something that is so obvi-ously apart that it receives only our fearful scorn. Yet of course, as we have seen, the alien's role is played out in different ways, in different science fiction. The alien as 'monster' threatening humanity, deriving either from extraterrestrial ori-gins, artificially constructed or a perverted version of what is held to be natural is one version. In other cases, the alien, far from threatening humanity, serves to represent our essential values. In this science fiction, the alien is held apart from the human, but only to provide a nostalgic message about what has been lost. Good examples are films like *The Day the Earth Stood Still* (1951), *ET* (1982) and *Close Encounters of the Third Kind* (1977). More recently, science fiction questions whether there is any original model of humanness from which the alien can be distanced (or alternatively seen to represent). In a world where traditional signifiers have been lost, we are all aliens whether human or extraterrestrial. Distinctions drawn from such binaries as alien/human are increasingly troubled. This science fiction breaks down divisions such as male/female, real/imaginary, human/other, literal/metaphorical, factual/fictional, plausible/incredible (Sobchack, 1987). The replicating hallucination of *Videodrome* (1982) is a good example.

It is no surprise that the science fiction alien assumes different roles. But more importantly this begins to suggest something interesting about our engagement with it. Sontag's detachment, which allows the vicarious enjoyment of the destructive Other, is no longer possible. There is nothing so obviously different to demarcate ourselves. In other words, the meaning of alienation is eroded if, as in certain science fiction, colonization is no longer the result of invasion by an identifiable Other. Science fiction 'no longer symbolically figures the alien-ation generated by a whole new economic world system, but rather our incorporation of that new system and our *absorption* by it' (Sobchack 1987: 252 – italics in original).

Yet this seems to be going too far. Paradoxically the absorption (and loss) of Otherness leads to a situation close to that created by the divine exceptional body, in which God's will prevented extraordinary outcomes from being seen as abnormal. Accordingly they were not something from which we could be alien-ated. But the freak, that body unclaimed by myth, religion nor science, is a liminal figure, but which causes us pause to reflect. Our alienation takes a different course. To paraphrase Umberto Eco (1994), we contemplate the loathsome object but are forced to consider our own nature, and pause to wonder whether it is, in fact, natural. It is neither a figure purely Other, nor obviously human. These are not the secure limits of the monstrous alien, nor essentialist visions of humanism. Instead the alien is increasingly implicated but in a way that we struggle with its boundaries and the traces of our identity. This then is the alien as freak. A figure which always 'positions itself somewhere between pure familiarity and pure otherness. . . . Taking its positions on the border between identity and difference, it marks that border, articulating it while at the same time disarticulating and confusing the distinctions the border stands for' (Beehler, 1987: 32). No longer then, can we be certain of the limits of normality. However we remain strangely drawn to their exploration.

One major area in science fiction that explores these issues of engagement is what has been called *body horror* (see for instance a special edition of the film studies journal *Screen* in 1986). Hurley (1991: 203) explains that body horror seeks to 'inspire revulsion – and in its own way, pleasure – through representations of quasi-human figures whose effect/affect is produced by their abjection, their ambiguation, their impossible embodiments of multiple, incompatible forms'. The term 'horror' suggests perhaps a different genre, but this would also imply a more detached, vicarious consumption of fearful spectacle in the way in which Sontag (1971) (mistakeningly) presents the 'thrills' of science fiction. Instead body horror introduces a state that disrespects 'borders, positions, rules' and 'that dis-turbs identity, system, order' (Creed, 1986: 45). It therefore emerges at a fertile intersection between horror and science fiction. The films of David Cronenberg immediately spring to mind. Cronenberg consistently has displayed freakish creatures, freakish human beings and occasionally merges the two. His films contemplate the effect of technology on the body, through teleportation, *The Fly* (1986), gynaecology, *Dead Ringers* (1988), sexual transgressions, *Crash* (1996), mutations, *Shivers* (1975); and the mind, via telepathy, *The Dead Zone* (1983), brainwashing, *Scanners* (1981) and hallucination, *Videodrome* (1983).

Body horror combines the spectacle of the horror film with the questions of engagement with the alien posed by science fiction. But what is alien is produced by the distortion of the human body. In these films the body is transformed from a (relatively) integrated entity, to an ongoing subject of metamorphosis. This may be provoked virally, through genetic mutation or indeed, through extraterrestrial influence. In John Carpenter's *The Thing* (1982) the alien combines human, animal and artificial elements in increasingly incredible ways. The scientists, who have been steadily dispatched by the alien and combined into its form, regard its capabilities with terrified bemusement. One display proves particularly spectacular, almost exasperated, a crewmember can only blurt out, 'You've got to be fucking kidding'. David Cronenberg (2000) calls these reactions 'an aesthetics of revulsion'. But this is an aesthetic defined by its absence; in certain situations we lack a developed aesthetic sense. It is this lack that his films trade upon. He notes that we have tried to incorporate an aesthetic sense towards ageing, but there is a problem if we do the same for disease, 'that's a fine cancer-ridden young man', he muses playfully. Similarly, and importantly for the body horror film, we have not developed an aesthetic for the inside of our bodies.

The four-part *Alien* trilogy

This aesthetic plays an important role in the Alien series of films, *Alien* (1979), *Aliens* (1986), *Alien 3* (1992) and *Alien: Resurrection* (1997). Moreover there are some interesting developments and differences in the portrayal of the Alien and its 'relationship' with the central character, Ellen Ripley. What occurs over the course of the four films is a loosening of the depiction of the alien as rampaging, predatory Other, to a mutual absorption of the alien and the human subject. In other words, what begins with the archetypal alien Other, ends with the human and alien being absorbed into mutual freakishness. Here, like the body horror films of David Cronenberg, the films gradually but steadily began to trade on the aesthetics of revulsion. Whilst Ripley begins by evading and ejecting the archetypal implacable monster, eventually she has to contemplate her part in its creation and existence. She must begin to develop a sensibility towards their engagement.

The first film, Ridley Scott's *Alien*, is often, perhaps somewhat glibly, called a 'haunted house movie in space'. And, indeed, there are some similarities with the typical horror genre movie. One by one the crew of a deep space frigate are dispatched by a largely unseen alien entity. Finally, in another horror staple, a lone female battles and defeats the alien. It is the survivor, Ripley, played by Sigourney Weaver, who becomes the focus for the three sequels. As the saga develops she finds it harder and harder to banish the alien. This is not simply because the beast is hard to beat or that it will not stay dead, although there are elements of this in the 'false ending' to *Aliens*. Instead the identity of the alien is increasingly blurred. Whilst Ripley is initially constructed in opposition to the alien, finally in *Alien: Resurrection* she is inseparable as the cloned offspring Ripley 8 of human/alien DNA. As she wearily points out in *Alien 3*, 'You've been in my life so long, I can't remember anything else'. Yet the unsettling of the boundaries of the alien Other begins in the first film. The alien lifecycle depends on a biological host to incubate its eggs. There is the suggestion that the form of the alien is somehow influenced by the characteristics of the host. In *Alien 3*, the alien incubated by a dog is a quadruped whereas the human-hosted aliens of the earlier films are bipeds. H.R. Giger's design of the Alien is a biomechanical hybrid of shiny surfaces and slimy secretions that serves to suggest both natural and, assisted by the script's depiction of shadowy military-industrial interference, artificial origins.

Creation in the *Alien* films is often read in terms of femininity and reproduction (e.g. Hurley, 1991; Vaughn, 1995; Constable, 1999). Certainly there is much here particularly if we examine Ripley's climactic encounters with the alien. It has often been noted that life on the *Nostromo*, the ship in the first film, appears largely ungendered. Both sexes work together in 'blue-collar' roles and live and sleep in unisex quarters. However in Ripley's final encounter with the alien she is finally sexualized. Unaware of the alien's presence in the escape pod, Ripley has stripped for hyper-sleep. She remains semi-dressed until she puts on a space suit in preparation for ejecting the alien into space. For a time the alien watches the oblivious Ripley from a crevice in the wall. It is at this point that the voyeuristic alien becomes an archetypal masculine predator, its previously inscrutable biomechanical appearance becoming focused around the phallic appearance of its mouth/tongue.

It is in *Aliens*, particularly James Cameron's *Special Edition*, that Ripley's status as mother – potential, actual and surrogate – begins to be stressed. This becomes a preoccupation in the subsequent films. The image of the masculine stalker that closed *Alien* recedes into the background, to be replaced by the vengeful mother. We learn that Ripley had a young daughter who had died in old age whilst she was adrift in space. Ripley's subsequent desire to protect an orphaned young girl, Newt, the lone survivor of the ravaged colony, is therefore placed within an essentialist framework of maternal instinct. Ripley's subsequent personal confrontations with the alien begin to be configured around these images. In *Aliens* she rescues the orphan from the Alien queen's nest by threatening and finally destroying the mother's eggs. The alien queen however pursues Ripley to an orbiting landing craft where the two battle until again, the alien is evacuated into deep space.

In *Alien 3* however these positions are immediately thrown into flux. The putative nuclear family of Corporal Hicks, Newt and Ripley is instantly destroyed. A fault in the life-support system leads to the death of all but Ripley. Crash-landing on Fiorina 161, a prison planet hosting a correctional facility for genetically deviant male sexual offenders, Ripley discovers that a stowaway alien has compromized the ship's hyper-sleep containers. Worse, Ripley has herself been impregnated. A chest scan reveals that an infant alien queen is being incubated within her body. Finally Ripley chooses to destroy both herself and the newborn alien by diving into a furnace, cradling it in her arms as it bursts from her chest. By *Alien 3*, reproduction has become a series of intersecting possibilities; human, alien and, as the nefarious company hope to harvest and re-engineer an alien child, artificial. No longer is the alien pure Other, instead it is increasingly implicated with other entities. In *Alien: Resurrection* Ripley's remains have yielded enough DNA to produce a clone. From this clone the alien embryo is surgically extracted. Both entities however have genetic material from the other. Ripley has increased strength and heightened senses, whilst the cloned alien queen has a human womb. The alien is now far from the oppositional monster of the first film. Both it and Ripley have become freaks.

In fact the whole appearance of *Alien: Resurrection* accentuates the freakish. There are some intertextual reasons for this. The previous work of the director Jean-Pierre Jeunet, in particular *The City of Lost Children* (1995) and *Delicatessen* (1991), is notable for the surreal physicality of their characters. Dominique Pinon and Ron Perlman, who appear in *Alien: Resurrection* are actors used repeatedly by Jeunet. Both have used their unconventional looks to play a number of marginal figures throughout their careers. Perlman's hunchback Salvatore in *The Name of the Rose* (1986) is most memorable, though his half-man/half-lion in the saccharin television series *Beauty and the Beast* (1987) is perhaps best forgotten. In fact there was a short-lived trend for major science fiction films to self-consciously relish the visually preposterous and outlandish. Luc Besson's *The Fifth Element* (1997) and Tim Burton's *Mars Attacks!* (1996) are both garish spectaculars that express themselves through the peculiar bodies on display.

However the freakish transformation of the Alien films is completed in one key scene. Walking through a medical laboratory, the cloned Ripley 8 finds the failed seven previous versions. These are preserved and exhibited in glass display tanks. Ripley wanders through this freaks gallery increasingly disturbed but nevertheless drawn to the multiple potentials of her alien/human self. But there are greater horrors ahead. Ripley 7 is still alive, a sickening mound of distorted flesh. In echoes of the earlier films, it tells Ripley to 'kill me'. After some hesitation and in much distress Ripley torches both Ripley 7 and the rest of the laboratory.

But Ripley's ontological shock at having to identify, and then destroy, something that is both her and not-her is not complete. The alien queen harvested from Ripley gives birth to a monstrous human/alien hybrid that rejects and destroys her birth mother but fixates on Ripley. Ripley in turn rejects and destroys her surrogate child. In the traditional denouement the alien is ejected into space. However the integral alien subject has been irrevocably lost and symbolically the alien child is pulled through a small hole in the crafts hull piece by piece. The vacuum relentlessly strips the hybrid of its layers of alien/human flesh leaving a final image of a recognizably human skull. No longer is the alien dismissed whole. The four films having steadily established irrevocable resemblances between

Ripley and the alien, her Other can no longer be completely ejected. The Other is now the same.

'That's it man, game over man, game over, man! Game over!'

Alienation suggests some sense of agreed normality from which we can demarcate abnormality. It requires strong borders. These offer a common rationality, 'the standard by which deviations, irrationalities are judged, through which exclusions are not only effected but discerned' (Dean, 1998: 16). Likewise for Sobchack (1987: 86) the milieu of science fiction is a contested space in which 'generic oppositions' are determined by a kind of contest between the 'human community' and some kind of 'alien or monstrous force'.

However science fiction does not always draw its 'generic oppositions' very clearly. Of course, there are many examples of science fiction in which the distinction between the human community and the alien force is often blurred so that it becomes difficult, if not impossible to tell alien and human apart. This is the classic scenario of such films as *It Came from Outer Space* (1953) and *Invasion of the Body Snatchers* (1956). But these remain accounts of colonization and false consciousness in which the victim is unaware of his/her possession. They may appear unchanged to their family and friends, but once all human, they are now all alien. The only hope is for the alien presence to be definitively exorcised. I have pointed to an alternative alien presence, a presence which dissolves the monstrous alien Other within an implicate state of freakishness. In this state, our pre-existing sensibilities are never entirely lost. Identification with the alien as freak is always present if, sometimes, sensed only obliquely. This figure exists in a semi-defined space between fear and attraction. Rather than alienation, this is a state of abjection. The abject, 'lies there, quite close, but it cannot be assimilated. It beseeches, worries, fascinates desire, which, nonetheless, does not let itself be seduced' (Kristeva, 1982: 1). This is an almost romantic tension, a wistful desire for the remote object whilst recognizing its inaccessibility and impenetrability.

Coda

Yes, a wistful desire. The perceptive reader will no doubt have sensed a certain feeling of ennui in the various editors' contributions to this collection. Some editors have become, shall we say somewhat alienated by the contents of this collection. We fear that, over the course of journal issue, conference and this book, we have slowly but relentlessly strangled the life out of one of our small, but nevertheless shiny pleasures. Martin Parker will struggle with some of these issues shortly. Despite the many contemporary opportunities to refocus our existence, choose from spiritualism, voodoo, environmentalism, New Age therapy, anti-consumerism, abduction narrative, management education, opening a delicatessen, etc., the alternatives remain still, just too alternative. We are still able to produce a level of engagement that produces the sort of stuff you hold in your hand.

A very small claim indeed. For a bunch of 'management' academics to indulge their private pleasures, in public, in print, and then backtrack sulkily is surely an abject state of affairs. Still let me backtrack further. It is time therefore to acknowledge the contribution of one Rajiv Patel whose teenage perspicacity not only involved going to see *Aliens* thirteen times, but getting enthusiastic about *Blade Runner before* it was released. So I happily admit that I'm writing about *Aliens* mostly because of Private Hudson's one-liners and alarmingly fragile military mentality. It reminds me that I still like this stuff. Let's break off now to recite a few lines.

References

Baldrick, C. (1990) *In Frankenstein's Shadow*, New York: Clarendon Press.

Baudrillard, J. (1988) *Xerox and Infinity*, Agitac: Touchepass.

Bauman, Z. (1987) *Legislators and Interpreters*, Cambridge: Polity Press.

Bauman, Z. (1991) *Modernity and Ambivalence*, Cambridge: Polity Press.

Beehler, Michael (1987) 'Border Patrols', in George E. Slusser and Eric S. Rabkin (eds) *Aliens: The Anthropology of Science Fiction*, Illinois: Southern Illinois University Press.

Bloomfield, Brian P. and Vurdubakis, Theo (1999) 'The Outer Limits: Monsters, Actor Networks and the Writing of Displacement', *Organization*, (6)4: 625–47.

Bogdan, Robert (1988) *Freak Show: Presenting Human Oddities for Amusement and Profit*, Chicago: Chicago University Press.

Bukatman, Scott (1994) 'X-Bodies: The Torment of the Mutant Superhero', in Rodney Sappington and Tyler Stalling (eds) *Uncontrollable Bodies: Testimonies of Identity and Culture*, Seattle: Bay Press, pp. 93–130.

Constable, Catherine (1999) 'Becoming the Monster's Mother: Morphologies of Identity in the Alien Series', in Annette Kuhn (ed.) *Alien Zone 2: The Spaces of Science Fiction Cinema*, New York: Verso.

Creed, Barbara (1986) 'Horror and the Monstrous-Feminine: An Imaginary Abjection', *Screen*, 27(1), Jan/Feb: 44–71.

Cronenberg, David (2000) 'Interview with David Cronenberg', *Mondo 2000*. Available at http://zappa.users.netlink.co.uk/mond2000.html

Dean, Jodi (1998) *Conspiracy Cultures from Outerspace to Cyberspace*, New York: Cornell University Press.

Dery, Mark (1999) *The Pyrotechnic Insanitarium: American Culture on the Brink*, New York: Grove Press.

Eco, U. (1994) 'Apocalyptic and Integrated Intellectuals: Mass Communication and Theories of Mass Culture', in R. Lumley (ed.) *Apocalypse Postponed*, London: British Film Institute.

Fiedler, Leslie (1978) *Freaks: Myths and Images of the Secret Self*, Harmondsworth, Middlesex: Penguin Books.

Halberstam, Judith and Livingston, Ira (1991) *Postmodern Bodies*, Indiana: Indiana University Press.

Haraway, Donna (1991) 'A Manifesto for Cyborgs: Science, Technology, and Socialist Feminism in the 1980s', in Steven Seidman (ed.) *The Postmodern Turn: New Perspectives on Social Theory*, Cambridge: Cambridge University Press.

Hawkins-Dady, Mark (1992) *International Dictionary of Theatre 1: Plays*, London: St James Press, p. 696.

Holland, Samantha (1995) 'Descartes Goes to Hollywood: Mind, Body and Gender in Contemporary Cyborg Cinema', *Body and Society*, 1(3–4): 157–74.

Hurley, Kelly (1991) 'Reading like an Alien: Posthuman Identity in Ridley Scott's *Alien* and David Cronenberg's *Rabid*', in Judith Halberstam and Ira Livingston (eds) *Postmodern Bodies*, Indiana: Indiana University Press.

Johnson, F. (1973) 'Alienation: Overview and Introduction', in Frank Johnson (ed.) *Alienation: Concept, Term and Meanings*, New York: Seminar Press.

Kristeva, Julia (1982) *The Powers of Horror: An Essay on Abjection*, trans. Leon S. Roudiez, New York: Columbia University Press.

Levine, G. (1979) *The Endurance of Frankenstein*, London: University of California Press.

Marx, K. (1975) *Early Writings*, Harmondsworth, Middlesex: Penguin Books.

Schacht, R. (1970) *Alienation*, New York: Doubleday.

Screen (1986) *Body Horror Special Issue*, 27(1), Jan/Feb.

Sobchack, V. (1987) *Screening Space* (2nd edn), New York: Ungar.

Sontag, S. (1971) 'The Imagination of Disaster', in D. Allen (ed.) *Science Fiction: The Future*, New York: Harcourt Brace Jovanovich, pp. 312–25.

Squires, J. (1996) 'Fabulous Feminist Futures and the Lure of Cyberculture', in Jon Dovey (ed.) *Fractal Dreams: New Media in Social Context*, London: Lawrence & Wishart.

Telotte, J.P. (1995) *Replications: A Robotic History of the Science Fiction Film*, Urbana: University of Illinois Press.

Thomson, Rosemarie Garland (1996) 'Introduction: From Wonder to Error – A Genealogy of Freak Discourse', in Rosemarie Garland Thomson (ed.) *Freakery: Cultural Spectacles of the Extraordinary Body*, New York: New York University Press.

Tomas, David (1995) 'Feedback and Cybernetics: Reimaging the Body in the Age of Cybernetics', *Body and Society*, 1(3–4): 21–44.

Vaughn, Thomas (1995) 'Voices of Sexual Distortion: Rape, Birth, and Self-Annihilation Metaphors in the *Alien Trilogy*', *The Quarterly Journal of Speech*, 81(4): 423–35.

Part IV

The gamesters of Triskelion

12 'Repent Harlequin!' said the Ticktockman

Digesting science fiction

Martin Parker

Ticktockmen and jellybeans

Science fiction and management?[1] What for? Why on earth should a respectable publisher like Routledge – the original publishers of the *International Library of Sociology and Social Reconstruction*, established by Karl Mannheim – agree to publish something like *this*? Why do these various editors and authors, academics at respectable universities funded by taxpayers money, want to attach themselves to such an obviously trivial project? What next, *Cowboy Films, Foucault and Accounting*, published by Oxford University Press with a preface by Clint Eastwood? What is the *point* of all this?

Harlan Ellison's classic short story ' "Repent Harlequin!" Said the Ticktockman' describes a skirmish between Harlequin, a jellybean-spilling deviant on a flying skateboard, and the Ticktockman, the Master Timekeeper in a scientifically managed world. This is a world in which 'The Ones Who Kept the Machine Functioning Smoothly' from 'the cubicles of hierarchy' impose 'order and unity and promptness and clocklike precision' on the ants below (1973). It often seems that the intellectual climate of the present age is best characterized as a skirmish between the performative and the trivial, between the Ticktockman and the Harlequin. On the one hand, we have the various forces of sensible utilitarianism – science, applied psychology, accountability, strategy, social policy, technology, and of course, management. All these words add up to a demand for knowledge that does something useful. What works, and what could work better? Like an army of determined civil servants, these disciplines process the world and turn it into a series of suggestions to the minister. The administration of the territory in our bodies, our minds, our organizations, our globe will be so much more efficient and effective once we understand, and follow, the precepts and protocols that are being gradually formulated. After all, everything is potentially manageable, and there is really no good reason why we should not want it to be so. From the inequities of global starvation to the problem of single parents, from the human genome to market segmentation strategies for older consumers. All that remains is to fill in the gaps.

And so to the trivial, a category that can only exist because of the demand for the performative. Faced with the gigantic apparatus of the performative, there seems to be an urge amongst some people to play in the narrowing gaps. They cut cows in half and pickle them, they express an interest in Bataille, they smoke themselves to death and believe it to be an act of senseless beauty, they write books with too many words in them, develop an obsessive interest in the life of the romantic poets, throw jellybeans around like confetti. Sometimes, when asked, these people will give an account of themselves in terms of voicing the Other. The search for the Other, difference, alterity is often a moral tale that can be told to make sense of inexplicable behaviour because it can sound like a form of joyous liberalism. But I'm not sure they always believe the story that they tell, they just need to tell it to be left alone. These people are pointless.

This is no neat Mexican stand-off though, simply because the performative does not recognize borders. Confronted by the senseless and the trivial, it tries to make it useful. It orders and organizes, comments and categorizes. The performative is the interfering neighbour who always knows better. Not content to stand and stare, or run away screaming, they come to help and advise. 'You don't want to do it like that, you want to do it like this.' But once you have let them through the gate, they won't go away. And pretty soon you won't be able to engage in acts of senseless beauty anymore. Instead you will make lists of jobs to do, consult your diary, underline the programmes you want to watch in the TV guide and disapprove when people spoil their ballot papers.

And I feel the need to get to the point. I am spilling my words like jellybeans when I don't have the time and you don't have the patience. Just what is the moral of this penultimate tale?

Digesting science fiction

Given the context (that this is almost the end of the book of essays about science fiction and organization that you hold in your hand) I should (in the interests of both politeness and marketing) stress the importance of this emerging area of enquiry. Clearly this is an area that needs more research. There is not much known about it and, if we did know more about it, then that would undoubtedly be very useful. There are a variety of useful things that might be done and I will list them.

First, science fiction could be used as a resource in management teaching. This would make management teaching better because lots of people like science fiction. Second, science fiction might help writers, teachers and students to be more imaginative. This would be a good thing because imagination helps people to think up new things, and some of these new things might be useful. Third, there are lots of references to organizations in science fiction, and this gives us some useful ideas about how people think about organizations nowadays. Fourth, since much science fiction is quite critical of organizations, if we want to be critical we might get some good ideas about how to do it more effectively. Fifth, this is a neglected area of research so more research is needed so that it is no longer neglected. Sixth (but not least), academic promotions are helped if the academics gets their names in print, and this is quite a marketable area which can guarantee a fair amount of publicity (Crace 2000) and likely career advancement.

But I am, for the sake of a jellybean metaphor, trivializing the chapters in this very interesting book. As one of the editors, this is impolite and self-destructive, so let me pick out some key themes, and stop being Harlequin (for a moment). I'll ignore the first and last of my odd list above – the first because this is not a book about pedagogy, the last because it is simply too vulgar. Let me start with the role of imagination. In some sense, SF is the most developed example of literary and visual creativity. Unlike many other genres, it allows (indeed requires) that the suspension of disbelief is taken very seriously indeed. McHugh's essay puts the matter rather nicely in terms of an SF 'methodology' which 'makes variables out of what everyday life often treats as ontological and epistemological "fixities"'. Where other genres take human beings, culture, physics, history, knowledge, technology or whatever for granted, SF is premised on the disturbance of at least one of these categories. As De Cock reminds us, this is John W. Campbell's 'what if?' premise for a publishable astounding story. Of course SF has its sub-genres too, its fixities if you will, but its wilful denial of (some aspect of) our common sense is what binds the genre together as a more or less meaningful category.

Now I think this means that SF is very much like science itself. Following the classic prescriptions of the hypothetico-deductive method, scientists perform precisely these kind of 'what if' experiments too. What if I took all the gas out of this container? What if it were possible to teleport from place to place? The difference is primarily one of cognitive rather than material execution, yet a great deal of what passes for science (theoretical physics, or evolutionary biology for example) is only dimly associated with actual experimentation. And in any case, as Haley's chapter suggests, perhaps imagination is more routine in the generation of material scientific problems than we might believe. From Archimedes onwards, we have stories of scientists who have been inspired by wild thought experiments, and more recently by writing and reading SF themselves (see Parker *et al.*. 1999). So, perhaps in methodological terms we could think about SF as a kind of theoretical science which routinely requires skills of advanced imagination. Philosophy is instructive in this regard. Take for example Plato's cave metaphor, Wittgenstein's explorations of private language or Deleuze and Guattari's use of Ray Bradbury's *Illustrated Man*. It would seem that 'thought experiments' are central to the philosophical imagination. Indeed, in John Hospers' classic *Introduction to Philosophical Analysis* he uses the 'case' of *Star Trek* teleport technology to explore the mind–body problem (1990). Respectability indeed.

So perhaps SF could stimulate social scientists to imagine what the world would be like if corporations grew employees in vats, or if what we call 'organization structure' was merely an archetypal metaphor that disguises privilege (as Tolliver and Coleman do), or if the 'alien' was part of us too (as Smith does). Ironically, this might not involve what David McHugh refers to as an 'escape from normal science' (by which he probably means dull habits of thought), but an attempt to invigorate the scientific imagination by making common sense sound implausible. How else could we imagine that aeroplanes might fly? Or that organizations could become virtual? Or even that the 'ideal type' of bureaucracy represented a new form of rationality? For social scientists to imagine at least twenty-seven improbable things before breakfast could be a useful habit of thought, and one that SF could almost certainly encourage.

But there is another theme to many of these chapters too, that of using SF as an empirical symptom of the present age, rather than bringing a new one into being. When McHugh calls social science and science fiction 'fashion conscious disciplines', he is suggesting that they are both areas that are attuned to contemporary cultural contexts. Being fashionable does not have to be a matter for criticism, just as being unfashionable should not automatically imply some kind of ivory tower ascetic superiority. It is interesting, for example, that so many contemporary SF films represent the big corporation as being a problem in itself, as encouraging immoral and illegal practices, as being populated by hard-hearted utilitarians who seem not to care overmuch about the consequences of their actions. Contemporary SF is replete with such images, and a very common narrative device is the rebellion of the oppressed against the technologies of the masters (as Tolliver and Coleman document in their chapter). The oppressed might be mutants, or genetically engineered, or cyborgs, or mere humans – but in most cases the skyscrapered military corporate state is positioned as the threat (Parker 2000b).

It would have to be a wilfully anti-contextual argument that then refused to acknowledge that these cultural products did not suggest something about contemporary anxieties. This is not to say that SF dystopias have some unproblematic relationship to an actually existing cultural imaginary. They are, after all, produced in specific sites, by specific people, for specific markets. But we should not ignore them on these grounds either. Consider Tolliver and Coleman's use of *Metropolis* as an early denunciation of Fordism – an SF version of Charlie Chaplin's *Modern Times*. Other chapters in this book do something similar – Maria Ferreira's use of feminist SF novels as a way of commenting on organizational patriarchy and environmentalism; Smith and Boje's (very different) explorations of the dystopic concerns evidenced in contemporary SF films; and Monin and Monin's exploration of the metaphors and morality of a technology obsessed world through a short story. In each case, the argument is partly that SF can be used like a piece of cultural market research, an 'expressive good' as Kavanagh, Keohane and Kuhling would have it. That is to say, an archaeological artefact that we can interpret for signs of the life of its makers. SF texts tell us something about the way that the world is, about the way that people see things, and perhaps about the organizational arrangements and spirit of an age. Of course, like all market research, any conclusions need to be treated with some scepticism. How SF is 'read' and 'represented' are contextual matters too, but this recognition does not disqualify us from reading.

Which brings me on to the third theme, the use of SF in sponsoring critical projects. This involves using SF as a weapon rather than a weathervane. For myself, this is probably the most powerful argument from utility, one that certainly dignifies this book as a contribution to some larger project of social emancipation. As McHugh suggests, there has long been a concern to legitimate SF (like much 'art') as a 'cultural redoubt' from which subversion, imaginative alternatives and criticism can flow. The metaphor here is an interesting one, because it relies on the idea that some kind of purity of purpose is protected through a degree of insulation from dominant thinking, and perhaps from incorporation by the corrosive mechanisms of the market. For centuries, utopian literature has employed this kind of bracketing in order to comment on the problems and prospects of the contemporary. In an age when we consumers are weary of prophets and politicians, and seem uninterested in drowned giants, so might SF employ similar devices in order to speak truth to power indirectly.

In this present volume we find utopian and dystopian visions both being self-consciously used to sharpen critique and focus ambition. Ferreira's speculation about future alternative worlds is certainly the most explicitly utopian chapter, with possible futures being used to cast a critical eye on some contemporary masculine common sense. The narrative drive here comes from the juxtaposition of imagined social orders with the manifest cruelty of the present day. Other papers work the other way around, but achieve similar effects. In the case of Monin and Monin's claim that certain technical metaphors reveal a pathological symbolic ordering, Boje's condemnation of the society of the spectacle, or Land and Corbett's assault on humanism, the narrative is to dramatize the asymmetries of the present through dystopic lenses. The space for utopia, or at least some form of reform, is then opened negatively as somewhere the reader might be propelled to avoid the world of *The Trial* or *1984*. In Boje's case, this can be clearly located as a form of ideology critique. The refutation of what he nicely terms 'pleasantville theory' allows us to 'peer beneath the veil' of our collective hallucination. When we see how awful things are, and become a class for ourselves, rebellion will surely follow. But whether the utopia is positive or negative, the principle of hope is reaffirmed by opening some kind of space between 'now' and the somewhere – the no-place – of utopia.

Finally then, the 'more research is needed' argument. Whilst this is not a matter explictly discussed in the essays in this book, it does underpin the very notion of books like this. Indeed, in terms of contemporary writing my original dualism between trivia and performativity was a little overdone, simply because there is a cross-over genre which has been on the rise for quite a few years. This is a genre that attempts to shuttle between the trivial and the performative. It is often called 'cultural studies', but variants of it can be found in geography, sociology, politics, literature, history and so on. Its aim is often to represent things, places and people that have been missed out or misrepresented by current orders of knowledge. For example, Dick Hebdige, in a classic of this genre, has argued that youth sub-cultural style can be a form of aesthetic resistance in itself (1979). The mission statement of this culturalism then becomes the search for political significance in the smallest details of everyday life. So we have 'work' on leisure, women, humour, bodies, popular culture, emotions, time, shopping, the disabled, sport, the working classes, fashion – an encyclopedic Chinese list of oddities that share some inexplicable unity (Foucault 1970: xv). And now, even in 'management', the home of the performative where the human sciences are concerned, we can see the emergence of a cultural turn which reciprocally attempts to expose the performative as trivial. (Or to colonize the trivial and make it performative.) From the various studies of culture and symbolism over the last few decades (Parker 2000a), to more recent work on gender, emotions, popular culture, the body and so on (Hearn *et al.*. 1989, Fineman 1993, Hassard and Holliday 1998; Hassard, Holliday and Willmott 2000) the move seems to be to (re)attach 'management' to 'everyday life'.

Whilst, in its most narrow conception, this becomes a matter of filling in gaps in knowledge – 'more research is needed' – this kind of research can also be driven by two related imperatives. One is dully predictable – the attempt to discover how a knowledge of a particular unknown variable can allow it to be better controlled. (The opposite of McHugh's SF methodology.) So knowing about culture allows for better motivational strategies, or knowing about women allows for more understanding of the management of diversity, and so on. The other imperative is to provide voices for the people and things that are deemed to be voiceless, somehow disenfranchised by commission or omission. Once they have their voices provided for them (through academic enquiry) then they can enter into the parliament of things, and the processes of democratic liberalism. The wider the net is cast, the less likely we are to miss something out. With regard to SF then, we would have a justification that widened 'management' to include all those texts and practices that might be relevant to the conduct of organization. If SF films and books have lessons to teach us, then we should attend to these texts and not, through myopia or cultural snobbery, miss these matters out of our growing encyclopedia. To put it another way, 'organization', 'management', 'business' and the like are simply too important to be left to the narrow imagination of conventional managerialism.

In summary then, these four arguments seem to be useful ways in which SF might be attached to organization theory – to stimulate imagination, to attune our cultural sensitivities, to sponsor critical projects and to fill in unfortunate gaps. This is not to claim that SF has a monopoly on these matters (no doubt we could do something with *Cowboy Films, Foucault and Accounting*) but simply that SF does undoubtedly provide a lot of things which are very good to think with. Its very distance from management provokes interesting questions and stimulates thought. Which inevitably seems to take me back to the performative, to my four arguments from utility (with two others waiting in reserve). Why is science fiction useful? Because . . . As soon as the question is asked the ticktock scientific management men move in and demand answers. It would be hypocritical of me to deny such responses. So, in conclusion, this is a ground-breaking and important book of essays which contributes considerably to our understanding of science fiction and organizations. It will be useful for advanced undergraduates, postgraduates and academics in management, sociology and cultural studies. Sales can be expected in the UK, North America and Australasia.

Now, what else is there to be said?

Science fiction and indigestion

I want to be clear. I do believe that these are all good arguments for legitimizing a book like this one and for answering pointed questions about pointlessness. Most of these arguments are explicitly or implicitly made extremely well by the essays that precede this one and I do not intend to be dismissive. (Though, I admit, this may be the resulting impression.) This is a very interesting book, and I would buy it myself. Yet this all leaves me feeling rather queasy. SF is an astounding collection of books, films, cartoons, video games, toys, pictures, fan conventions, costumes, bookshops, comics and so on that has occasionally perplexed, distracted and pleased me for many years. It scrapes the profound depths of the cultural food-chain, borrows relentlessly from everywhere, raises its eyebrows at everything, and always claims far more than it can deliver. So why should I want to deliver it giftwrapped into the mouth of management? Having it taken seriously by literary critics or sociologists is bad enough, but by management?

The problem here is one of resisting digestion, of making something so worthless, so obscene, so alien, that it can not be incorporated within the urgent and persistent demands for utility. De Cock's quote from Philip K. Dick puts the matter very nicely indeed. ' "But are you writing something serious?" Note the word. Fuck. If they couldn't get us to write serious things, they solved the problem by decreeing that what we were writing *was* serious.' Fuck indeed. Why should SF have to bear such a weight? Why should SF be *for* anything? The problem, as I indicated above, comes from the Ticktockman's question. As soon as it is asked, as soon as an account is demanded, then the proper response is framed by the question. What is it for? What can it do? Once I am made accountable for the utility of my ideas, then trivial defences must fall. Such is the relentless nature of the performative demand for more data, more information, more knowledge. As Munro (2000) shows, there is no obvious way out of this impasse. It is constitutive of identity itself, and must be answered as part of my legitimation for this book, for these publishers, for you the reader. There must be a serious point to all this, otherwise why has all this effort, this ink and paper, been expended?

This is why I was pleased when De Cock hopefully asserted, 'of course we will never be able to simply "apply" Dick'. In a way, he had already begun the process of application, but the tone of his chapter is intended to make us believe that such a machinery had not been set in motion. Land and Corbett are less optimistic, suggesting that cyborganization theory might be able to offer some fleeting insight, but only 'before it is assimilated'. Resistance is futile, assimilation is inevitable. Indeed, Fitchett and Fitchett's chapter argues that it is already too late, because even the future has become a commodity form that can be traded like any other (Frillons 2011, YanL 2014). Perhaps they are right. Even the most difficult and arcane of matters seem to be digestible by management. Another Chinese list. Postmodernism, cyborg anthropology, Dilbert cartoons, Marxism, simulacra, semiotics, game theory, information theory, feminism, pro-feminism, men's studies, sexuality, queer theory, complexity theory, photocopier art – not to mention markets, trees, strategy, numbers, animals, machines, people, ethics and so on. All this is grist to the mill, and nothing seems indigestible. Nothing provokes stomach-ache or vomiting.

Georges Bataille's distinction between 'general' and 'restricted' economies is relevant here. Whilst by the general economy he refers to all the patterns of waste, abundance, loss and expenditure in the widest sense, the restricted economy is that which is concerned with specific forms of production, utility and equilibrium – with balancing the books (Richardson 1994). Bataille's assumption is that the restricted economy (which economic man usually understands as the Market) tends to digest and efface the effusions of the general economy. Rather like Weber's value rationality versus technical rationality, or Habermas' more indigest-ible distinction between the lifeworld and the system, we are left with the idea of a creeping process of colonization and a general restriction of possibilities, human and otherwise. For Baudrillard, much influenced by Bataille's analysis, 'frontal resistances' to this process of commodification and socialization are futile (1983: 41). Instead, he writes of two more indirect strategies. The first is the interception, transposition and recycling of media messages, a practice which salvages the detritus of the dominant code for cargo cult purposes. This is a strategy employed by 'groups traditionally structured by identity and significance', of (subcultural) groups who 're-code' for their own purposes (see, for example Hebdige 1979). It is a utilitarianism opposed to the dominant, to the hegemonic, but a utilitarian-ism none the less – and hence can be incorporated into the restricted economy by easily transforming its use value into exchange value (the conjunction of SF, management and Routledge, for example; see also Hebdige 1979 for other examples).

The other strategy, the one Baudrillard is better known for, is the dumb unreflective defiance of the masses themselves. This is a mass, a silent majority, which is brought into being by the technologies and restrictions of the social, but that digests everything with a manic hyper-conformity, and hence even digests the ordered protocols of the social itself. The mass will consume 'anything what-soever, for any useless and absurd purpose' (Baudrillard 1983: 46). It would seem then (moving back to Bataille for a moment) that the general economy of excess, of magic, eroticism and spectacle takes its eventual revenge on those who demand only narrow utility. This second strategy relies on the assumption that the restricted economy simply cannot hermetically insulate itself from the general. There is, in the end, no fixed discrimination between the high and the low, the great tradition and the freakshow, or perhaps management and pulp fiction. Everything gets digested, and in the end it all turns to waste. This is an attitude to consumption which refuses utility, and cultivates indifference to bright eyed utili-tarianism. 'It is not a question of positive action of the revolutionary sort. All that I can do is to create this zone of strategic indifference. . . . It's a militant, non-spectacular sacrifice, the opposite of action as it is usually understood' (Baudril-lard 1993: 195–6).

But how can an author, as they are writing, cultivate or sponsor indifference to their writing? How can valuable words, four arguments from utility, and so many fascinating possibilities be solicited to turn to waste so quickly? How can usefulness be avoided?

Let me put the problem of digestibility another way. When your ideas can be summarized in a few sentences, then the game is up. I see no way to write something here that cannot be condensed into such a tasty morsel. I want (like Bataille and Baudrillard) to write something with cruel spikes, or something that floats away, or something so dense that it refuses to open. Yet I have summarized their ideas in a few paragraphs. The problem, of course, is starting from here – in this book. If I really wanted to write something else, then I would not be publishing with Routledge, but perhaps writing a science fiction story myself. At least Piñeiro didn't try to do anything else, and the shuffling coughing silence that greeted his 'paper' at the conference that preceded this book said an awful lot about what counted as knowledge, even in that libertarian context. Georges Bataille's obscene fictions were originally published under pseudonyms, with false dates of publication – a strategy that is only partially adopted by Piñeiro, and not at all by this author. Instead I merely and self-consciously celebrate triviality, futilty and senseless beauty. Baudrillard terms this the 'final somersault of the intellectuals'. It is an attempt to 'exalt insignificance, to promote non-sense into the order of sense' (1983: 40). It is of course, just another trick we can turn to make ourselves sound paradoxically useful before the masses (you, me, us) hyperconsume their way to genuine non-sense; before the general economy turns this book into toilet paper. I might be pissing in the wind, but it does seem the only strategy that I (somersaulting intellectual) have to offer. Indeed, perhaps the best trading card that SF has to play is that it is, in the Ticktockman's terms, a disposable product. Since SF is (largely) still regarded as trash, just pulp fiction waiting for the refuse collectors, then hopefully this commentary might become disposable too. And who, in their right mind, would want to digest such rubbish? It contains nothing of nutritional value.

So, let me summarize myself in a few sentences, and let that be an end of it. David McHugh eventually ends his chapter by celebrating being 'hip just for the fun of it'. If SF is merely a style, an aesthetic, then of taste there is no disputing. As Oscar Wilde well knew, putting on the style, for no other reason than the fun of it, is a fine and pathetic way to avoid answering the Ticktockman's questions without posing any of your own (see Higgins' introduction to this volume). Demanding accounts of style seems inappropriate, if only because such questions have reasons (intentions) that imply a logic of communication, and generalized ideal speech situations are not what style usually intends to achieve (despite what Hebdige 1979 argues). Instead, it represents a kind of fascination with certain surfaces, and a disdain for the seriousness of depths. An example of this might be Warren Smith's claim about the simultaneous repulsion from and attraction to freaks, aliens, monsters and so on. They in some way solicit us as freakish too, and our inhuman condition is reflected back to us through exposing the limits of its ordinariness. This is not a moral project, one that is intended to conclude by giving aliens a vote in the galactic parliament. It is more like a preference for difference rather than repetition, an aimless engagement with becoming other, experiencing what has not yet been experienced.

Neither of these responses are particularly useful, and hence they are pointless. But here we begin to see that accusations of 'pointlessness', such as the ones I began with, necessarily imply an outside from which accounts of utility can be solicited. They imply that preferences, for style, for freaks, for spectacle should be grounded in some manner. Yet such preferences can be, in a sense, immanent to themselves and are hence (as they stand, and without addition) impermeable to the external gaze. They do not admit of 'explanation', beyond an unadorned claim of taste. When wearing the Terminator's mirrorshades the best gesture is a shrug, or a blank reflecting stare. 'But this isn't the strategy of a responsible, moral subject, it's the strategy of an object. You make yourself inert like an object, devoid of responses, thus gaining an enigmatic strength' (Baudrillard 1993: 191).

Management requires transparency, accountability, usefulness – and I would rather that SF were not seen as any of these things. I would rather that it were not attached to management, even though I and my co-editors have just done it. Or better, I would like the mirrorshades to reflect back on management, and for their blankness to make management stutter for a moment as it recognizes its own freakishness. Or cough as it swallows a jellybean.

And so, like one of those dadaist machines that destroy themselves, this chapter must end as it began, as mission impossible. The book's introduction and this 'conclusion' have a certain symmetry here, as well as a forced smile in common. This is the paradox of wanting to deny that this splendid book does anything useful, and hoping that it will self-destruct in five seconds, whilst at the same time spilling words and hoping it sells enough copies to make it into paperback. As one of the Ticktockmen, I repent.

Notes

1 Thanks to Valerie Fournier, Rolland Munro and my co-editors for comments on an earlier draft of this chapter, to Fred Botting for some indigestible food for thought, and to Andy Sawyer for the copy of a half-forgotten story.

References

Baudrillard, J. (1983) *In the Shadow of the Silent Majorities*. New York: Semiotext(e).

Baudrillard, J. (1993) 'Interview with Nicole Czechowski', in M. Gane (ed.) *Baudrillard Live*. London: Routledge, 191–6.

Crace, J. (2000) 'Aliens Ate My MBA', *Guardian* (Education Supplement), May 9, 12.

Ellison, H. (1973) ' "Repent Harlequin!" Said the Ticktockman', in *All the Sounds of Fear*. London: Panther, 129–43.

Fineman, S. (ed.) (1993) *Emotion in Organisations*. London: Sage.

Foucault, M. (1970) *The Order of Things*. New York: Pantheon.

Frillons, I. (2011) *Who Wants to be a metaManager?* Capital-Human Editions.

Hassard, J. and Holliday, R. (eds) (1998) *Organisation-Representation: Work and Organisations in Popular Culture*. London: Sage.

Hassard, J., Holliday, R. and Willmott, H. (eds) (2000) *Body and Organisation*. London: Sage.

Hearn, J., Sheppard, D., Tancred-Sherif, P. and Burrell, G. (eds) (1989) *The Sexuality of Organisation*. London: Sage.

Hebdige, D. (1979) *Subculture: the Meaning of Style*. London: Methuen.

Hospers, J. (1990) *An Introduction to Philosophical Analysis* (3rd edn). London: Routledge.

Munro, R. (2000) 'After Knowledge: The Language of Information', in S. Linstead and R. Westwood (eds) *The Language of Organisation*. London: Sage.

Parker, M. (2000a) *Organisational Culture and Identity*. London: Sage.

Parker, M. (2000b) 'Manufacturing Bodies: Flesh, Organization, Cyborgs', in J. Hassard, R. Holliday and H. Willmott (eds) *Body and Organisation*. London: Sage, 71–86.

Parker, M., Higgins, M., Lightfoot, G. and Smith, W. (1999) 'Amazing Tales: Organization Studies as Science Fiction', *Organisation*, 6/4: 579–90.

Richardson, M. (1994) *Georges Bataille*. London: Routledge.

YanL, B. (2014) *Firmnet: A Map*. Parcelsus vOpus.

13 Cyberpunk management

Erik Piñeiro

> The future exists first in Imagination, then in Will, then in Reality.
> (R.A. Wilson, *The Trick Top Hat*, 1979: 530)

East Junction Enclave, Dupont State
The Northern Dupont Territories
XXI.XI.XX–XVI

Regarding

Ms Tonssafgusv, chief editor, has asked me to consider Reipino's report on YanL's new vOpus. Here follows my opinion.

Comment

Rike Reipino is a sad case of total market blindness. Not only does she strongly criticize the work of one of this decade's most successful authors, daring to suggest that YanL has misunderstood the classics of Baudrillard and Virilio, but, even worse, she brings to her aid the old invalid ghost of Karl Marx, whose theories are now as provoking as a packet of potato-flavoured capsules.

She has once again fallen victim to her own antediluvian mind-structures, failing to sense any of the actual trends in society. Moreover, she seems incapable of understanding the change in writing fashion that has taken place during the last decade, or even longer. Her style is no more compelling than the already mentioned capsules.

What we want today are enlightening articles of the inspiring How-to kind. Exactly what YanL is providing us with. There's only one thing wrong with YanL's book: no mention of sex or drugs. The three earlier chapters in her series contained some interesting statistical figures on drug use among the winners and, even if she refused to spice up her personal opinion (which

---

would have added to controversy and enlivened the discussion), she did create a most entertaining debate. Of course, this flaw is not even mentioned by Reipino, who probably sees it as a rare asset.

Hyatt's scoring

(based on her 2016 scale, min: 0–max: 10)

Colourism	2
Neatness	1
Psychedelic Blend	0
Ease of Experience	1
Multimedia	0
Spirituality	1

(This must certainly be a new record, even for somebody with the reputation of Reipino.)

Publication

I do not recommend this report to be published in our January issue. Or in any issue of *The Art of Management*, for that matter.

ON WINNING THE RACE

By R. Reipino

Rike Reipino
Master of Sciences, Ph.D. Student
Royal University
Department of Industrial Management
Democratic European Confederation

On Winning the Race, Yan López, Birgitte
Paracelsus vOpus Editions, 2016
San Tyago
South Dupont Territories

Brigitte Yan López [space here for a shortvid of YanL at the Beaumont Hall presenting the book] has come out with a new virtualOpus. This work completes her famous series about the art (?) of becoming an agent in the Firmnet. In the earlier numbers she was under strong fire, much of the criticism concerning her ability to give any advice at all in such a secretly kept subject. Some of the most radical analysts claim Firmnet (the circle of initiates) does not exist as an actual society but that it is a grandiose hoax with its roots in the 1980s and 1990s SF tradition of Cyberpunk. This would not be the first time a writer's invention achieves spectacular levels of believers (think of Donnelly's Atlantis) and in our society of the sellable the Firmnet is probably not the only true-claiming meme with fictional origins. Anyway, YanL has attended to these ideas and in this fourth chapter the delicate matter of who is who in Firmnet and how to fish for contacts in that evasive world has been totally ignored. Not satisfied with this measure she has gone even further, writing in the introduction to this new vOpus that the aim of *Firmnet, a Map* (YanL, 2014) was not to represent the exact actual situation of that circle but simply to draw a sketch where the important bits are 'the relating lines, not the details' (she seems to have failed to see that, according to the trends, there are only details).

So, once her back is covered, YanL sets out for a new adventure: *On Winning the Race*. This vOpus, very much as the title suggests, is a collection of advice and examples for those interested in becoming members of the fictional class of number-one managers.

On Winning the Race is a rather uncontroversial piece of work that can be summarized in a few maxims that all aspiring managers should follow: forget efficiency, concentrate on Profit; market, market and market: it's show time; it is painful but absolutely inevitable: invest in e-security; obtain your own territory, without it you are not even going to make it to the Gate. The last step is, of course, to cross the Gate and be admitted in Firmnet, but 'this is altogether another story' (p. 34).

What YanL actually does is to dedicate her new vOpus to the treatment of a few other memes that were, if not conceived, at least accentuated in the same period and same dominion as Firmnet. These memes are different in nature to Firmnet, since they do not relate to an existing (?) entity but to values that have been raising in importance and hype, becoming today worthy of starring in a vOpus dedicated to teach inferior humans how to take the step into the higher form of evolution: the superManagers.

The vOpus is a perfect didactic example of how to teach Semiotics and its closely related cousin Memetics. YanL has produced yet another work whose significance does not lie in the truth and exactitude of her affirmations, but on the construction of symbols that acquire a floating meaning based on, yes, on vOpus like *On Winning the Race*. This circularity can be traced back to language itself, as the works of the classics claim (Derrida, Foucault, Baudrillard, Czarniawska) but, evolving from those early years of the information age, it has become the supreme way of making sense. But YanL does not create any new symbols, that is too risky, she chooses instead to gourmandize on the sweet mission of selling what wants to be bought, an activity not especially infrequent amongst authors nowadays.

Starting with the first symbol to be encountered, the one that gives the vOpus its foundation: superManagers (metaManagers, Frillons 2011; supraManagers, Tjinksy 2016, the list of terms is long and rather monotonous). But the symbol superManager does not come alone, a complete set of followers is there to support the flagship. These valets have before served other Lords, but now Ultracapitalism has enlisted them in its army. They are no less than Morality and Aesthetics, which themselves have produced a new generation of values to the glory of Ultracapitalism: expensive, hip, fast, ego, decadent, baroque, isolated.

It is quite amusing to recognize most of these values in the works of the Cyberpunk tradition and, indeed, some people have insisted on elevating Gibson, Sterling and the rest of the Neuromantics to Messiahs or, at least, visionaries. They were officially presented with the opportunity of forming a new religion when Telepresence millionaire Hujik II offered to fund the whole process at the end of 2012 (rumour had it he was not allowed in Firmnet and, as a result, overdid his amphetamine dose) but they declined the proposal.

At the same time, it feels rather unpleasant to notice that she makes no reference whatsoever to the articles and books on Management and Science Fiction that were published in the same period as the Cyberpunk volumes. The Management and Science Fiction movement (if I dare call it so) of the late XX century never became as influential as the later Exotic Management, mostly because of its academic strictness, but nevertheless it explored the possibilities of learning something about management from the study of the Science Fiction field. The reference void feels unpleasant but none the less evident. Unpleasant because she totally ignores a body of work clearly related to hers and evident because she cannot let anyone understand that this is the fact. Since she claims to present the concepts that 'are flourishing today, the keys to unlock the new gates to success' she must do her utmost to avoid any resemblance with austere academic works from another century like the 'Organization as Science Fiction' issue of the magazine *Organization*, the interdisciplinary journal of organization, theory and society (volume 6, number 4, November 1999); or the 2001 Routledge edited collection on science fiction and organization. It cannot escape anyone that these correct and unfashionable names are not the companions YanL wants for her vOpus.

Very well, but how does YanL suggest that one is to act to reach earthly salvation, the top of the tops, the Everest of social climbing? YanL does not talk about 'earthly salvation' even though she has indeed been called the mystic of Ultracapitalism because of her writing style. In her vOpuses she makes constant references to Jung and the Archetypes, Oriental religions, the Alchemists, Native American and Siberian shamanism and other assorted New Age sources of inspiration that are once again so much in vogue.

It is the use of these populist references and metaphors that makes me suggest that YanL is not so much in the educational business as in the memetical one. Her aim is not to actually teach anyone how to arrive at the Gate but to contribute to the construction of today's values. The sell rates she has been enjoying since the first of her works in the series indicate the high density of vertical-mobility wannabees who wish to believe they understand the inner workings of the managerial profession. This is not by any means a new situation, neither the existence of verticalers, nor their hunger for easily digested formulae to reach the top. Only the contents of those formulae change, YanL suggesting four fundamental elements in the path to the Olympus: Profit, Market, e-Security and Territories. She has not invented anything new, she only rides the wave (giving it further strength) created by the new moral and aesthetic values.

The goddess Profit

Enter goddess Profit. Exit non-profit organizations, artisans, traditions, anything that might catch your attention and divert it towards earthly matters. Thou shall not serve any other Master. Profit is Amon-Ra reincarnated, the Shiva of Ultra-capitalism, the ultimate maker of sense and Firmnet is Its church.

The question of whether there actually exists a group of humans in control of the Firmnet (which was YanL's thesis in *Firmnet, a Map*, 2014) is not of import-ance. The Firmnet exists: it is the gigantic impenetrable mesh of proprietorships and interests that effectively separates real personal experience from the financial sphere. It is the supreme alienating force.

YanL explains how Profit has risen among other lesser gods to the throne of Midgaard: '[There have been three eras in the evolution of Profit] the first one has been called Steamcapitalism' – she coined this term herself in *Distilling Profit* (YanL 2011) – 'but could also have been called "the beginners mistake". A few visionaries tried to elevate Profit to its rightful place in society but did so in a rather coarse way, something for which humans were not ready [. . .] Socialism grew stronger and slowly forced Profit to retire, at least from the visible position as head of Prosperity. This marked the beginning of the second era, Capitalism. This time Profit took a more subtle approach, enrolling lesser (and not as pure) gods to stand in the spotlight and take the criticism of those primitive humans incapable of understanding the sign of times. It first chose Efficiency which would turn to be a long lasting positive alliance. It cleared FW Taylor's theories of its humanistic aspects and reduced it to clean beautiful mechanics' – here YanL loses her line of thought and gets messed up in aesthetical valorizations – 'the monad became a dyad: Profit & Efficiency. Other theories and other values were intro-duced in this new cult: Evolution and Natural Selection, Usefulness, Dedication, Human Resources Management, Neurological Engineering [. . .] All these lesser gods were needed to make sense of the situation, to give a meaning to decisions that had to be made to reach the next era [. . .] until Profit, arguably around 2006, was capable of standing alone as the only god once more, giving a start to new flamboyant era of Ultracapitalism.'

It is surprising (although not so much in YanL's case) to attend a lecture on the history of Capitalism and not hear the name of the author of *Das Kapital*. There is a good reason for it, one that springs directly from the Spirit of Profit. Even I have to acknowledge that the name Karl Marx is not going to boost sales. Ultracapital-ism disarmed his theories by assimilating them as *à-la-mode* rhetoric and letting the infallible machinery of fashion roll over them. The perfection of this method cannot be doubted as Marx's work is presently considered not only uncontro-versial but incontestably dull. Admittedly, it is true that his prophecies on the evolution of society and the end of Capitalism were wrong. Capitalism did not end with the arriving of Socialism, even if (as YanL herself suggests) it did slow down the march into Ultracapitalism. But his analysis of the proletarian situation is today as prophetic as ever. To compare the living conditions of the anonymous masses of the second XX-decade with that of the working class in Marx's time may be disrespectful, but both situations show a strong similarity in form, especially after the abolition of retirement pensions and social security with the advent of the Corporate Territories. Only this time the importance of the management of meaning has been much better understood and communication technologies make it possible to flood society with symbols. EVR (Enhanced Virtual Reality) is the new opium of the people. Poverty, drug addiction and spiritual starvation are increasing, very much in pace with Alienation, and Marx's basic idea that (Ultra)Capitalism is not capable of solving the problems of humanity is still valid.

But let us move on with YanL and her climbing manual. Anyone seeking for vertical mobility in these times must, YanL claims, dedicate all her/his attention to the sacrament of Profit. You should be able to 'distil its essence' and direct your attention towards this final Mercurius, the spirit of life. Old concepts, such as Reorganization, Re-engineering, Downsizing or Empowerment are revived and the 'new' ones presented: Distillation, Stripping and Visualization. All of them are old wine in the rediscovered bottles of New Age. YanL has been called, as I mentioned before, the mystic of Ultracapitalism, something that I feel prone to agree with, but, in her defence, it must be said that she has never claimed (yet) to write under divine inspiration. She seems to be interested solely in the positive influence that New Age ideals have on most members of our society.

But not only does she drink from the sources of New Age. To defend her theory of the development of Capitalism into Ultracapitalism she brings up other actors. One of them is the existence and style of Silicon Valley, one of the 'glorious past cradles of Ultracapitalism'. She has not interviewed people that actually lived there (after all, there were not many survivors after the Great One), but refers instead to written material. In doing so (not talking to actual Siliconners but collecting information from the written records) she shows yet another proof of her intelligence: 'Written and audio-visual records are the ones that create the symbols, the myths, the legends, they are the fuel of Simulations' (*On Winning the Race*, 2016: 14). I'll talk more about Simulations in the next section, but let us see what the end-of-millennium readers were fed about Silicon Valley:

> I imagine a manifesto for Silicon Valley today: Get lean, get stripped down, live on nothing. Bare bones. Focus. Be a fighter. Ration yourself daily one Snickers, one jackoff, and one Dilbert cartoon. Forget about love that nourishes. Forget about food that satiates. Forget about long conversations that only get good in the middle of the night, when that third bottle of wine gets uncorked. Forget about poetry: the whisper, the leaf, the tuck of hair. Forget about politics: the bilingual-ed revolt, the damns diverting more water south. Get ready for ultracapitalism.
>
> (Bronson, 1999)

YanL is a good author and understands her art. Not only does she bring in a populist New Age style, mobilizing Jung and the archetypes, the Alchemists and their cosmological vision of mankind and a smorgasbord of Oriental religions, she also mobilizes more serious academic authors such as Baudrillard and Virilio. In both cases she misinterprets their ideas, something that is, considering society in its present circumstances, difficult to blame her for. Though it has occurred to me that the explanation might be even worse, that she has actually understood their message but found it not fit for the purpose of *On Winning the Race*. This has forced her to step into the machinery and create a more suitable meaning. Both authors were in their times considered as social critics, though perhaps Virilio was more dedicated than Baudrillard to the search for a means of understanding society than merely describing it. However, both were concerned about the direction humanity was taking under the rule of Capitalism.

It's ShowTime

Baudrillard coined the term 'Simulations' to refer to the growing jungle of symbols with no connection to personal experience or real perceptions that were flooding the information society. He was already there at the Kuwait war, the first of the real real-time armed conflicts, and raised the alarm for the indifference with which TV watchers received the news. The war had become a digital tale, a new grand Wagnerian opera in the exploding night skies of Baghdad to the music of missiles and the cut voices of the pilots in the radio. It cannot escape anyone how this phenomenon has been growing ever since, when the news, the very symbol of objectivity, have been replaced by dramatized documentaries and soap operas featuring real(?) actors. Gang wars in the Noncorp Territories; the addicts' fall to hell, mostly out in the Noncorp Territories as well; the Great One in San Francisco, with cameras flown in under the collapsing buildings; and the infamous nuclear tests out on the Pacific Islands. All these events are being served in glittering packages designed in VR studios in London and Berlin, filled with a charm, glamour and music they have never possessed but that today form part of their sublime nature.

In the Middle Ages, that which was true was written in the Books. That is to say, the work of Aristotle, though some other thinkers, such as Plato and Saint Augustine, were also considered. Put very simply, then rationality arrived and truth was only that which was logically correct. And now, truth is only that which can be sold. This is the radicalization of Baudrillard's Simulations – the chain of justification stops at Profit, and meaning springs from It.

YanL has understood this well, what she seems to have missed (intentionally or not) is that Baudrillard was a critic, not a prophet. He wrote of 'Seduction', which was an attempt to ease Capitalism's harsh understanding of Nature and the aggressive social relations it created. Even this has been misunderstood. YanL does indeed talk about Seduction, but she mobilizes it as an ally to Ultracapitalism. She engages in an act of metonymical confusion, claiming Seduction is to be found at the origin of marketing. Marketing's final goal, she says, is not to sell a product but to seduce the consumer, give him/her a pleasure he/she would not find anywhere else. So, by a trick of her magic wand, she has transformed raw marketing (all kinds) into a disinterested act of hedonism, and praises Baudrillard for his visionary faculties!

But the manipulation of ideas from the Capitalist decades does not end there. There is one step left, since so far she has only presented and defended the essence of marketing but has not yet told the would-be topManagers (Guillian, 2014) what concepts should be used in the campaigns. In accordance with her style in the rest of the work, she is very uncontroversial when listing the 'winning values', advising her readers to concentrate on 'design, baroque, decadence and, above all, on the king of aesthetic values, Speed'.

All this information is not only uncontroversial but is even a bit passé. Design will always be there, she seems to have forgotten that it is not a value but a form. Decadence, on the other hand, is a value, and is what might give content to coolness and design. It has been very much in vogue during the last decade and is intimately related to the legalization of all kinds of drugs in the Noncorp Territories and the extended use of opium derivatives in the Corporated Territories. But the first signs of decadence devaluation are visible everywhere nowadays. Nine out of ten intelligent-billboard images used to be about some kind of drug, this is not the case any more. Now they share the time on a 40/40 basis with detergents and soaps. Two years ago, the final in the Corporate Ice-Hockey-Aussi-Rules League was the most widely tele-exped event but this year the corporate championship in table tennis has displaced both the CIH-AR and the CEFL finals. Not only has decadence lost its edge as an aesthetic value, but its significance in our society has already been the subject of a few marketing books (Huan 2012, 2016; Johnson and Walker 2013), which makes YanL's contribution in this matter rather uninteresting.

Her analysis of Speed is just as uncontroversial, but it is nevertheless interesting to study how she distorts Virilio's ideas to fit the wishes of the market. In this case, as with Profit, she sets out to give meaning to and legitimate a value that has taken over in our society. And as with Profit, she does this by giving Speed a history. But once again, she misunderstands (or manipulates) one of the classics. I refuse to think that the actual Speed frenzy has its genesis in the works of Paul Virilio (as YanL seems to claim), and this for two reasons. His books are a reaction to an already existing Speed creed (back in the 1970s), and anyway he was definitely against that ever-increasing belief in Speed as the saviour of mankind.

I want to insist on the harmful consequences of her work, even though this will not better my reputation as an argumentative academic. Very few people today read the original work of Virilio, unlike that of YanL, who is read by thousands and who is the master of the myth. Virilio is not here anymore to explain his ideas, society will only know what YanL and others have written about him. And if anybody actually falls to the temptation of reading him, most probably she/he will understand his theories through the lens of what the legend says about them.

Virilio did write about Speed, and did foresee many of our society's values, but he did not like it. He was a hard critic of the direction western society (the equivalent, though not geographically, of our Corporate Territories) was taking. He raised the alarm for the coming of the total transit without destination, the ultimate Speed towards nowhere, the frictionless movement at the end of the line.

It is only the result of an unfortunate irony of history that he now is considered the 'prophet' of Speed. Well, not the result of an unfortunate irony, but more of the conscious labour of writers like YanL whose goal is to sell and who will write anything people demand. And what people demand are myths, legends, hybrids (as described by Latour in his brilliant but forgotten 'We Have Never Been Modern') that can help them to cope with the extensive work of purification carried out by the ruling classes to keep the structure standing.

For instance, technological hybrids are being mass-produced today. Carefully designed and manufactured gadgets with senseless functionality that form the base on which we humans live. Ortega y Gasset, before the Second World War, already stated that 'man has interposed between himself and nature a zone of pure technical creation' (Ortega y Gasset, 1996; own translation). Humankind cannot evolve its norms and values outside its own physical circumstances. These circumstances have always been defined by the practical use of our technological capabilities. As Virilio reported half a century ago, technological advances have more and more been directed towards the development of a whole fauna of dromological objects: things that can carry us (both physically and virtually) faster and faster, further and further, in a global trip to nowhere. We need stronger and stronger kicks to feel anything, we have become Speed addicts. Supersonic travel, terra-bandwidth transmission, instantaneous universal access, non-material presence are all at the end of the line. They cannot take us anywhere; they can now only exist as transportation means to the hipness, the cool style, the sunglasses at night.

Our society's Speed addiction has not gone unnoticed by YanL (nor by the many other situation-analysts). She states clearly that 'to reach the sublime state of perfect Profit, one has to become a servant of Speed'. Given today's situation, it is perfectly impossible not to agree with this statement. But this is hardly any news for those who have followed the development in the pages of *The Art of Management*. This journal, a bastard and undesired offspring of the ideas of an obscure group of academics in Stockholm at the beginning of this millennium (Guillet de Montoux, Gustafsson and Fern, mostly), has been the showcase for all the fashion waves for the last two decades and has, as such, displayed a vast array of articles on the cult of Speed, mostly climbing manuals with a similar audience and style as *Winning the Race*.

e-Security and the Territories

The last part of her vOpus is dedicated to today's most widely known facts about management. It is embarrassing that somebody with the experience of YanL can get entangled in such banal matters at such length. Nobody, interested or not in vertical mobility, has failed to understand the importance of e-Security. The kids out in the Noncorp Territories seek fortunes in the jungle of corporation data;

engineers in the corporations invest two-thirds of their time fighting intrusions of the most varied kind (Samuel, 2014); two of the corporations in the 10-top Linked Index provide e-Security solutions. Where has YanL been the last two decades?

The recommendation about the Territories ('get one!') is as non-informative as the advice of not leaving the door to your Profit-generating knowledge open. Of course it is necessary to own territories to be considered a worthy corporation. Has anybody thought otherwise after the last international convention in Cancun 2010 was totally neglected in favour of the simultaneous Second Intercorporate meetings in Lagos?

YanL misses the chance to engage in a (interpretative, historical, semantical) discussion about the meaning of e-Security and the Territories and offers instead recommendations of no more novelty than 'make sure you do not run out of water bottles' or 'do not venture in the Noncorps after dark'.

Conclusion

YanL has delivered yet another readers' digest on what is popularly known as the Art of Management. The novelty in this case is the attempt to create an explanatory myth of the rise and dominance of both Profit and Speed. *On Winning the Race* is an attempt to give both concepts transcendental meaning and a place in evolution. Whilst they obviously have a place in evolution, since they exist, whether or not their offspring Ultracapitalism is 'the perfect social condition' and has its origins in divine inspiration is most arguable.

All kinds of communicative acts are memetic: means for the transmission of concepts, the flow of values, symbols and theories in society. This vOpus is an explicit example, and not one of the brightest. Its message is a praise to Ultracapitalism, a social system responsible for the actual disastrous condition of humanity (not the least its decadent acceptance of the situation); and its style a populist potpourri of uncontroversial fashionable trends.

As for the daring advice to vertically-conscious managers – Profit, Speed, e-Security and Territories – I will refrain from further comments.

References

Bronson, Po 1999, *Wired Magazine*, Number 7.07.

Disch, Thomas M. 1998, *The Dreams our Stuff is Made of – How Science Fiction Conquered the World*, New York, The Free Press.

Frillons, Isabella 2011, *Who Wants to be a MetaManager?*, third edition, UpperCastilla Capital-Human Editions.

Gibson, William 1984, *Neuromancer*, New York, Ace Science Fiction.

Gibson, William 1993, *Burning Chrome*, London, Voyager (HarperCollins Publishers, 1986).

Gibson, William 1994, *Virtual Light*, New York, Bantam PaperBack (1993).

Gibson, William and Sterling, Bruce 1996, *The Difference Engine*, London, Vista (1990).

Guillet de Monthoux, Pierre 1998, *Konstföretaget – Mellan spektakelkultur och kulturspektakel*, Stockholm, Bokförlaget Korpen.

Guillian, Faster 2014, *TopManagers Intimate*, FreeBase, Willbe vOpus.

Gustafsson, Claes 1994, *Produktion av av allvar – Om det ekonomiska förnuftets metafysik*, Stolkholm, Nerenius and Santérus Förlag.

Huan, Yee Long 2012, *Market by Violence*, Medellin, Extreme Editions.

Huan, Yee Long 2016, *Smashing the Competitors*, Medellin, Extreme Editions.

Johnson, Peter and Walker, Frontec 2013, *Intensive Positioning*, Sunburned, Foundation for Teaching vOpus.

Landon, Brooks 1997, *Science Fiction after 1900: From the Steam Man to the Stars*, New York, Twayne Publishers.

Ortega y Gasset, José 1996, *Meditación de la técnica – y otros ensayos sobre ciencia y filosofía*, Madrid, Revista de Occidente en Alianza Editorial (1939).

Samuel, Rebecca 2014, *Management Figures*, Alexandria, Ministry of Business, United Fruit Corp.

Stephenson, Neal 1993, *Snow Crash*, New York, Bantam Books.

Sterling, Bruce 1997, *Holy Fire*, New York, Bantam.

Taylor, Frederick Winslow 1967, *The Principles of Scientific Management*, New York, Norton Library (1911).

Tjinsky, Valeria 2016, *How I became a SupraManager*, Putingrad, Capital-Human Editions.

Virilio, Paul 1986, *Speed and Politics: An Essay on Dromology*, Columbia University, New York, Semiotext(e).

Virilio, Paul 1996, *Försvinnandets Estetik (Esthétique de la disparition)*, Stockholm, Bokförlaget Korpen (1989).

Von Wright, Georg Henrik 1993, *Myten om framsteget*, Stockholm, Månpocket.

YanL, Birgitte 2011, *Distilling Profit*, Selenia City, Paracelsus vOpus.

YanL, Birgitte 2014, *Firmnet, a Map*, Selenia City, Paracelsus vOpus.

Wilson, R. A. 1988, *The Trick Top Hat*, a Dell Trade paperback, New York, Dell Publishing (1979).

Wittgenstein, Ludwig 1998, *Filosofiska undersökningar*, Stockholm, Månpocket.

Index

MEMORIAL UNIVERSITY OF NEWFOUNDLAND

3 1162 01240026 4